YOUR DR___MS
A - Z

S. W. THAVERNER

Debpma Books International Ltd

ISBN: 0-9546898-3-6

Published by Debpma Books International Ltd.
Ryecroft, Manor Park Road, Glossop, SK13 7SQ
Copyright© 2003 strictly reserved.
Printed and bound by Antony Rowe Ltd, Eastbourne

INTRODUCTION

Dreams are a communication of body, mind and spirit in a symbolic communicative environmental state of being. I know that you are thoroughly confused. Please let me explain it in a more down to earth language. Our brains are in constant activity. Different states of consciousness like "awake", "asleep", "alert", "drowsy", "excited", "bored", "concentrating" or "daydreaming" cause different brain wave activity. Our conscious mind, or let me put it this way; the part with which we think, in other words, our "window" into life, only takes up a very small portion of our brain activity. It has been estimated that our conscious brain activity is only 10% of the total capacity of our brains.

Other areas of our brain control other functions such as breathing, heartbeat, converting light to vision, sound to hearing, balance when we walk, taste, smell, feeling and so on. These functions also have their own percentages of brain activities as well and it is also considered to be a small percentage of the total capacity of our brains.

Another area controls imagination. This area is widely an undiscovered frontier. Imagination is more than dreaming of a new car or picturing someone with their clothes off! When you look at clouds and see shapes, or wood grain and see images, this is the "order from chaos" part of your imagination. The mind cannot deal with chaos very well, in fact it will resist it and sometimes manufacture order. (very important to the dreaming process). This too occupies a small percentage of the total brain activity. Then there is memory. Memory is vast! And I believe it occupies more of the brains resources than most people believe.

And then there is the activity called dreaming. I think that to a certain extent, we dream all the time. Even while awake! But the process is functioning in our subconscious minds, out of view from our "window". Our subconscious mind, which is an area of our mind capable of picking and storing information endlessly without the knowledge of our conscious thinking minds. If defined precisely, they may not be referred to as dreams technically, but the activity is very closely related.

During certain cycles of brain activity while asleep, we can "view" these dreams (i.e. the information which have been picked up by our subconscious minds) and record them in our memory. This is why we sometimes remember them when we wake up. It will not be possible to "see" or "interpret" these images during the day because our conscious mind is occupying our entire attention and concentration. But while we drop off to sleep at night our conscious mind "switches off" while our subconscious mind remains active. It is during the activities of our subconscious mind during sleep that the information which has been picked up during the day (it could even be yesterday, last week or even last year) is passed to our memory.

We often obtain weird pictures in our dreams due to the fact that our conscious mind cannot interpret what it is receiving. Our subconscious mind does not possess a distinct way of communicating to us. All it can do is to transmit the information to our conscious mind in exactly the same way it has acquired it. The confusion arises when we are trying to understand it with our conscious rational thinking. This is why the interpretations of dreams are of utmost importance.

Ah, but would it not be nice if it were that simple! Dreams are easily influenced by factors in your life and spirit, and these influences create "categories" that are almost infinite. We do broadly categorise them in terms like "prophetic, standard, physical and nightmare" (to name just a few). And these we study each on their own, in order to gain benefit from them. I look at it in this way: Our mind and spirit, together with our brain, is actually the greatest computer ever devised! To understand its "background" processing is to learn more about ourselves, God, our future and each other. Many things can be gained from dreams, better health (mental and physical), entertainment and even financial gain! (i.e. dreaming of an invention or idea). Now that you know some of the basics about dreaming and what (theoretically) dreams are, you should have a better grasp on how to understand and use your dreams.

In this book we have compiled a comprehensive analysis and researched document which we are sure you will reap the maximum benefits from it. We would like to point out that it has been extremely interesting to put together different analyses to form the book. We have learnt a lot while compiling this book and you will be amazed at the different meanings which may even prompt you to wonder what could possibly be going on in your day-to-day activities.

We would also like to highlight the fact that recurring dreams have practically no useful meanings. These types of dreams are usually the backfiring of the various strong impressions which have been picked up by your subconscious mind during the day. We would also like to point out that recurring dreams could occur according to a strong thought which you are keeping in your mind. Suppose you are a salesman who detest being sent to a particular area during the course of your work. You will always have resentments when you are sent to that particular area. If, suppose you are sent to that area on four different occasions you may find yourself cursing that area or even your supervisor on four different occasions. Remember that your true feelings will not simply be dispersed into thin air. It will obviously be echoed somewhere. Bear in mind that it has been picked up by your subconscious mind. The bottom line is that the same information is being picked up by your subconscious mind on different occasions.

Another type of dream, which has no meaningful interpretation, is what we call a nightmare. Nightmares occur due to strong impressions being held in the conscious mind. Usually these impressions are fearful impressions. Let us take for example, somebody who is due to sit for a very important examination. The fear of failure may overwhelm that person up to a point of frenzy. Never for a moment think that these emotions will just dissolve. Every action will produce a reaction. The reaction may manifest itself as a violent dream which we consider as a nightmare.

Nightmares can occur for various reasons such as cases which involve marital problems, litigation, insecurity, apprehension, domestic violence and so on. We must never ignore the fact that our subconscious mind is perfectly capable of picking up distant information about hostile and vicious thinking which other people may be plotting against you. You are totally unaware of what is going on but your subconscious mind does. This is what is commonly termed as a psychic attack. It is worth noting that every human being possess what we call an aura. The aura is a positive mental atmosphere of dynamic force, just like a psychic suit of armour which naturally shields its owner from unwanted and adverse influences. Your subconscious mind fights these vicious attacks without your knowledge. As mentioned earlier, there will always be a reaction to an action. As a result, the psychic attacks which are being propelled towards you from your "enemies" are picked up in the aura and your subconscious mind reacts accordingly. The end result is the production of those wild fantasies called nightmares. Dreams which are carrying meaningful interpretations are the types of dreams through which our subconscious mind perceives a variety of information which concerns our surroundings, our family, our friends, our health, our habit and every aspect which you will obviously find useful in the event that you receive additional information regarding same.

We are sure that you will be able to discern numerous meanings which will be parted to you through your dreams. At last you have reached the stage where a complicated area of your life can be brought to light. It may or may not be entirely accurate to your particular situation. But it is obvious that you will be able to shed much light on an obscure activity which has been ignored for so long. Even so, it may not be possible to cover the vast range of individual situations which may arise in each particular dream. There could be cases where your dreams may not be matched to an interpretation from this dictionary. In this particular case it will be very helpful for you to look up the meanings of the most significant objects which appeared in your dreams. Good luck to you and your transformed new life.

A

ABANDON

1. To dream of being abandoned by relatives portends freedom from the most recent anxiety you may have been experiencing. To be abandoned by friends signifies a personal desire to accomplish a long overdue objective.

2. To dream of abandoning a task, journey, a sporting event, a project, studies and anything, which does not involve the abandoning of human beings, portrays a lack of initiative on your part. Assess yourself and make a special effort to accomplish any outstanding tasks you may have. Or else you risk missing the deadline, if any, and you may face unforeseen consequences.

3. To abandon any of your relatives, or kids, friends or even work mates means you have an unconscious desire for a promotion at work or an improvement in your studies. Pursue this desire because it is within reach even if there is no indication whatsoever.

4. If you find yourself abandoning your pets and personal belongings you adore, you may have to be a little extra cautious with your romantic relationship as this may signify light trouble ahead.

ABNORMALITY

1. If you dream of anything which looks to be abnormal in a dream represents something which you instinctively feel is wrong. This may not necessarily be the case. All you need to do is to revise any latest instructions you may have been given either at home, school or at work. There is a strong possibility that you may have wrongly understood. You will have to shoulder the entire blame in the event that you make an error.

2. To be aware of something abnormal warns you of the fact that you should be paying particular attention to areas in life which are not conforming to your ideals. You may be trying to attempt something which is beyond your means at the moment.

ABORTION

1. To witness an abortion (in the case of a woman), in a dream means you have to take an account of your own self and reject any bad feelings and emotions you may have towards anybody, as this will lead to a conflict.

2. In the case of men, you will need to make a decision to get rid of what is no longer needed.

ABROAD

1. To dream about being or travelling abroad signifies that you will soon be free from any recent setbacks either at home, in your studies or at work.
2. To be travelling abroad against your will means that you may have to face a difficult decision soon.

ABSENCE

1. A dream about someone being absent under any circumstance means that you will have to be prepared for an event which will happen unexpectedly.
2. In the case where you are absent in an event which you would have liked to attend, portrays delay in some undertakings.
3. To be absent on purpose portrays total failure.

ABSORPTION

1. To dream of being totally absorbed in what you are doing indicates your ability to be totally focused. Successful outcome is expected in your next undertaking.
2. If you dream of witnessing matter being absorbed into any other material signifies confidence.

ABYSS

1. To see an abyss in your dream indicates that you possess internal psychic ability to handle spiritual issues.
2. To find oneself in an abyss in your dream signifies that risky action needs to be taken in an endeavour which you have no idea what the outcome will be.
3. To dream of finding somebody else in an abyss shows that there is a fear of losing control of a particular situation or fear of some type of failure.

ACCIDENT

1. Dreams of being injured, murdered or killed occur relatively often and need to be analysed to the specific circumstances of the dream. Most often it is a sign of receiving a warning to be cautious or to be aware of hidden aggression.
2. To be witnessing an accident in your dreams highlight anxieties to do with safety or carelessness, or fear of taking responsibility.
3. To narrowly miss an accident in dreams is a sign of spiritual growth and you may avoid an interference from any authoritative source within your circle.

ACID

1. Using acids in dreams means that there is a caustic influence in the dreamer's life but may be improving.
2. To be avoiding contacts with acid means that the dreamer should take special care not to be involved with heavy financial planning within the next quarter.
3. To dream of somebody being injured with acid means that there is a necessity to become aware of something which must be used with caution, depending how, and on whom it is being used.
4. To dream of yourself being injured with acid indicates that you have to watch out for an act of corruption against you or your integrity.

ACORN

1. To dream of acorns signifies that there is a vast growth progression which will result from small beginnings. Your strong point in such a dream is strength.
2. To dream of acorns in water or rain means the emergence of a new idea in your present undertaking.
3. Decayed acorns in your dream show a need for patience in dealing either with yourself or with others.

ACTOR

1. To dream of a famous actor/actress is a sure sign that you have to become aware of your unconscious desire for your ambitions.
2. To dream of yourself playing the role of an actor/actress suggests that you have high hopes for your undertakings but unfortunately you are not taking the necessary actions to push through. Please make the necessary moves.
3. To dream of a deceased actor/actress suggests that you may be liable

10

to take responsibility for actions resulting from someone else's decisions. Watch out!!!

ADDER

1. To dream of an adder signifies that you may lose control on a particular person or a particular situation which is present in one form or another. There may be a situation where another person you rely on, cannot be trusted.
2. To dream of an adder chasing, biting or even squeezing you is a sign that you have to take up matters related to your sex life. This may mean that you will have to take up unresolved matters relating to sexual activity or fear of sexual activity.
3. To watch somebody else being hurt with an adder in your dream shows a sign of depravity or deceit on your part.

ADDICTION

1. To dream of yourself being addicted to anything like alcohol, cigarettes, sex or even sporting activities indicates you have a need to recognise your abilities and be on the lookout not to over do something which has got to do with an important decision in your work or studies.
2. To dream of others being addicted to any of the above substances shows that you may be worried that someone else or something may be taking you over.
3. To dream of being addicted to someone is a warning that you are unconsciously avoiding responsibility. You should stand up to any challenge as this will be a sure sign of self-improvement.
4. To dream of a fear of addiction is a sign of self-esteem and authority on your part.
5. To dream of a group of addicts shows that you have a lack of understanding in somebody else's behaviour in social situations.
6. To dream of others avoiding addiction may signify that you could be a victim of a fabricated gossip.

ADDRESS

1. To dream of seeing your address on a letter may mean a present situation whereby you may have to take consideration of your current lifestyle. If on a parcel means a strong and healthy lifestyle.
2. To be writing or gluing an address on either a letter or a parcel may be significant that you have to take an overdue course of action regarding social issues.

3. To dream of addressing a group of people is a warning that you should share your knowledge with others. Believe me it will be for your own benefit.
4. To dream of an address you know means safety in your attempts to do anything.
5. To dream of seeing your previous address written on anything signifies that you need to analyse old behaviour or attitudes and ensure that you do not get back to them.
6. To dream of a new address suggests the need for change and challenge.

ADVERTISEMENT

1. To dream of an advertisement on a billboard may indicate that you might have to change some working practices to avoid delays and loss.
2. To see an advertisement on television is a sign that you will most probably have to change your way of thinking regarding working issues. This may mean a change of the way you think about your superiors or subordinates.
3. To dream of yourself featured in an advertisement indicates expectation to be more active and open about your activities.
4. To dream of someone you know in an advertisement may have a two-fold meaning. That person may have the ability to help you in your activities or he/she may be alerting you of their need for help.

ADVICE

1. If you receive advice in a dream means that there is a possibility that you need guidance in your next important undertaking.
2. If you dream of accepting an advice means that there is a need to be doing something which you are not keen to do.
3. To dream of refusing an advice you consider unacceptable demonstrates the strong character in you and it is an indication that you should not be apprehensive to displease someone by refusing any proposals you find not acceptable.
4. To dream of giving advice is a sign that you are aware of information which can be helpful to others.

AFFAIR

1. To be having an affair in your dreams happens literally often. This is usually in the form of a sexual relationship. This indicates the need to come to terms with your own sexual needs and desires. But not to worry. It is very often not something to do with an actual act of

indecency. It is also an indication of your need of social affection.

2. To witness your partner being involved in an affair in your dreams is a signal of a lack of attention to family affairs. It may be a wise move to pay a closer look at how things are handled at home.

3. To dream of any member of your family having an affair in a dream is a sign that whoever is involved may be in need of social or financial assistance.

4. To dream of witnessing an affair about people unknown to you means that you are seeking an understanding of issues regarding work or studies-related subjects. It could be a challenge before you eventually figure it out.

AEROPLANE

1. Dreaming of aeroplanes parked at their bays represent a sudden change of your life pattern.

2. If it is taking off means that you are about to take action regarding changes which involves a certain amount of risks.

3. If it is landing indicates the success of a new venture or the favourable outcome of a calculated risk.

4. If you are in the aeroplane denotes a successful move towards independent being.

5. If the aeroplane crashes in your dream signifies extreme delays in your ambitions within the next quarter.

AIRPORT

1. To dream of being in an airport signifies a transition of your life which could be in terms of work-related changes.

2. If you are leaving the airport is an indication that you should be making a fresh start regarding an issue still pending.

3. To find yourself alone in an airport is significant of a need to reassess your authority as other people may undermine it.

4. To be in an airport for no apparent reason signifies a transitory stage for new experiences.

ALCOHOL

1. If you dream of alcohol signifies a forthcoming and pleasurable influence either at home or at work.

2. To dream of yourself being drunk is an indication that you will experience confusion in your next decision regarding social affairs.

13

3. Refusing to take alcohol in your dreams is a sure sign that you are maintaining a strong character and you will be pleased with yourself how you handle situations whereby somebody else may try to impose their desires upon you.

ALIEN

1. To dream of something considered to be an alien demonstrates the need for better understanding of things which you are a bit naïve about.
2. To be confronting an alien in your dream signifies a strengthening character to attempt to handle something beyond your capabilities.
3. To be frightened of an alien in your dreams portends a lack of energy and charisma to face your next challenge.
4. To dream of yourself being an alien signifies growth in your inner power.

ALIGNMENT

1. To dream of aligning anything shows an inner desire for you to solve an outstanding social problem. You will succeed.
2. If whatever you are trying to align keeps getting out of alignment shows delays and even failure to solve outstanding problems.

ALIMONY

1. To dream of paying for alimony signifies financial burden. It will not last but will be irritable.
2. To be receiving alimony is a sign that you will not be as smooth as expected in handling either a social or a financial issue.

ALLEYWAY

1. If you are passing through an alleyway during dreams, it does not matter whether you are walking or running or strolling, means you should refrain from any temptation to share confidential information even to somebody you trust.
2. Trying to find an alleyway without success is a good indication of your success of avoiding unnecessary troubles out of no conscious efforts of yours.

ALLIGATOR

1   To dream of an alligator is a serious omen that someone may be spying on you. Be careful.

ALONE

1. Being alone in your dream does not necessarily mean that you are alone in the actual sense. It is rather a sign which represents the need for independence. Try as much as you can to handle various issues on your own even if you are not confident. The chances are that you will succeed.
2. To see somebody else alone may signify the necessity to handle your own emotional make-up without the help of others.

ALTAR

1. To see an altar in your dreams means there is a need to give yourself up to something that is more important than the immediate situation.
2. To be standing at an altar means that you will need to sacrifice something in order for you to benefit in material gains.
3. A damaged altar means that extra efforts than you imagined are required for accomplishment of your present or forthcoming endeavour.

AMMUNITION

1. To dream of ammunitions is a sign that you should rely as little as you can on other people to reach accomplishment.
2. To be using ammunitions in your dream is a sign that you are feeling insecure. Pay special attention not to be taken in by fast talking colleagues.

AMPUTATION

1. When you dream of fear of amputating one of your own limbs is a sign that you are carefully approaching an interrogation of some sort which you will triumph.
2. To dream of amputating someone else's limb is a sign that you have to watch out in case you try to deny others their right to self-expression.
3. If you dream of having amputated one of your limbs is significant of a journey or an interview which you will have to cut short.
4. To see other peoples' limbs amputated is a sign that you may be losing power or ability over one or more of your responsibilities. You should refrain from being complacent.

ANALYST

1. Dreaming of any kind of analyst is significant of a certain level of prudence which needs to be taken when handling issues in social or official meetings. Particular care should be taken not to be offensive.

2. To be an analyst yourself, in your dream represents awareness that you are not acting appropriately to a particular situation in your life. Be frank with yourself and see that justice is done.

ANCHOR
1. When an anchor appears in a dream it generally means that you are stable and there is the necessity to remain stable in emotional situations.
2. If you dream of an anchor being dragged means that there are external situations which you are trying to handle which is too complicated for you. You will have no option but to sit back for sometime and allow time to bring things to your favour.
3. An anchor is not meant to float. But in dreams this can happen. If you happen to see an anchor floating without the help of any external objects means you may be deprived of existing tranquillity.

ANAESTHESIA
1. To be anaesthetised in a dream highlights the fact that you are trying to avoid painful emotions, and feeling overpowered by external circumstances. It also indicates that you are trying, or being forced, to avoid something.
2. To be handling anaesthesia on behalf of somebody else may signify the need to be open-minded and let events unfold around you before proceeding any further.
3. To be trying to acquire anaesthesia in your dream can signify an indication of declining health conditions, but usually only part of your body.

ANGEL
1. Dreaming of angels indicates that you are searching for a superior figure which gives comfort, love and support.
2. To dream of being an angel yourself indicates that you may be trying to introduce religious concepts into your life.
3. A dead angel signifies the end of a comfortable tenure in office. You may be in for a harder, maybe more rewarding career but less satisfactory.
4. Quarrelling with angels is significant of a judicial matter with an outcome which may not be entirely in your favour.

ANGER

1. To find yourself in a state of anger in a dream can often represent other passionate emotions. This demonstrates the need to express your emotions appropriately, without fear in your day-to-day activities.
2. Trying to calm down an angry person has a two-fold meaning: If you succeed in doing so, demonstrates the ability in the level of authority which you never thought you had. If not there could be a need for sexual desire which will remain unfulfilled.
3. If somebody is angry with you in your dream, it may mean that you are a steadfast person hence, do not bend to other peoples' will.

ANIMALS

1. Animals in dreams usually represent a variety of different aspects of the personality which need to be understood on an intrinsic level.
2. An Animal with a cub: This will represent motherly qualities. Hence there could be unforeseen pregnancy among close relatives or acquaintances.
3. Baby animals: The dreamer will be dealing with the childlike side of his or her personality, or possibly children known to him or her.
4. The hurt young animal: The dreamer may perceive a difficulty in facing a mature person.
5. Eating the animal: This dream represents a difficulty which will be a result of something you created yourself.
6. Petting the animal: Somebody around you may be in need of help. Pay a little more attention to your everyday activities and you will eventually discover who the person is.

Sometimes you will need some sort of understanding of your own psychological needs. Most often, animals will appear which will symbolise different aspects of yourself such as:

1. **Bear:** This is the affectionate aspect of your personality which is dominant at this time.
2. If it is recognised in the dream that the bear is masculine, the image may then be of an authoritative person, which means you are at your highest level of your authoritative qualities.
3. **Bull:** Usually the bull in your dream denotes the negative side of your behaviour, such as destructiveness, fear or anger. However, on the positive side, the bull is recognised as sexual passion or creative power.

4. **Slaying the bull:** Indicates initiation into the world of the mature adult who succeeds in mastering his instincts.

5. **Cat:** To dream of cats is to link with the sensuous side in human beings, usually in women. The elegant but also the powerful aspects of a woman may also be perceived as the cat.

6. **Chameleon:** The dreamer is recognising either in himself or others the ability to adapt and to change according to surrounding circumstances.

7. **Cold-blooded animals or reptiles:** This represents the unfeeling and inhuman aspect of often-hypocritical people around you. Be cautious towards people you trust during the next two weeks.

8. **Composite animals:** To dream of composite animals could indicate some confusion in sorting out what qualities are needed in a given situation.

9. **Cow:** This signifies that you will have plenty to eat and drink. It also carries a connotation of satisfied sexual desire.

10. **Deer/Reindeer:** The deer and the reindeer have a strict hierarchical structure. The dreamer therefore will be proud of an accomplished feat.

11. **Deformed animal:** You will come to the awareness that some of your impulses are offensive, or revolting. Make a special effort to calm down in situation where you find yourself boiling with anger.

12. **A dog that the dreamer owned or knew at some period of his life:** Try to bring back memories associated with that period of your life because it holds clues to a present situation which you may have been trying to sort out.

13. **A dog guarding gates:** In dreams this indicates the safety of your surroundings, relatives and acquaintances.

14. **Domestic animals:** When you dream of domestic animals is an indication of the receipt of a solution which is long sought.

15. **Elephant:** To see an elephant in a dream is to recognise your qualities of patience, long memory, strength and fidelity.

16. **Fox:** If you dream of a fox signifies certain inclination on your part to be cunning and sly.

17. **Frog:** This implies the ability to transform for the better, any particular situation on your part or under your responsibility.

18. **Goat:** To dream of a goat is symbolic of your rejuvenated energy and vitality. It is advantageous to pursue, at this stage, something even if for the moment, has no apparent solution.

19. **Hare:** Your level of intuition is at the maximum. Pay attention to your instinct regarding any subject. Whatever you are advised by your

imagination will most probably be correct.

20. **Hedgehog:** The hedgehog can represent evil and bad manners, or literally your inability to handle a "prickly" situation.

21. **Horse:** The horse in a dream represents the energy at the dreamer's disposal. A white horse depicts the spiritual awareness of the dreamer; a brown one, the more pragmatic and down-to-earth side, while a black horse is the passionate side of the dreamers nature.

22. **A grey horse:** is taken to indicate death.

23. **A winged horse:** Depicts your ability to change any unpleasant circumstance to your favour.

24. **A dying horse:** There is a severe weakening of your dynamic power that carries you forward. Too much pressure may be being experienced in your life.

25. **A horse harnessed to a cart:** The dreamer may be concentrating too hard on thoroughly utilitarian objectives. It may be extremely helpful to take a break and avoid stress.

26. **If a woman dreams of being kicked by a horse:** may indicate an ill feeling of her relationship with a man.

27. **A horse clearing all obstacles:** This is a sure indication of a long standing problem solved.

28. **Hyena:** The hyena is generally taken in dreams to signify impurity and infidelity on your part.

29. **Jackal:** The jackal is associated with the graveyard, and therefore with Death. You may learn of the death of a close acquaintance.

30. **Jaguar:** The jaguar's main qualities are its speed and balance. It stands for the balance of power between the dark and light forces. You are emotionally strong at the moment.

31. **Kangaroo:** This animal being somewhat exotic, often stands for motherhood, and also strength. You will gain a measure of superiority over colleagues in any given situation.

32. **Lamb:** The lamb is the innocent side of man's nature. It is said that evil cannot withstand such innocence. You will triumph over psychic attacks you are unaware of.

33. **Leopard:** The leopard represents cruelty and aggression. If you are in a position of authority avoid being abusive.

34. **Lion:** The lion stands for strength and courage. It can also represent the ego and the passions associated with it. If the dreamer is struggling with the lion there should be a successful development as long as the dreamer is not overpowered, or the lion killed.

35. **A man-eating lion:** Shows that an aspect of the personality has slipped

out of control, putting both the dreamer and his surroundings at risks of theft-similar incidents.

36. **Lizard:** The lizard appearing in a dream is indicative of your ability to react positively to somebody else's negative thinking.

37. **Lynx:** The main quality associated with the lynx is its keen eyesight, thus in a dream it can often portray your ability to attain your objective.

38. **Mole:** The mole is often taken to represent the powers of darkness, can often signify the blind and unconscious determination of the dreamer to succeed.

39. **Monkey:** To dream of a monkey is a sign that you may be too easy-going in whatever issues you may be handling. Do not adopt an aggressive attitude but it may be advisable to rather adopt a firm approach.

40. **Ox:** An ox represents strength as well as power. To dream of an ox is to demonstrate the ability of strength and power if your job entails negotiations or if you have a forthcoming job interview.

41. **Pig:** The pig is taken in Western belief to indicate ignorance, stupidity, selfishness, and gluttony. So do not evaluate things only on the bad side. Instead, it is a wonderful warning alerting you not to be casual in handling day-to-day matters as this may hold you accountable.

42. **Wild Boar:** Watch out!! You may be evading an issue that should be challenged and dealt with more daringly.

43. **Rabbit:** Rabbits appearing in a dream can mean one of two things. The obvious connection with fertility could be important or it could be that the trickster aspect of your personality could be coming to the fore.

44. **A white rabbit:** This is significant of your inner spiritual world and as such act as a guide. You are beginning to become a wiser person as a result of your mature approach to handling social factors.

45. **Ram:** The ram is a symbol of masculine energy and power. To dream of a ram is symbolic of your inner determination to succeed. You have the drive to accomplish.

46. **Rat:** The rat signifies the diseased and devious part of the dreamer or of his situation. It can also represent something which is repulsive in some ways. The dreamer may be experiencing disloyalty from a friend or colleague.

47. **Reptiles:** To dream of reptiles is indicative that there is an element of disease which is not at a high scale but needs attention. Maybe a medical check-up is advisable just to ensure you are on the safe side.

48. **Seal:** Dreaming of a seal is a strong indication of your intention to be

20

anonymous or evasive in certain situations.

49. **Serpent (snake):** The serpent is a universal symbol which can be male or female. It can signify death if it is aggressive in your dream. If friendly it signifies rejuvenation.

50. **Sheep:** The sheep represents the symbol of being subtle. It indicates the need to be gentle even in situations where tempers are flying around.

51. **Sinister Animals:** Any threat from strange animals indicates the fears and doubts you have over your ability to cope with family discontentment. This is an issue you can handle but need more confidence.

52. **A snake in the grass:** This denotes disloyalty, trickery and evil.

53. **Squirrel:** Squirrel represents the hoarding aspect of your personality. Maybe you feel insecure at the moment but hoarding is unnecessary as you are in no serious lack.

54. **Tiger:** The tiger signifies royalty, dignity and power and is both a creator and a destroyer. You are actually emotionally and spiritually balanced.

55. **Toad**: To dream of toads is significant of the power of the dreamer of having the ability of transforming something unattractive to something beautiful.

56. **A toad and an eagle:** This dream is significant of your ability to make a justified judgement in social and romantic affairs.

57. **Unicorn:** The unicorn is a symbol of purity and strength. You may be at your peak performance at home or at work.

58. **Vermin:** *(See rat).*

59. **Whale:** The whale, because it is a mammal which lives within water, indicates the power of resurrection and rebirth in your ability to overcome what you may consider a serious problem or setback.

60. **Weasel:** The weasel is significant of the devious, more criminally oriented side of yourself. It is important at this stage of your life to be cautious against being influenced into fraudulent dealings.

61. **Wild animals**: Usually, wild animals stand for danger, dangerous passions, or dangerous people. There is a destructive force threatening your safety. The best approach is to avoid mental pressure by talking out either your workload or marital shortcomings.

62. **Wolf:** Dreaming of wolves may indicate that you are being threatened by others, whether singly or by the pack. You may have cruel sadistic fantasies without taking responsibility for them.

63. **If wolf is wounded:** The dreamer may be suffering either emotional or spiritual wounds.

64. **Zebra:** This animal has the same significance as the horse, but with the additional meaning of balancing the negative and the positive in a very dynamic way.

ANVIL

1. Depending on the circumstances in the dream, the anvil can represent the basic force of nature. You are about to succeed in something which is not totally approved by colleagues. They are helpless to deny it to you.
2. If damaged, it is symbolic of losing something which was not yet given to you.

APE

1. To dream of apes and monkeys is a warning that you lack self-confidence in a forthcoming job interview, or examination, or a promotion or even a new responsibility.
2. If the ape is dead is significant of your diminished opportunity to improve in any given circumstance, be it in studies or in sports.

APPETITE

1. When an appetite is particularly noticeable in a dream it usually represents a desire which is unfulfilled. This will not necessarily be a physical desire, but could be emotional or spiritual.
2. To be hungry or thirsty in a dream is indicative of lust and sexual desire.
3. If your appetite cannot be satisfied in your dream means your inability to succeed in emotional issues particularly romance.

APPLE

1. In dreams this can represent fruitfulness, love and temptation. You have to pay particular attention against infidelity on your part.
2. If you are eating an apple indicates the wish to be trying to acquire specific information or knowledge, something you will gain.
3. Apple blossom is a Chinese symbol of peace and beauty. Spiritually people suggest a new beginning and a freshness of approach.

APPOINTMENT

1. Dreaming of going on an appointment indicates that you need to have an aim or a goal. The dream is bringing to your notice that you definitely need to do something to gain achievement.

2. Missing an appointment suggests you are not paying enough attention to details about any of your given commitments.
3. If you are fixing an appointment for somebody else signifies that there is something which has to be accomplished within a certain time limit.
4. Cancelling the appointment means that you need to keep, or make use of your time in the most effective way before it is too late.

APRON
1. Dreaming of an apron in general means the cosy and peaceful atmosphere prevailing in your family life.
2. However, if the apron is dirty indicates the possibility of a relatively light problem which is being kept from your knowledge.
3. If torn, signifies hardship within the next two weeks and possibly even through the next month.
4. If you are the one wearing the apron may indicate the need for skill. You may have the perception that you are handling things successfully but in fact there may be a little more to go.
5. If worn by someone else may mean that your home may need protection against psychic attacks.

ARC
1. Dreaming of an arc is a warning that you need to concentrate on a particular part of your life. You may be trying to pursue different uncompleted tasks at the moment which is not effective for you. It may be better to concentrate on them and tackle them one by one.
2. If the arc is incomplete, it shows a psychological inclination of paying attention only to a segment or portion of what you are trying to deal with at the present time.
3. A wide arc shows that there is dynamism available which will enhance the growth or promotion of the dreamer.

ARCADE
1. Dreaming of being in an arcade is a good sign of accomplishment if it is not at night.
2. If your intention is to get to the arcade but you never managed to get there signifies the delays of completing any projects you have in mind at present.
3. To be in an arcade at night is symbolic of failure of what could have been a very fruitful venture.

ARCH

1. When you dream of arches or doorways, you are often moving into a different environment or way of life. You have to go through some form of initiation, training or sacrifice in order to succeed.
2. If passing freely through the arch means that you are in the process of passing a test. You may be being protected by authority.
3. A white arch means that you will have to make a fresh start to accomplish your present task.
4. If you have to bend down to go through the arch means that you may be subject to inquiry before something new is granted to you.

ARCHER

1. To dream of an archer is a sign of maturity and there is the need to be extra careful especially in handling matters which are linked to the sea.
2. To dream of being an archer yourself is a warning that you should not overdo your principles linked to safety.

ARCHITECT

1 Dreaming of architects or architectural designs is a plain sign that you are actually under pressure in any given form either at work or at home. You may need more concentration in order to make sensible judgements.

ARENA

1. Dreaming of being in an arena either as a player or as a spectator highlights the fact that you may need to make the decision to move into a specifically created environment, one which gives more room for self-expression and creativity. Changes of your environment may be imminent.
2. An arena may also signify your focused attention in an area of conflict. This conflict may need to be brought out into the open in order to cultivate a peaceful solution.
3. An arena can also signify ambition. If you have ambitious goals it will be beneficial to pursue them.

ARGUS

1. Dreaming of an Argus is a very good sign that long-awaited good news will finally be received.
2. It can also signify long-term peace.

24

ARMBAND

1. To dream of armbands is an indication that a minor incident is prevailing. It may not be possible to avoid it altogether because it will not be your fault. But to be on the look-out for it will definitely give you the moral to handle it wisely.
2. To be wearing armbands in your dream is a sign that, for the time being, you may not be as successful as expected in your quest for either a promotion or a personal objective.

ARMCHAIR

1. Armchair signifies relaxation and comfort. To be seated in a comfortable armchair is a good sign that your present endeavours are being handled up to standard.
2. If you dream of either an old or damaged armchair, or if you are disposing of your old armchairs is an indication that you may be threatened by somebody who is well acquainted to you.
3. Dreaming of buying new armchairs means that there is an unconscious urge for you to reach financial independence. It may be a good idea to focus on your career development.

ARMOUR

1. If you are in armour in your dream it could be that you may be overprotecting yourself to the point of paranoia.
2. To dream of others in armour is a clear indication that you may be aware of confidential information regarding other people. You may need to show respect by safeguarding this information.
3. You may also be protecting yourself from something you feel is threatening you. Your way of protecting yourself may, however, be outdated and inappropriate in the present circumstances. Seeking advice about how to improve your security may be the best approach at present.
4. Armour also signifies chivalry, protection and the need to protect or be protected from hostile attitudes of others.

ARMS

1. You use your arms in all sorts of different ways, and in dreams it is often significant to note what is actually taking place. You may be in need of wisdom in confronting your adversaries.
2. Arms-in the sense of weapons – *see ammunitions.*

3. The arm signifies action. Do not be lethargic. Be on the move and you will reap the benefits.

ARMY

1. To dream of an army is significant that you will be pleasantly supported with financial assistance to complete the project which needs funds beyond your means.
2. To be enrolled in an army depicts emotional strength. This is a good time to pursue issues which need convincing others. It is also a good time for politicians to pursue their goals.
3. To dream of a battered army is a sign that you are lacking the courage to face circumstances which are inevitable. You do not need special training or special assistance. All you need is to be bold and get on with it. The sooner the better for you to relieve yourself of pressure.

ARREST

1. To dream of being arrested shows that you have restraint on your natural self-expression. You may not be a good speaker but it will certainly help to speak yourself out, no matter what others may think or do.
2. To dream of arresting someone else would indicate your instinctive disapproval of something which you do not yet fully understand. You have to study the respective issue in detail before giving a verdict.
3. To be involved in circumstances regarding arrests is an indication that you are unsure of your motives in an action you are contemplating. You need to stop and think before you proceed.
4. To be released following an arrest is significant that there is a need for authority within a specified area of your life be it at work or at home.

ARROW

1. If you dream of shooting arrows means that you are aware of the consequences of actions, either your own or other peoples', which can't be recalled or revoked.
2. To dream of arrows being shot towards you may indicate that communications which you make could be damaging to other people. You could either hurt or be hurt by directness.
3. Buying or possessing arrows as weapons suggests you possess the power, energy and expertise to complete or achieve a given objective.

ARTIST

1. To dream of an artist is a sign that you are attaining spiritual growth. You may be chosen to lead due to your cautious approach.
2. To dream of being an artist with remarkable skills portends your ambition to succeed. It may take a while in achieving your objectives. But succeed you will.

ASCEND

1. To dream of something ascending means that you are becoming conscious of being able to exercise the need for control over passion or sexual pleasure.
2. If you are climbing stairs, going up in an elevator or lift means you are making a movement towards waking or becoming more aware of events which have been going on right under your nose for some time.
3. To watch other objects ascending is significant that you are making an escape from anxiety or being down to earth; and you are cultivating the will to free yourself from constraints.

ASCENSION

1. The act of Ascension is a breakthrough to a new spiritual plane which transcends the state of being human. It is an awareness that you are now reaching improved levels of concentration which is vital to your success.

ASCETIC

1. To dream of an ascetic, shows some conflicts with natural issues. There may be an avoidance of contact through fear or the need for restraint. This is due to lack of self-confidence. All you need is to study the particular situation thoroughly and you will be enlightened.
2. In a dream to meet an ascetic, or holy man demonstrates the need to recognise the part of yourself which is in need of attention. This could be your sexual life, romance or work commitments.

ASH

1. Ashes in a dream often indicate penitence and sorrow. You are aware that you have been over anxious and stupid within a situation, and that there is little left to be done. That situation has outlived its usefulness.
2. Scattered ashes may indicate the end of an event or the departure of a person you know.
3. Cleaning up ashes portends your ability to use your experience which will enable you to make the best of a situation.

4. To find what you consider being your most personal item burned down to ashes represents mortality. You may learn of the passing away of an acquaintance.

ATTACK

1. Being attacked in a dream indicates a fear of being under threat from external events or internal emotions.
2. If animals are attacking you, this means that you are turning your own aggression against someone who may be innocent.
3. If the dreamer is the attacker he needs to defend himself by positive self-expressing attitudes and he needs to make attempts to destroy some urge or feeling of vengeance in himself.
4. To be dispelling an attack from other parties show a spiritual or psychic threat from discontented friends.

AUDIENCE

1. To be dreaming of standing in front of an audience, you probably have to deal with an important issue in your life. Such issue is likely to have a bearing on your social comfort.
2. If you are in the audience then it is very likely that you are witnessing an emotion or a process of change within yourself, something that you intended to achieve.
3. Refusing to be facing an audience means that you need to carefully consider some aspect of your life particularly one which takes place in public.

AURA

1. To perceive an aura in a dream indicates how powerful you consider yourself and others to be. To perceive the aura of yourself is significant of your inner power which is now at its peak.
2. Repelling the aura of somebody else is a sure sign that your strong emotional integrity will be respected by others.

AUTUMN

1. Autumn gives you the sense of something coming to an end. You will have to admit that something good in a particular situation can be brought in and made use of but the rest must be given up. Do not hold on unnecessarily to something which does not have a perfectly defined objective
2. If autumn is approaching to an end signifies the need to consider the cycles that occur in your own life and whether some of these can be

brought to an end. It may be helpful to consider abolishing certain patterns you find are not contributing to your well being any longer.

3. The beginning of autumn in your dream is a message that you will soon have to part with certain events you enjoyed lately.

AVALANCHE

1. If you witness an avalanche in your dream, you are experiencing a destructive force.
2. If you are being washed away in an avalanche, you are being overwhelmed by circumstances.
3. To witness others trapped in an avalanche demonstrates the need to regain control over circumstances which could be going out of hand.

AXE

1. To dream of somebody using an axe against you means that you are being threatened by someone's psychic power.
2. To dream of using an axe indicates that you need to become aware of destructive forces around you.
3. If you are using the axe destructively means that you have to come to terms with your mental state. Do not have the impression that you have to use destructive means to deal with a destructive situation.
4. If you are using the axe to clear debris or any obstruction means that you possess the power to conquer hostility in your everyday activities.

AXLE

1. To dream of anything spinning about its axle is a good sign that you are stable in the existing life circumstances.
2. If the axle is damaged, you will be faced with various hold-ups when trying to complete official proceedings. Fortunately those delays will not last.

B

BABOON

1. To dream of baboons portends strength. You have the strength to handle responsibilities but it seems that you lack self-confidence.
2. To be attacked by baboons depends on who wins. If you succeed in defeating the baboon is a sure sign of succeeding in your next major project. If not, you face hidden delays.
3. If you are fleeing the baboon demonstrates your shyness to face formal proceedings.

BABY

1. Nice dream if the baby is healthy and playful. You will finally overcome any situation having an adverse bearing on your career.
2. If the baby is ill, you are subject of gossip either in your neighbourhood or workplace.
3. To be feeding the baby is a sign that you will soon be satisfied with an agreement under your supervision.

BACHELOR

1. To dream of meeting a bachelor indicates that you are searching for freedom either within your emotions or in your love life. It could be that your romantic life is facing pressure at the moment. It may be very helpful to adopt an easy-going attitude for now.
2. If the dreamer is a male, he may be wishing for the freedom to achieve something he might find difficult in partnership.
3. If you dream of being the bachelor, it means that you are not making an effort to tackle a present issue which will have a significant effect on your destiny. Try to have clarity of mind and make that important move.

BACK

1. Dreaming of seeing someone's back suggests you are vulnerable to the unexpected.
2. If you dream of turning your back to someone signifies that you are rejecting the feeling of someone who may be in need of your help.
3. If you constantly fail to identify someone whose back is turned towards you suggests that you may be at the bottom of an argument soon to erupt.

30

BACKBONE

1. If the backbone is particularly noticeable in the dream shows that you are well organised in your pre-defined structure for any of your given commitments.
2. If the backbone is bent you should reconsider your character, as it carries the connotation that you lack some firmness.
3. If fractured means that you are being overruled.

BACK STREET

1. To suddenly find yourself in a back street in your dreams with the intention to make a short cut signifies your desire to be independent.
2. If you are in a deserted back street signifies an urge to take command over issues you have previously ignored.

BACKWARDS

1. To dream of going backwards indicates that you may be withdrawing from a situation or slow to learn from it. You may need to realise that to continue in a particular situation will stop your progress.
2. To dream of looking backwards signifies your detrimental habit of resentment. You should note that it is not helpful to keep a grudge over an issue. It only helps to worsen things and it prevents you from seeing a brighter horizon.
3. If somebody has to look backwards to address you is significant that you should take note of what is happening in your life at this time and determine the exact reasons for this.

BACKYARD

1. If you dream of retreating to your backyard, it represents loneliness. It is not serious though. Someone whom you enjoy his/her company may have to depart temporarily.
2. If you are using the space of your backyard to either make an extension or for storing equipments is significant of your ability to progress in leadership.

BACTERIA

1. To dream of either yourself or someone else being infected with bacteria is a sign that you do not have to struggle to meet the requirements of any given circumstance.

BAD

1. When you dream of something being bad you are being made aware that you do not necessarily have to be facing something bad in the normal sense. But it is significant of bad practices in which you may be indulging.
2. To dream of feeling bad can have the impression that you are off balance in some ways. You may be waiting for a verdict of some sort.
3. Your thought processes may be corrupt. Pay special attention not to be involved in deception.
4. If you dream of food turning bad you are not taking sufficient care of your inner needs.
5. A bad smell in dreams could mean that your environment may be prone to changes which will not be appreciated.

BADGE

1. To have your attention drawn in a dream to a badge makes you aware of your right to belong to a group. Do not be left behind. You may be the one who will benefit the most.
2. To be wearing a badge is significant that you may be singled out for particular recognition, possibly because you possess certain qualities.
3. Dreaming of producing or manufacturing a badge carries the possibility of a promotion at work. If at home there will be a marked improvement in the available facilities.

BAD NEWS

1. Dreaming of receiving bad news is indeed not a pleasant omen. To receive bad news in a dream is significant of things which look perfectly right with your eyes, are in fact not as you think they are.
2. If you are the one delivering what is considered to be bad news to your recipient is a sign that you may need attention to either achieve or complete something in which you think you need no help.

BAD TEMPER
See anger

BAG

1. To dream of bag(s) signifies that the dreamer may be having problems with the feminine elements in his or her environment.
2. Depending on the type of bag, e.g. a handbag, a shopping bag, a school bad etc., you may be hiding certain aspects of yourself from public

32

consideration.

3. Finally, to own the bag portends an element of risk which you will have to take to reach accomplishment.

BAGGAGE

1. To be carrying extra baggage in a dream signifies that you may be carrying an extra load, either emotional or practical. You may be expecting too much from yourself or from others. Your results will be below your expectation.

2. Also the dreamer may be under some psychological stress, and may have to decide on leaving behind the most trivial aspects of his/her waking life.

3. To be in possession of excess baggage is significant of your conscience being loaded due to something which you may have committed and you may be reproaching yourself inwardly.

BAILIFF

1. When a bailiff appears in your dream it signifies that you doubt your own ability to manage your own resources.

2. If you are the target of the bailiff means that you have overstepped the mark in a particular way and must be accountable to authority.

3. If you are the bailiff means that you have put yourself at a risk by not fulfilling one or more of your obligations. Unless you take responsibility, you will be "punished" in terms of material loss or status.

BAIT

1. To be putting down bait in your dream can be an indication of your doubts about your own ability to attract a partner, be it romance or a business partner. Do not have the impression that you have to either entrap or ensnare the partner. Proceed with a normal approach.

2. If you find that you need bait as a commercial item is significant that you are not making enough progress in your quest to achieve. Push harder.

BAKER

1. Dreaming of a baker is an alert that you have within yourself the ability to alter your approach or attitude to situations in your life to make significant progress.

2. If you are the baker in your dreams suggests that your creative ability may need to be enhanced or lightened in order for you to achieve success.

BALANCE

1. When you dream of trying to maintain your balance to prevent yourself from falling from a difficult position means that you have a good leadership character.
2. To dream of trying to balance a financial account means you are pursuing something which remains unrecognised by your superiors.
3. To have the feeling that you are looking for the balance of a quantity of goods indicates you have more mental abilities than you thought you had.
4. To find yourself unbalanced in the sense of equilibrium portends a sense of injustice.

BALCONY

1. To dream of being on a balcony indicates that you are searching for a higher status than you have at present.
2. To dream of being underneath a balcony indicates that you are aware of other peoples' need for status.
3. When you dream of being elevated onto a balcony is significant of recognising your spiritual competence or progression.

BALD

1. To dream of someone who is bald indicates that you are being made aware of a degree of dullness in your life. In fact it is a good dream which will push you to alter certain practices and make life more interesting.
2. To dream of yourself being bald can be somewhat confusing. It usually suggests a loss of intellectual prowess, but can also symbolise improved intelligence.

BALL

1. Attending a ball in dreams suggests a need for freedom, but in fact you are at your best mental state at present.
2. If you are playing with a ball means that you are conscious of your need for both structure and freedom. You need to celebrate special occasions. A ball as in a formal party allows you to do just this.
3. If the ball is deflated there will be diminished power or authority within your responsibility.

BALLERINA

1. The appearance of a ballerina in a dream shows an urge for you to strike a balance between your workload and social life.

34

2. If you are dressed with the intention to perform as a ballerina means that you have creative powers to face tricky situations.
3. To be graduated as being a ballerina shows an urge to achieve a higher self-esteem.

BALLOON
1. A balloon in your dream can indicate a forthcoming festive occasion or a desire for sex.
2. An over-inflated balloon may indicate an exaggeration in your indulgence in certain events or substances such as foodstuff and other beverages.
3. If the balloon bursts indicates a delay of an event in which you will play a prominent role to achieve recognition.

BALLOT
1. To dream of casting a ballot in any given situation portends the importance of maintaining a sense of individuality so as to avoid disappointment.
2. Counting ballots signifies a lack of free will and open attitude in discussion.

BALLPOINT
1. To dream of using a ballpoint pen in a dream signifies confidence in your next commitment.
2. If the pen runs out of ink is an indication that you have unconscious fears to approach someone in authority.

BAMBOO
1. Dreaming of bamboo is a sign that the dreamer is one who possesses enduring strengths.
2. To dream of bamboo in a stack is a sign that what is achieved may not be maintained if you are not careful.

BANANA
1. The banana signifies the male dominance. If green, it can suggest strength and in control.
2. If ripe it signifies masculine sexuality.
3. If, in the case of a woman, it can signify the possibility of pregnancy of either herself or acquaintances.

BAND
1. If the image of a band is that of a stripe then there is some limitation

within your circumstances which needs to be noted.

2. If, however, the image is that of a group of musicians, this would indicate the need for teamwork. You may not approve of it, but you will have to accomplish whatever which is under your responsibility through teamwork.

3. If you are a member of a musical group then there is an appreciation of harmony on a psychological level which will help to establish long lasting social peace.

BANDAGE

1. If a bandage is being applied on you in a dream this shows the beginning of a healing process amidst the possibility of a slight degree of hurt feelings or emotional injuries.

2. If you are applying the bandage on someone else it signifies that you may have been made aghast by some difficulties within your life and need to pay attention to your ability to be healed.

3. If the bandage is coming off you may have overcome the difficulty, or you may have been careless.

4. Bandages signify preservation as in the bandages of a mummy, So, in this instance the dreamer can analyse what he wants to preserve in his life and act accordingly.

BANK

1. Dreaming of yourself in a bank means that you have a sense of security, without which you cannot venture into the world, need to be properly managed and monitored.

2. If you are handling any document which has got something to do with the bank signifies certain fear of venturing into an activity which has to do with financial implications.

3. A bank indicates a secure financial place. If you dream of receiving financial benefits from the bank indicates your social stability amidst setbacks.

BANKER

1. Money and personal resources tend to be the things with which most people have difficulty, Our need for an authority figure to help us deal with problems that arise are usually symbolised by the banker or bank manager in dreams.

2. Your intense desire to acquire financial stability is also symbolised by a banker. But the trick in this dream is a warning that you have to knock to get the required results. Whatever is your merit will not come to you by itself.

3. In dreams a banker can also symbolise your capacity to handle things

which requires management qualities.

BANKRUPTCY

1. To dream of an Establishment filing bankruptcy is a sign of lack on your part. You may lack either financial resources or courage to generate more financial resources.
2. To be filing bankruptcy yourself shows a lack of courage for you to face things which you are perfectly capable of doing so.

BANNER

1. If the banner in the dream is a commercial one, it represents the need to have something which you may previously have ignored or rejected.
2. If the banner is an old fashioned one as used in medieval battles, it indicates a need to consolidate thoughts and actions regarding your career.
3. A torn or destroyed banner symbolises a deflected psychic attack towards you without conscious efforts of your own.

BANQUET

1. If you dream that you are serving at a banquet, you should be careful not to deny yourself the good things in life, by giving too much away.
2. If you are attending one you should recognise your need to be nurtured into a new activity until you are thoroughly confident.
3. To find yourself missing a banquet in dreams symbolises that you are under-utilising your mental faculties.

BAPTISM

1. To dream of being baptised indicates a new influence entering your life patterns. It may be difficult at the beginning to determine whether it is a good or bad influence. But it is very important to safeguard in case it is a bad one.
2. To dream of baptizing someone means that you have to pass on knowledge to other people in order to benefit from your own knowledge.
3. To dream of witnessing a baptism ceremony indicates your sensitivity to higher being in the sense that you have the ability to attain spiritual growth.

BAR

1. When you dream of a bar, such as an Iron bar, you should look at how rigid, or aggressive you are in your behaviour. You may need to be more subtle when handling issues where opinions differ.
2. If you dream of standing at a bar may represent a barrier to your sexual enjoyment particularly in the male.
3. To dream of owning the bar *(or public house),* is a symbol of your spiritual power, as well as power in your everyday life.

BARB

1. To be surrounded by barbed wire in a dream indicates that you are being prevented from moving forward by either your own, or others, hurtful remarks.
2. To be entangled in barbed wire in your dream is significant that you are trying to be too smart. Equally you may be trying to force other people to do something against their will.

BARBECUE

1. To dream of a barbecue gathering signifies your jubilant expected outcome in any circumstance to come.
2. To dream of participating in a barbecue is significant of your lack of alertness to identify discontentment among colleagues as a result of your actions.

BARBER

1. When you dream of visiting a barber you are, in effect, considering a change of attitude, thought or opinion about yourself for the better.
2. To dream of being in the company of a barber means that you may be under an adverse influence which is becoming apparent in your life and which needs to be changed.
3. To be the barber yourself indicates that you have a new idea, backed by a new inspiration to be in control.

BARE

1. If the dreamer is bare he or she is becoming aware of his or her vulnerability. You may be vulnerable to criticisms out of no fault of yours. Pay very careful attention to do things which have properly been authorised and do not proceed with things out of your own accord.
2. To dream of a bare landscape denotes a lack of happiness or perhaps of fertility.

3. To dream of a bare household is symbolic of a new challenge coming your way which you will have to be determined to overcome it.
4. To dream of bare wardrobes or larders is a message of the necessity to make a move to bring financial comfort in your life.

BAREFOOT
1. Depending on the circumstances of the dream, to be barefoot can indicate poverty. It is a warning to be more prudent with your spending.
2. To be barefoot and not able to find ones shoes shows a lack of suitability, an awareness of inappropriate behaviour. Watch out for your indulgence.
3. Being barefoot at appropriate places such as in your room or on the beach indicates wisdom. A good decision on your part is prevailing.

BARGAIN
1. To dream of being engaged in some sort of bargaining signifies a strong character and you should be satisfied with the way you handle your affairs at work.
2. If you dream of having lost the advantage of your bargain to your opponent is a sign that you may have to re-assess certain issues before presentation for consideration.

BARGE
1. To dream of a barge indicates a strong desire to be promoted or to achieve any sort of advancement. It is important at this point in time to access the most advantageous way forward.
2. Dreaming of a sunken barge denotes a lack of initiative on your part. You can achieve but you need to be pushed forward. If you allow this to happen you may end up accomplishing something but with no recognition.
3. To be in command of a barge signifies your command and prowess. If you are not being recognised for your skills there is a good chance that you may have to leave your present activities and proceed on your own in order to be successful.

BARMAN/MAID
1. To dream of a barman or barmaid signifies the need for you to take a break from stressful commitments. Mind you it will give you a wonderful boost to enable you to continue.
2. To dream of being a barman on duty suggests the tendency for you to

be greedy in some aspects. Pay attention not to hoard certain commodities only to find them useless in the end.

BARN

1. To dream of a barn is a good sign that you will soon have plenty of what is much needed at this stage of your life.
2. Dreaming of an empty barn is a sign that you are not doing enough to reach that goal you have set to yourself sometimes back.

BASE

1. If, in your dream your attention is drawn to the base of an object, you may need to go back to the starting point of a project in which you are involved in order to consolidate a smooth progress.
2. To dream of base metal indicates that you are dealing with something which is somehow inferior and needs refining in some ways.

BASEMENT

1. To dream of being in a basement signifies a need to be more conservative in handling your personal affairs in front of others.

BASIN

1. Using a basin in a dream suggests the need for purity. Something is not going too well either at home or at work. You may need to be a little more open to confront the setbacks sensibly.
2. To be buying a basin suggests the need to be on your guard against being materialistic or someone else being too dependent on you.

BASKET

1. To dream of a basket, particularly a full one, is to dream of full fruition and abundance. A feat achieved or will be achieved.
2. To be attempting to fill a basket can mean that you are trying to increase your talents and abilities.
3. If the basket is full of bread it can represent sharing, something which will earn you big respect.

BAT

1. Because popular belief has it that bats are frightening, to dream of bats indicates that there are forthcoming events or news which will not be pleasant to you.
2. Dreaming of a baseball bat or other such implement will give an

indication of your attitude to controlled aggression but you need not be too involved.

3. To dream of being attacked by a bat shows the need to confront fears. You may have fears which are baseless. All you need to do is to face these fears and be contented with yourself that they were empty ones.

4. To be using a cricket bat is significant that you will display a degree of competence within your responsibilities.

5. Using a tennis bat in a dream is a sign that you will have to take appropriate measures to earn recognition for things which are accomplished through your expertise.

BATH

1. To dream of being in a bath may indicate the need for cleansing of some old feelings. If you are disturbed by some unpleasant feelings please make a special effort to rid yourself of them.

2. Dreaming of bathing someone shows a need to safeguard against intimate relations outside your marriage or engagement.

3. Dreaming of buying a bath shows a necessity for you to gain improvement in your way of thinking regarding recurring problems, if any, at home. It is detrimental to view things on the bad side only. You may live to regret it.

BATON

1. To dream of a police baton represents a measure of authority you are expected to gain.

2. To dream of a drum baton or stick signifies the need for self-expression in a more forceful way than normal.

3. To dream of any other ordinary baton symbolises a change in the course which you will have to take in order to achieve progress.

BAY

1. To dream of a seashore in the form of a bay shows your inclination to concentrate on more sexual activities. A point of warning though is that you must watch out against infidelity.

2. To be keeping something at bay indicates a need to be on your guard against malicious intents from people you trust.

3. A parking bay means the slow attainment of something you desire.

BEACH

1. To be on a beach shows your inclination to be a little too careless about the reality which confronts you in terms of financial gains. Pay more attention so as to identify a channel with financial benefits.
2. Depending on your actions and state of mind in the dream, dreaming of a beach usually means relaxation and creativity.
3. If you are on a deserted beach you will have to watch out in case your happiness is robbed from you. This is likely to be in the form of treachery.

BEACON

1. To dream of a beacon symbolises the need for you to abandon a long-held grudge about somebody you detest.
2. To be installing a beacon is a warning that your emotions may be flaring and that you may need some guidance of some sort.
3. A lighted beacon signifies that an end to an itchy problem will end sooner than expected.

BEADS

1. When you dream of beads for instance a rosary, you are making a connection with continuity. You are in fact in a position to solve a situation which has been baffling others for some time.
2. To dream of counting beads indicates the failure of a favourite project.

BEAN

1. To be storing beans in a dream may show a fear of failure, or lack of confidence in your ability to carry through an objective, the need to create something in the future.
2. To be planting beans would suggest faith in the future, and a wish to create something useful.
3. Buying beans shows that you have the ability to use a reserve of power to achieve whatever you desire.
4. Disposing of beans can signify immortality and magic power.

BEAR

1. To dream of a live bear indicates aggression against you. You may have to watch out not to offend other people.
2. To dream of a dead bear is a sign that you have to be careful not to display your financial position in front of others, which may give rise to bad intentions, whether or not you are financially healthy.
3. Being attacked by a bear in your dream symbolises a need for improving security features at home or in the office.

4. If you are attacking the bear it symbolises strength. You have to pursue an objective which is still lagging. The time is now right.

BEARD

1. To dream of a man with a beard means you must guard against cover-up and deceit. Don't do it even if the temptation may be strong.
2. To dream of yourself carrying a beard suggests the need for you to fight your way so that your opinions will be respected.
3. It is not strange for a woman to dream and find that she has suddenly acquired a beard. This symbolises a loss of her dignity to some extent. She will have to be prudent to what she says or does.

BEATING

1. In dreams the act of beating something or someone represents your need to overpower by aggression and brute force. Ensure that all other options have been exploited before this one is chosen.
2. To be beaten either physically or in a game indicates your willingness to submit to the will of others. Remember that you have a right of your own. Stick to your own mind and stand on your feet.

BED

1. To dream of going to bed alone indicates a desire for safety and security. There may not be real threats but it is prudent to ensure that you are not at risk.
2. To dream of a bed made up with fresh linen indicates the need for a fresh approach to thoughts and ideas that really matter to you.
3. To be going to bed with someone else can represent either your sexual attraction to that person or indicate that you have no fear of being intimidated by anyone.

BED-WETTING

1. To dream of wetting the bed indicates anxieties over lack of control. In some cases it may also indicate a problem with sex or sexuality.
2. You may have worries about correct behaviour in society or of being condemned for improper behaviour.
3. Bed-wetting can in dreams suggest a need for freedom of personal expression.

BEE

1. To be stung by a bee is a warning of the possibility of being hurt. It is not serious though because it may be in terms of idle gossip.
2. Being attacked by a swarm indicates you are creating a situation in handling an issue either at home or at work which may become uncontrollable.
3. To dream of a queen bee registers your need to feel, or be, superior in some ways. You may possibly feel the need to be served in your chosen purpose by others. You are also aware of the need for hard work.

BEEHIVE

1. Dreaming of a beehive shows your ability to control a chaotic situation should the need arise.
2. To dream of tending a beehive is an alert of the need for you to have good management of your resources. Being complacent will later prove costly.

BEETLE

1. To dream of a beetle is symbolic of delays beyond your control which are expected in your present endeavours.
2. To be clearing beetles from your surroundings is indicative of something to be achieved through hard work.
3. To be overcome by beetles in your dream is not a favourable dream in the sense that you are likely to be ordered around by someone who is less knowledgeable and experienced than you are.

BEGGAR

1. To dream of being a beggar represents your own feeling of failure and lack of self-esteem. You must rid yourself of these negatives by adopting a more positive attitude in your everyday activities.
2. Sometimes when you dream of being a beggar is a warning not to limit the expression of your emotions and thoughts. In most cases you take the tendency to keep inside what you feel must be voiced out. Please don't do it.
3. To dream of someone else as a beggar indicates your need to become aware of your ability to help others less fortunate that yourself.

BEGINNER

1. Being a beginner in any field denotes the atmosphere of adventure. To dream of being a beginner in any given field is a sure sign of prosperity ahead.

2. If you are the person guiding a beginner in any given field denotes superiority or authority which will soon be within your areas of responsibility.

BEHAVIOUR
1. To dream of displaying a decent behaviour signifies the total control of your ability to face any given circumstance with ease and confidence.
2. If you find yourself with a bizarre behaviour in your dream it is a tip that you are irritated with certain aspect of your waking life but you are still faced with the big question of how to take it up without offending somebody close to you.
3. To dream of others behaving nicely to you indicates a rise in your rank.
4. If you dream of others being rude to you is a warning that your personality is being abused. You should be careful not to let the guilty one off the hook while trying to make justice.

BEHEAD
1. To dream of witnessing a scene where the convict is being beheaded is a sign that you may have to be called upon for questioning regarding an issue which is under your responsibility.
2. If you are the one subject to being beheaded it shows that you have great inhibitions to participate among a crowd of people in authority.

BEHIND
1. To be behind someone in a dream indicates that, on a subconscious level, you may be considering yourself to be inferior in some ways. Rise and take command when necessary even if you still lack the sense of authority.
2. To be behind someone in a dream also denotes the fear of being left behind for either promotion, sporting events or even discussions which you feel you have a valuable contribution to make.
3. To find yourself behind something which really obstructs your vision and movement is a very good warning that someone is working against you. You will have to assess the areas where you encounter unexpected delays to help you identify your adversary.

BELL
1. Traditionally, to hear a church bell tolling in a dream is a warning of disaster or of death.
2. A doorbell in your dream signifies an urge to communicate with

someone who is distanced or estranged from you.

3. To hear what sounds like a school bell is a good omen in the sense that you will perceive approaching danger.

BELLY

1. To be paying attention to someone else's belly in a dream is a warning that the person is in need of emotional help and you may be in the position to help.
2. If your own belly is displayed in your dream is a warning that you need to confront someone in order to achieve an objective of your own.

BELT

1. To dream of a belt which attracts your attention represents your attitude to being bound by old attitudes, duty and so on. You may have to evolve a little bit in order to make further progress.
2. To dream of an ornate belt can represent a symbol of power or office.
3. An old and shabby belt in your dream is a warning not to be fooled by outdated material.
4. A large leather belt is an insignia of power, and can represent either the power you have, or the power you can obtain.

BET
See Gambling

BIBLE

1. If you dream of a Bible or other religious book it usually means that you are aware of traditional moral standards. You need a code of conduct which will help you to survive. In some sense you may need to change some practices in your everyday life to avoid a major setback.
2. To be either reading or preaching from the bible denotes your desire to be in command over something which you are not yet fully prepared to do so.
3. Receiving a bible in your dream signifies spiritual growth in the sense that you will suddenly turn out to be a respected by others, superior to you.

BICYCLE

1. To dream of riding a bicycle shows the need to pay attention to personal effort or motivation to ensure progress.
2. To be buying a bicycle means that you could be looking for financial freedom without responsibility. Come on! You won't get something

for nothing. If you try to be free from financial constraints you will have to take responsibility to manage it or risk losing it.

3. To dream of falling from a bicycle is a sign that you may soon lose an existing facility you enjoyed.

BIGAMY

1. To dream of being a bigamist indicates not being able to decide either between two loves or two courses of action. You are being presented with two alternatives both of which have equal validity.

2. When you dream you are married to a bigamist you need to be aware that you are being two-timed or deceived by someone very close to you.

3. Spiritually, bigamy can represent the choices one has to make, possibly between right and wrong. You will have to display a clear conscience and choose what you consider will enable you to steer well clear of problems.

BIRDS

1. Birds in dreams usually represent freedom, imagination, thoughts and ideas which by nature need freedom to be able to become evident.

2. To dream to be among birds is a sign that you will be pleasantly surprised by something which will enhance your way of living.

3. To dream of feeding birds means that you may soon acquire material possessions.

4. **A caged bird:** can indicate restraint or entrapment.

5. **A bird flying freely:** represents aspirations and desires soon to be accomplished.

6. **A display of birds' feathers:** indicates the dreamer should view him/herself in a more positive way.

7. **A flock of birds:** indicate some confusion over your financial and spiritual aspirations. You need to strike the balance between the two.

8. **A golden-winged bird:** has the same significance as fire and therefore indicates materialistic gains.

9. **A highflying bird:** This indicates spiritual awareness that you have to seek knowledge in your desired field in order to make substantial progress.

10. **White/Black birds:** This is significant that you have to ensure that justice is done in anything you handle to enable you to emerge victorious.

11. **A pet bird:** Personal circumstances and emotions can have a profound effect on your self-management.

12. **Chicken:** Watch out in case you display stupidity and cowardice in a situation where you have the ability to be in total control.
13. **Cock:** The cock is the symbol of a new day and of vigilance. It symbolises the need for you to be more upfront and courageous.
14. **Crow:** Dreaming of a crow can represent wisdom and deviousness.
15. **Cuckoo:** Something new and fresh is on your way.
16. **Dove:** The bringer of calm after the storm. This signifies your persisting troubles will finally be over.
17. **Duck:** In a dream this can often denote some kind of superficiality or childishness.
18. **Eagle:** Because the eagle is known to be a bird of prey, in dreams it signifies domination and supremacy.
19. **If the dreamer feels threatened by the eagle:** Somebody else may be threatening your peace and comfort.
20. **Falcon**: As a bird of prey it typifies freedom and hope for those who are being restricted in any way. It can represent victory over lust.
21. **Goose/Geese:** The goose is said to represent watchfulness and love. Like the swan, it can represent the dawn or new life.
22. **A flock of geese:** This often represents your powers of intuition and to give you a warning of disaster.
23. **Wild goose:** There may be a sinister event which will soon unfold in your life.
24. **Hen:** The hen denotes providence, maternal care and procreation. When a hen crows in a dream it is symbolic of a virtue of domination.
25. **Ibis:** The ibis, sometimes taken to be the stork, is the symbol of perseverance and of aspiration. These are good qualities you have nurtured. Keep it up.
26. **Kingfisher:** To dream of a kingfisher is to dream of dignity and calmness. These are also good character traits of respect.
27. **Lark:** There is the need to be more transparent in your way of handling things at home.
28. **Magpie:** Because of the belief that magpies are thieves, to dream of one may indicate that an associate is attempting to take away something that the dreamer values. Also the magpie can signify good news.
29. **Ostrich:** The ostrich denotes that you are trying to run away from your responsibilities.
30. **Owl:** You may learn of the death of someone dear.
31. **Parrot:** The parrot signifies intelligence or skills.
32. **Peacock:** A new courage and strength will be established in your psyche to accomplish something which is still outstanding.

33. **Pelican:** There are two meanings to the symbolism of the pelican. One is sacrifice and devotion and the other is careful and maternal love.
34. **Penguin:** The penguin is thought to represent adaptability but also possibly stupidity.
35. **Pheasant:** To dream of pheasants generally foretells of prosperity and good fortune to come.
36. **Phoenix:** The phoenix is a universal symbol of rebirth, resurrection and immortality (dying in order to live).
37. **Quail:** The quail represents, amorousness, sometimes courage and often good luck. In its negative form it can also represent witchcraft and sorcery.
38. **Raven:** To dream of a raven is a warning that you are focused too much on the bad side of everything.
39. **Seagull:** The seagull is a symbol freedom and power.
40. **Sparrow:** The sparrow represents business and industry. You should be prospering nicely if you are somebody who deals in any commercial activity.
41. **Stork:** The stork is a symbol of new life and new beginnings.
42. **Swallow:** The swallow seen in a dream represents hope.
43. **Swan:** The swan sometimes denotes a peaceful death.
44. **Turkey:** The turkey is traditionally a food for celebrations and festivals. To dream of it can therefore means that there may be good times ahead.
45. **Vulture:** The vulture often represents destructive aspects of life. Do not be frightened. It simply means that you will encounter delays in things which you may have to try by trial and error.

BIRTH

1. Birth signifies a new life. You have the desire to move forward and the best approach, it seems, is to re-assess your situation and start all over again if necessary.
2. In the case of a woman, to dream of giving birth signifies materialistic gains, courage and advancement.

BITE

1. If you are bitten in a dream may suggest that you are experiencing aggression from someone else or conversely, you may have aggressive instincts which are not under control.
2. To be biting someone or something such as a fruit in a dream indicates

your need to participate more fully in social issues which you have avoided up to now.

3. To witness somebody being bitten is a sign that you may be at the receiving end of a malicious attack which does not imply physical harm.

BIZARRE

1. Dream images are often bizarre in that someone may be doing something that is very odd, or something may have an odd or grotesque appearance. This is usually because it is important that you remember the image in order to understand.

2. The mind is capable, within dreams, of creating what may apparently be nonsensical. It is only on consideration that the dreamer recognises the relevance of the image in his everyday or working life.

3. In spiritual terms the bizarre is most likely to be the product of misunderstood information.

BLACKBIRD
See Bird

BLINDFOLD

1. If you have been blindfolded in a dream, shows that a deliberate attempt is being made to deceive you.

2. If you are blindfolding someone else, you are not being honest in your dealings with other people. This may be through ignorance on your part.

3. To dream of removing a blindfold from your face is significant that you may need to retreat from fully-committed activities and take some time to recuperate.

BLINDNESS

1. If you are suffering from blindness in a dream there is an unwillingness for you to accept criticisms. Criticism sometimes may help you in your progress. Constructive criticisms, of course!

2. To experience partial blindness in your dream suggests an internal restriction within your way of living. You will have to watch out in case you allow financial or other constraints to restrict you in any way.

3. To be nursing somebody with blindness signifies your ability to stand against things which are not in your favour in your career.

BLOCK

1. In dreams, a block may present itself in many forms. You can experience

it as a physical block; that is something that needs to be climbed over or gotten around, a mental block, for instance not being able to speak or hear, or a spiritual block such as the figure of an angel or a demon appearing in your dreams.

2. Blocks appear in dreams when you need to make a special effort to overcome an obstacle to progress.
3. A physical block in your dream mostly means that a preventative measure needs to be taken. A warning.

BLOOD

1. From time immemorial blood has represented the life carrier or the life force. To dream of a violent scene where blood appears, indicates that you are being self-destructive in some ways.
2. If you are having to deal with blood you need to be aware of your own strength in the sense that you are able to withstand resistance against you on a fairly high level.
3. If you have been injured and someone else is nursing blood on you signifies that you need to look at what help is necessary for you to overcome any existing problem.
4. To see blood on yourself is a sign that you have to assess whether or not you are not subjected to emotional abuses.
5. If you dream of blood circulating through the body is a good sign that you will be having vital force to take command of your next important endeavour.

BOAR

1. A boar in a dream indicates inferiority. You are warned not to be taken as low-ranked in an official gathering.
2. To be keeping a boar as a domestic animal in your dream is a sign of lust. It may be wise to evaluate whether you may have an excess of certain desires.
3. To be sacrificing a boar in your dream with the intention for feasting indicates an improvement to a lasting problem.

BOAT (SHIP)

1. To be on a boat/ship in your dream is a sign of glorious prosperity ahead if the boat is on calm waters.
2. If it is on stormy seas it indicates achievements after long and arduous efforts.
3. To dream of being alone in a boat means you need to assess whether you are spending enough time at home. It could be that your beloved

ones may be missing you badly.

4. To dream of being on a big ship is a warning of how you are handling a relationship which comprises a group of people. Beware not to be too authoritative.

5. To dream of missing a boat is a sign that you are hesitant to take opportunities when they arise.

BODY

1. To dream of admiring your body in your dream is a sign that you may be adopting a sense of selfishness and greed. Watch out against this.

2. To be admiring somebody else's body or conversely hating your own figure is a sign that you may not be reaping the most from an activity which you are contributing the most.

3. If you are in the process of toning up your body in your dream is a sign of forthcoming social responsibilities.

BOMB

1. To dream of bombs usually indicate some form of tense situation which you will have to handle sooner rather than later to avoid extreme complications.

2. Exploding a bomb indicates the need for you to be more positive with regards of how you view things in general.

3. Defusing a bomb suggests that you should be more cautious in handling a situation to avoid making it worse.

4. To be avoiding a bombed area is a sign that you are apprehensive of a certain event which, in reality, will not have adverse effects on you.

5. To witness a bomb exploding is a sign of apprehension of your involvement in an unfolding official event.

BOND

1. To dream of a savings bond (in the banking sector) is a good sign which shows that you have a sense of commitment to a person or a principle and that you are capable of making promises which you can honour.

2. To dream of bonds in the sense of "binding things together" indicates that you will be submitting to something with the intention of accepting defeat.

3. If you are doing the binding signifies a strong desire for you to outclass your competitors in some sort of challenge you are facing.

4. If you are being bound to either someone or something is a sign of

52

restriction. You may find that your freedom of expression in your daily life is being restricted to a certain extent.

BONE

1. To dream of bones usually indicate that you need to be aware not to underestimate anyone or anything in any way. You may have a price to pay for that.
2. To dream of a dog eating a bone means you need to consider your basic instincts. You may have to pay close attention to senses and feelings from your imagination at this time.
3. To dream of finding bones indicates that there is something essential you have not considered in a particular situation.
4. To dream of a skeleton indicates that you need to reconsider certain verdicts you have given regarding a particular situation.
5. If you are burying bones of any kind is a sign of maturity to handle diplomatic issues.

BONFIRE

1. To be lighting or tending a bonfire in a dream indicates a need for cleansing some aspect of your life. Assess whether there is something or a certain practice which you do not totally approve and stop at your earliest.
2. Feeding a bonfire in your dream is a sign that your emotional feeling needs a boost. Put that pressure down and feel more of what life brings.
3. If you dream of either a dying or extinguishing bonfire is a longing desire of yours to be over with a situation which, in reality, will be over soon.

BOOK

1. Dreaming of books is a sign that you posses high aspirations to tackle your objectives. Prosperities are guaranteed if you pursue your present goals.
2. Dreaming of old books is significant of something you are about to inherit.
3. Dreaming of account books indicates the need or ability to look after your own resources. Watch out for abuses.
4. Buying books is a sign of a decision you will make which will be a very good one.
5. A book, particularly a sacred one such as the Bible, signifies hidden knowledge. You are being left out of certain events because others are concerned not to offend you.
6. Dreaming of selling or lending your books is a sign that your are a

person of good generosity. The only warning is that you have to be cautious in helping those who are really in need.

BOOKSHOP

1. In general, dreaming of a bookshop entails spiritual growth whereby you will become a person of high integrity.
2. To be inside the bookshop is a sign of academic achievement.

BORDER

1. To have your attention drawn to the edge or border of something can indicate changes you will make in the material world in connection with your social life.
2. To be standing on a border between two countries would show the need to be making great changes in life; perhaps physically moving your place of residence.
3. Crossing a border in either between two countries or between two premises is a sign that you may need to make decisive changes in the way you think and feel about your social life.
4. Restricting others from crossing any border of any sort signifies that the time has come for you to make an important decision at home.

BORROW

1. To dream of borrowing anything from others signifies a lack of emotional and romantic aspect in your life.
2. If others are borrowing from you is a sign that you should be on your guard from being cheated in whatever channel available.

BOTTLE

1. This depends on the type of bottle perceived in your dream. A baby's feeding bottle would indicate the need to make successful progress in your career.
2. A bottle of alcohol indicates a happy or festive occasion ahead.
3. A medicine bottle might symbolise the need not to exaggerate in anything you handle.
4. A broken bottle could indicate either aggression against you or failure.
5. Opening a bottle could mean making available resources you have, but may have been suppressed.

BOUQUET

1. To be given a bouquet in a dream shows that you recognise your own

abilities but also expect others to recognise them.
2. To be giving someone else a bouquet indicates that you will reign superior over others in your quest to achieve supremacy.

BOW

1. To be bowing to someone in a dream indicates your sense of inferiority. It is a warning not to give in to others just because they are loud talkers.
2. If others are bowing to you is a sign of either a promotion or increased status.
3. To perceive a bow, as in Cupid's bow, in a dream indicates the need to fulfil a lack of romantic activity in your daily life.

BOWL

1. A bowl of food in a dream represents comfort and prosperity in your career.
2. A bowl of flowers represents a pleasant surprise.
3. A bowl of water represents your emotional steadfastness. You are a strong character but yet a bit reluctant to speak out.

BOX

1. To dream of packing things in a box indicates that you are trying to get rid of feelings or thoughts with which you cannot cope.
2. To dream of various types of boxes may represent different aspects of the feminine personality in your life. You could be surrounded by women who may exert an influence on what you achieve within the next two weeks. Just ensure positive influences.
3. To be trapped in a box represents a level of individuality which, at this moment in time, is a good trait to avoid external influences.

BOXER

1. A boxer in your dream represents courage and strength on your part.
2. To dream of being a boxer yourself is to represent success you will achieve through taking a risk.

BRAIN

1. To dream of the brain being preserved indicates the need to take care in intellectual pursuits. You may be pushing yourself too hard.
2. To dream of using your brains hard to figure out a puzzle or to work something out is significant of a desire for you to reach great heights. You will, if you persevere.

3. To dream of something like a brain operation/transplant, or any treatment which is oriented towards the brain is a warning of failure ahead. It is best to make careful analyses and evaluations before proceeding with any project you have either started or plan to start.

BREAD
1. To be sharing bread in a dream represents your generosity to share your basic experience and knowledge to others.
2. If the bread in a dream is foreign or tastes bad you may be unsure of what you really need out of life. You may be doing the wrong thing in some area of your life.
3. To be buying bread is a sign of success in some ways. But you have to ensure not to pursue your goals by pursuing bits and pieces of unfinished desires. You should take them one by one.

BREAK
1. To dream of something being broken symbolises loss or damage.
2. If a favourite object is broken you must make changes and stop falling back on the past for your solutions.
3. If you dream of breaking a limb you may be prevented from moving forward or carrying out a certain action.
4. If you dream of breaking something, appropriate action needs to be taken in order to avoid setbacks in official dealings.
5. To dream of taking a break from either work or social burdens is a warning that you are not pushing hard enough to attain a very important goal in your life.

BREAKFAST
1. Dreaming of having breakfast is a good sign of abundance. You may attain abundant financial resources.
2. To dream of missing your breakfast for whatever reason is significant of your need to make careful planning about how to tackle your everyday duties. You may be doing them the wrong way round.

BREASTS
1. For a man to dream of breasts usually indicates his unconscious desire for accomplishment and this shows that usually, in such circumstances he may have to seek help from relatives or very close associates to accomplish something important.
2. To dream of exposing your breasts is significant of your urge to get out from under stress.

56

BREASTPLATE

1. To dream of wearing a breastplate represents your desire to protect love and social values.
2. To dream of someone else wearing a breastplate forewarns of your inclination to offend somebody else emotionally.
3. To be either polishing or simply taking care of a breastplate is a sure sign of your own valued self-esteem and strong ambitions which must be pursued.

BREATH

1. To become aware of one's own breath in a dream indicates a warning that you have to ensure that you are in perfect health conditions. Even if you feel healthy it may be advisable to check anyhow. To be aware of somebody else's breathing indicates the need for more understanding and patience when attending to other peoples' views.
2. To dream of the ability to breathe under absurd conditions such as under water is significant of your attempt to be trying to reach too far before you clear the nearest hurdle.
3. If in your dream you find yourself encountering difficulties to breathe is a sign that you may have or has the intention to embark on a daunting career.

BREEZE

1. To dream of a light, relaxing breeze indicates that at least for the moment everything should be going perfectly well in your life.
2. If the breeze carries discomfort along with it, it signifies incompleteness in some of your views or the bad habit of looking at things negatively.
3. If, in your dream you find that you have the ability to control the forces of the breeze is a very good sign of power and achievement.

BRIBERY

1. To be aware of being bribed in your dream by somebody else portends your willingness to give in to undesirable dealings if the prospect looks good. Please don't.
2. If you are bribing someone is a sign that you should not use your authority to the level of being abusive.
3. If you are conducting investigation in a case of bribery signifies good luck in your career or studies.

BRIDE

1. When a woman dreams of being a bride, she is often trying to reconcile her need for relationship and her need for independence and responsibility.

2. In a man's dream a bride indicates his understanding and clarity of whatever commitments he has ahead.
3. To dream of being a bride at a wedding, especially your own, indicates your desire to achieve material possessions. Beware of heavy borrowings.

BRIDEGROOM

1. To dream of a bridegroom usually indicates the desire to be married or to find a partner. It often shows the desire to be more responsible or to take on responsibility for someone else.
2. To be a bridegroom in your wedding portents good luck in your social life which is stable at the moment.
3. To be attending to a bridegroom in his wedding is your unconscious desire to be in control. Ensure that you are in control in anything you undertake at the moment if you desire a fruitful outcome.

BRIDGE

1. To dream of a bridge indicates the crossing from one phase of your life to another.
2. If the bridge is strong you will be making excellent progress in your proposed project or idea.
3. If it is weak it portends some social delays and setbacks.
4. If the bridge is damaged it signifies that you will have to start whatever endeavour all over again in order to achieve success.
5. If it is a wooden bridge but strong it signifies short term success which needs to be followed by a concrete plan to sustain it.

BRIDLE

1. To be bridled in a dream, as in being yoked to something, indicates the need for restraint and in control.
2. If the bridle is made of flowers it indicates a more subtle or diplomatic way of imposing control.
3. If the bridle is harsher, such as one of metal and/or leather, you perhaps need to be harder on yourself or on someone you love.

BRIGHT

1. To experience brightness in a dream means that you are hiding certain aspects of your life or daily activities.
2. Your positive aspects of your life are strong at the moment and you have strong influence over a wide range of activities and other personalities.

BRINK

1. To be on the brink of something in a dream literally means you are on the edge of either succeeding or failing in something.
2. To be on the brink of falling means that you are on the verge of failing in one or more of your activities.
3. If you find yourself on the brink of success in your dream it signifies more effort needs to be done on your part to ensure success. An urge for you to move is required.

BROADCAST

1. If you dream of taking part in a broadcast means you are aware of needing to reach a higher level in your life status. You are ambitious and you should pursue your goals.
2. To dream of listening to a broadcast means you should pay attention to a message that other people are trying to get across to you.
3. To dream of a broadcast which is not in your favour, means that you should try to restrain yourself from showing irritation when attending to other peoples' views.

BROCHURE

1. Dreaming of brochure is a good sign of displaying the ability to show knowledge in an argument and consequently winning the argument.
2. If you are distributing brochures in your dream is a sign of persuasion. You may need to persuade others to help you achieve your present feat. But be selective when you ask for help.
3. If somebody else is giving a brochure to you means that you have to assess your present situation and verify whether you are not being left out in something important at work.

BROTHEL

1. If a woman dreams of being in a brothel, something is for sure. Somebody is using her for his or her selfish ends. Be strong, identify the person and get out of it without any fuss.
2. If a man dreams of being in a brothel means he has a lack in his life, which is not necessarily sex-oriented, but other aspects which he is weak to face.
3. To dream of being simply in the vicinity of brothels is a warning not to try to either achieve or possess things through the easy way or through short cuts.

BROTHERHOOD

1. Dreaming of belonging to a brotherhood indicates your need to belong to a group of like-minded people. This could be something in the nature of a trade union, or of the Freemasons.
2. It could be that you may need to be more active in your spiritual activities such as groupings for the Sunday services.

BRUTALITY

1. To dream of being brutal in your usual behaviour may mean that you have a need to deal with fears which are not well founded in order for you to make progress.
2. To dream of being brutal to someone specific is a sign that you have a lot on your conscience which you are finding it difficult to talk them out. This could lead to stress. Please do not keep things inside.
3. If somebody else is being brutal to you means that you should be watchful for animosity feelings from colleagues.

BUBBLE

1. Dreaming of bubbles means that unexpected assistance will be received to help you accomplish present commitments.
2. If you dream of simply playing in bubbles means that you have to take care to prevent an abrupt end to your present happiness.
3. To find yourself having to wade through bubbles in your dream signifies your ability to succeed but it seems you are sitting back a bit too lousy.

BUCKLE

1. Dreaming of a buckle has the symbolism in that it can represent the holding of high office or status.
2. Adjusting your own buckle signifies honour and can be a symbol of loyalty or membership.
3. To be fastening a buckle in a dream shows that you are the person who accept responsibility for what you do.
4. To be unfastening a buckle in your dream is significant of your ability to shrug off criticisms which, in return, will not affect your feelings.

BUD

1. To dream of a bud is significant of the inclination to start a new way of life, new experiences or new emotions.
2. To dream of a dying or shrivelling bud indicates the failure of a project.

BUDDHA

1. In dreams the Buddha represents denial. You may face an uphill task to clarify an enquiry of any sort which is supposed to benefit you as a result. You will fall very short of the co-operation of others.
2. If you dream of being Buddhist you may need to be more tolerance regarding any differences you may have at home or at work in order to reach a favourable conclusion.

BUILDINGS

In your dreams, various buildings have various meanings and we will take different buildings as follows:

1. **Boarding House:** To dream of a boarding house indicates that you may not be feeling secure within your living conditions.
2. **Castle:** Dreaming of either inside a castle or owning one signifies social and financial comfort.
3. **Courtyard:** To dream of a courtyard signifies safety in your daily life.
4. **Church:** Happiness in your life will reign.
5. **House:** If you are aware that the house is not empty, that there is something in it (e.g. furnishings) it shows some of your aspects of courage and determination.
6. If someone else is in the house it suggests that you may be feeling threatened by an aspect of your own personality.
7. If there are different activities going on in the house it indicates there is a conflict between two parts of your personality, possibly the creative and the intellectual.
8. To dream of the front of the house portrays steadfastness.
9. Going into or out of the house means that you may have to decide whether you need at this time to be more introverted or more extroverted.
10. **An impressive & luxurious house:** You should be more adaptable to your environment in order to achieve.
11. **Moving to a larger house:** There is need for a change in your life, perhaps to achieve a more open way of life, or even for more comfort.
12. **Being outside the house:** Beware in case you leak confidential information.
13. **A house where you were born:** You need security to a certain extent at home and at work.
14. **Working on the house e.g., cementing, repairing, etc.** Relationships may need to be worked on or repaired, or perhaps you need to look at health matters.

15. **Igloo:** Because of its shape, the igloo stands for completeness. It is warm on the inside and cold on the outside and therefore signifies the difference between what you have and what you need to accomplish.
16. **Pyramid:** The pyramid is considered to be a focus for power, so for one to appear in a dream is to be concentrating on the achievement of power within.
17. **Tower:** Any image of a tower is representing the personality, and the Soul within. The tower represents strength. Mentally you are strong and you possess extreme persuasive powers.
18. **Warehouse:** Warehouse being primarily a storage place has the symbolism of abundance within your capacity.

Components of buildings:

19. **Balcony:** You all have a need for support within your life and a balcony indicates both support and protectiveness. Hence, it represents your stability in your present life.
20. **Construction or demolition:** You all have the ability within you to construct a successful life, and equally an ability to self-destruct. A dream that highlights construction or demolition gives you access to those qualities and abilities.
21. **Doors:** If opened it signifies your desire for sexual fulfilment. If closed it signifies a missed opportunity.
22. **The front door and back door:** Those doors signify entrance into a new and prospective venture.
23. **Breaking down the door:** signifies an unwillingness to face issues about sex.
24. **Opening and closing the door:** Watch out in case your sex life is ignored, because this is such an important aspect of your relationship.
25. **Refusing to open the door:** Refusing to open a door in your dream signifies an intention for you to retain important information maliciously.
26. **Barred door:** You need self-protection against physical assaults.
27. **If a person forces his way in and destroys the lock:** Pay attention to a plan on your agenda which may not necessarily work as planned.
28. **Making a get-away through the back door:** This is a sign that you will have to find another solution for something other than the one you have in mind.
29. **A knock on the door:** This is a warning that your attention should be focused on little things which you consider are not important to you.
30. **Elevator:** Going down would suggest a more attentive self-assessment

with regards to the way you tackle your objectives. You may be lethargic.

31. Going up would suggest general improvements.

32. **Getting stuck:** To be stuck in an elevator signifies deliberate attempts by others to frame you.

33. **Hall:** Going through a hall portends your weakness in the sense that other people can defeat your constructive arguments to attain their selfish ends.

34. **The kitchen:** Dreaming to be in the kitchen suggests your ability to develop your creative powers towards financial goals.

35. **The sitting room:** To be in the sitting room would suggest your ability to accomplish something according to your satisfaction.

36. **The basement:** To be in the basement signifies heavy workloads which you will have to delegate in order to be effective.

37. **Empty rooms:** Something, such as comfort or support, is lacking in your life.

38. **Stairway:** Climbing the stairs is indicative of more effort that you must make in order to have access to facilities which are rightfully yours.

39. **Going downstairs:** This depicts clear objectives, proper planning and prosperity in your existing commitments.

40. **Walls:** A wall signifies a block-to-progress. A difficulty you have or will come up against.

41. **Windows:** To dream of looking outwards through a window suggest that you have a tendency to look at things only on the outline. You are either too lazy or shortsighted to care to make a detailed analysis.

42. **Looking inward through a window:** Please look carefully at your own self before making criticisms of others because you may end up criticising negative values which are found within you.

43. **Opening a window:** This is a good dream as it portends your willingness to participate in teamwork and you are, at present, open to transparent consultation.

44. **Closing a window:** This dream portrays laziness to a certain extent. You may have the wish to accomplish but you are not making the necessary efforts.

BULL

1. To dream of the bull represents ignorance. You may be limited in specific knowledge which prevents you to be successful in handling a situation.

2. If the bull is chasing you signifies your lack of stubbornness to prevent yourself from being pushed around at the will of others.
3. If you are in command of the bull in your dream portends your ability to demonstrate your mastery qualities to push forward towards achievements.

BULLET

1. To dream of bullets is to be aware of aggression and a desire to hurt. If the bullet is being fired at you it may be considered to be a warning of danger.
2. If, however, you are firing the bullet there is an awareness of your vulnerability.
3. Buying or selling bullets shows a conscious move on your part to be secured. You may be a bit apprehensive at the moment.

BURGLAR

1. To dream of a burglar is a sign that you have to watch out in case someone is spying on your daily affairs. Whatever the reason may be unclear.
2. To dream of being burgled is a sign that you have to pay close attention not to lend your resources without a proper principle.
3. To dream of being a burglar yourself show your tendency to be greedy.

BURIAL

1. To dream of being buried indicates your fear of being defeated in any given event or a bid for promotion or election.
2. To be attending a burial is significant of the possibility of your being invited to a wedding ceremony.
3. If you are responsible to organise a burial is significant of your responsibility to accept liabilities for something which will go seriously wrong. Be especially attentive to safety.

BUS

1. If you dream of being in a bus shows that you may have to come to terms with the acceptance of a new procedure which may be implemented against your willingness.
2. To dream of driving a bus shows your desire to be in command through a promotion which may still be a long way to come by.
3. Getting off the bus at the wrong destination signifies your lack of devotion to complete something. You have the tendency to start something and drop out half-way all the time.

BUTCHER

1. Dreaming of a butcher signifies the need for you to make clear distinctions from the good and the bad. You may be under heavy influence to give approval to something which you know is wrong.
2. To dream of being a butcher shows that you possess some destructive streak in yourself. You may have to view things more positively in order to be a real winner.

BUTTERFLY

1. On a practical level when seen in dreams, the butterfly represents light heartedness and freedom. Happiness reigns in your present life.
2. If seen to be in an irritating position, the butterfly indicates a lack of ability to settle down or to undertake a protracted task.
3. If it lands on you in your dream the butterfly is warning you of a forthcoming bit of luck or relief.

C

CAB

1. To dream of being in a cab in your dream portends your superiority in handling your daily responsibilities.
2. Being a cab driver shows you have delayed commitments which could prove costly if not attended to in time.
3. Missing your cab to your destination portrays a tendency for you to dodge your responsibilities. You may be held responsible if you are careless.

CABARET

1. To dream of a cabaret shows a need for you to be extremely watchful about how you manage your time in your daily life. Beware of excessive indulgence.
2. To be participating in a cabaret shows your need to break free from certain commitments even if you do not yet have suitable replacements to take care of those responsibilities.

CABBAGE

1. To dream of harvesting cabbages show your creative talents at their peak. You may benefit enormously by trying something out of the ordinary.
2. Buying cabbage suggests your failure to interpret correctly, statements which have got to do with legal elements. It is advisable to seek advice in case you receive formal or official documents.
3. If you are either selling or giving away cabbages portends your ability to rise comfortably in rank or you will be moderately satisfied with any sort of official applications or requests.

CAFÉ

1. To dream of being in the vicinity of a café signifies your association with a fairly large group of people which means that you may acquire a certain degree of popularity and support from others.
2. To actually be in the café or having the sense of owning it is a warning that you have to be cautious that whatever powers or authority you have or have been granted to you, is well safeguarded from abuses.

CAGE

1. To dream of caging an animal is a warning of unforeseeable restrictions and delays in certain situations.
2. To dream of being in a cage yourself portends your frustrations. If you have existing frustrations be cautious not to voice them out in an offensive manner.
3. Constructing or buying a cage signifies that you could be allowing others to hold you back in some ways.

CAKE

1. Dreaming of a wedding or birthday cake is a good one which signifies a forthcoming celebration regarding something well accomplished.
2. If you dream of baking cakes is a sign of the need to care for others or to grant others some much needed assistances.
3. Buying cakes in your dream signifies generosity. Some nice gestures will be received from someone dear.

CALCULATOR

1. To dream of using a calculator in a dream is significant of your inclination to rely too heavily on others for help regarding things which you can manage on your own.
2. To dream of calculators simply appearing in your dream portends great skills on your part which you will be asked to share.

CALENDAR

1. If a calendar appears in your dream is significant that your attention may be drawn to the past and this is limiting your ability to handle present things toward a fruitful solution.
2. Unfolding or hanging a calendar in your dream is very significant of your time not being used efficiently. Take heed in case you may be pursuing non-relevant goals.
3. If you find the need to make reference to calendars in your dreams is a warning that you are not moving fast enough in your endeavours even if you have not yet been warned about it.

CAMEL

1. Dreaming of a camel is a superb dream which signifies your ability and strength to pursue your goals without fatigue. If you have started or plan to start some sort of project, this is the best time to do it. Mind you, you are at your peak at present.

2. Riding a camel in your dream signifies your door which is open to opportunities but you may not be in tune to tap the potentials. You should wake up and be more alert before it is too late.
3. Guiding a camel on a long journey portends your willingness to be persuaded into activities of betting and gambling. Success will yield but you have to exercise control over spending.

CAMERA
1. To be using a camera in a dream means you need to pay close attention to events or occasions which may prove to be a very valuable source of information to help you solve certain things.
2. To dream of being filmed indicates that you need to look more carefully at your actions and reactions to certain situations. You have to exercise rationality.
3. If the camera is damaged signifies difficulties in trying to make a breakthrough to get recognition for your abilities. At this point in time it is a disadvantage if you are a salesman.

CAMPING
1. To dream of being in a training camp of any sort signifies your need to make small sacrifices in order to achieve vast benefits.
2. Dreaming of being in a leisure camp signifies your ability of achieving a great deal without much effort.
3. If you dream of being enrolled in a military camp portends a tough road towards achievement.

CANAL
1. Because a canal is a man-made structure, a dream about a canal usually indicates that you are inclined to be rigid in so far as control of your emotions are concerned.
2. Being on the canal through any means suggests that you are introducing too much structure into your life at the expense of your creativity.
3. To find yourself swimming in a canal signifies the need for you to structure your available knowledge in order to be able to create a workable system to push you upwards. It can be done.

CANCEL
1. To dream of making cancellations portrays your unconscious lack of self-confidence. You tend to fall out each time you are about to succeed. Please make more self-commitments.

68

2. If you dream of cancelled events or flights is a sign that you have to make up for previous disagreements in order to make progress.
3. If you dream of coming to a planned activity only to find it cancelled is a sign that you have to be careful of blackmailing.

CANCER
1. To dream of someone with cancer indicates that you are out of harmony with your body. It indicates that you have some fears of some sort at present.
2. If you dream of having cancer yourself, suggests that you have fears relating to delayed work commitments which you thought you had completed.
3. To dream of nursing someone else with cancer is a sure sign that you will be reliable on commitments even in difficult moments.
4. To dream of the astrological sign of the zodiac "cancer" is a significant of your ability to be successful in enriching your knowledge in Intuition.

CANDLE
1. To dream of candles indicate that you are trying to clarify something that you do not fully understand. You may find it an uphill task but the solution will eventually come to light. Dreaming of candles on birthday cakes signify a change in your life for the better.
2. Lighting a candle in your dream signifies using courage and fortitude or generating the boldness to ask for something you need.
3. Lighting several candles (not birthday candles) signifies forthcoming prosperous events in your life.
4. To be extinguishing candles in your dreams portends satisfaction after a difficult "struggle" to attain excellence.
5. To dream to find your candle(s) extinguished by the wind or other external factors beyond your control signifies a minor accident or possibly very sad news.

CANDLELIGHT
1. To dream of being in candlelight for whatever reason (other than at funeral services) signifies the opportunity to attain spiritual power and physical control through specific training.

CANE
1. To dream of canes is significant of your ability to either achieve or maintain orderly principles to enable you to achieve self-improvement.

2. To dream of using the cane on others, e.g. your children is significant that you have the tendency to use authoritative measures which may not prove the best option to attain your goal.
3. If somebody is using the cane against you and you succumb, it may signify failure in your forthcoming commitment.
4. If you are showing great resistance against somebody using a cane against you shows your strong character of possessing the ability to talk frankly and refusal to be used. Bravo!

CANOE
1. To dream of a canoe would indicate that you are handling your emotions in isolation. You have to make a move to make changes but only by your own efforts that you will achieve it.
2. Riding a canoe in your dream is a sign that you may be at risk of some sort. Please make an assessment especially at work to ensure no hiccups. It may be advisable to check on the safety features at home especially security checks.
3. If you find that in your dream the only way to traverse a canal is by a canoe it portends a difficult situation whereby you may have to accept something reluctantly or decide something against your will.

CANOPY
1. Dreaming of sheltering under a canopy shows your ambitious goal of becoming a great person. It will materialise with hard work and it will take some time.
2. To be buying or constructing a canopy is a sure sign that you will overcome heavy pressure from higher authorities.

CAP
1. If you dream of wearing a cap it is a signal that you may be limiting your creative abilities and providing what is best for others other than yours.
2. If you dream of a cap but not wearing it, it signifies that you will uncover secrets which have been deliberately kept from you.
3. If you are either selling or giving away caps in your dream signifies assistances will be timely received.

CAPITAL
1. To dream of one's financial capital would imply a need to conserve resources.

2. Dreaming of a country's capital city indicates you should look at your attitude to the wider issues in that country or your connection with that city in the sense that you make the best of your environmental facilities to progress

3. To dream of capital letters could indicate that you need to pay more attention to what you consider to be important issues in your life. There is a matter which needs sorting out.

CAPSIZE

1. To dream of a capsized boat signifies a loss of material or financial possessions.

2. If you dream of struggling to prevent a boat from capsizing shows your ability to survive against things which are beyond your control such as recession which may result in a degree of loss on your part.

CAR

1. To dream of being in a car usually alerts you to your own motivation and self-determination towards achievement.

2. To dream of driving the car can indicate your need to achieve a goal in order to prove yourself beyond any reasonable doubt.

3. To dream of being a passenger could indicate that you have handed over responsibility for your life to someone else. You could be refraining from accepting your full responsibilities in any respect.

4. Dreaming of being alone in a vehicle indicates independence and a sense of much needed tranquillity.

5. Dreaming of a car crash suggests fear of failure in life, while a car on fire denotes stress of some sort, either physically or emotionally.

6. To drive recklessly in a car either by yourself or someone else, marks a lack of responsibility in your haste to achieve something in the sense that you are leaving important details behind.

7. If your car is being overtaken means that you have a feeling of being left out of something which you consider very important. This is only your feeling. In reality it may not be the case.

8. To dream of reversing a car signifies that you may have to reverse a very important decision which, as a result, you will feel a bit low.

CARDS

1. To dream of giving or receiving a card such as a birthday card alerts you of the need for a specific kind of communication with the addressee. You may have common goals worth discussing.

2. Writing Christmas greetings or birthday cards signifies the arrival of a good occasion with a good reason for celebrations.
3. To dream of playing cards highlights your courage to take risks. Calculated risks which alerts you to potential dangers.
4. If you are dealing cards in your dream there are several meanings pertaining to the suite or number drawn: **Hearts** indicate your emotional activities.
5. **Diamonds** represent financial well-being.
6. **Spades** represent conflict, difficulties and obstacles.
7. **Clubs** represent action, work and intelligence.
8. **The king** represents your human success and mastery.
9. **The Queen** indicates emotional depth, sensitivity and understanding.
10. **The Jack** represents creativity or an adolescent energy.

CARRIAGE
1. Dreaming of a carriage, such as a horse-drawn one, portrays your inclination to refrain to adapt to modern thinking. It is time to get out from the old ways as this could jeopardise progress.
2. A train carriage suggests that you may soon be taking a journey that is slightly more public in character than a car journey.
3. To dream of boarding a train carriage signifies your inclination to make progressive changes in your life in the near future.
4. If you find yourself travelling alone in a carriage signifies a symbol of majesty, power and authority.

CARRY
1. To dream of carrying objects suggest your need to pay attention not to scrap something useful and mistakenly keeping its counterpart which may be useless.
2. To dream of carrying someone is a strong warning not to accept responsibility for someone else because this responsibility will be a burden.
3. To dream of being carried is a sign that you should be more involved in activities which entail more responsibilities in order to be recognised and henceforth, make progressive steps towards fulfilling long standing desires.

CART
1. To dream of a cart generally signifies slow progress in your endeavours.
2. If you dream of riding on a cart means a lack of determination and

motivation to accomplish. You should shake yourself out of this lazy mood.

3. To dream of guiding a cart suggests that you may be let down by someone you heavily rely on.

CARTON

1. Dreaming of full and heavy cartons signify an abundance which you should shortly expect.
2. If the cartons are empty signifies the danger of either a demotion in your job, somebody may attempt to swindle you, or putting your financial resources in projects which are non-viable.
3. If you dream of a crushed carton signifies the need for you to be on your guard about proposals which seem very convincing.

CARTRIDGE

1. An ink or printer cartridge signifies your ability to maintain a high level of confidence in negotiations.
2. An empty cartridge signifies the abrupt end of something which will be a disadvantage to you.
3. A full or usable cartridge signifies your role in contributing towards the successful outcome of something at home or at work.
4. To dream of finding an empty firearms cartridge signifies that the worst of a situation you may be involved in, is over.

CASK

1. Since a cask is usually handmade, to dream of one indicates that care must be taken in dealing with whatever feelings you may have regarding certain disagreements you may encounter.
2. To dream of a full cask indicates your ability to be creative and progress towards recognition.
3. An empty cask means that you are unaware that you may be losing out on something.
4. A bottomless cask represents your luck in succeeding without too much efforts at this point in time.

CASTLE

1. Dreaming of a castle represents a very lucky facility or favour through which you will achieve your objectives.
2. If you dream of finding yourself trapped inside a castle portrays your difficulty to be open to other people. If you refrain to be conservative

you may receive unexpected assistances.
3. To find yourself in a deserted castle in your dream signifies difficulties ahead towards accomplishments.

CASTRATE

1. If you dream of being castrated is a warning that you should address certain fears in order to spare yourself from an emotional breakdown. The sooner you clear the doubts off your mind, the better.
2. To dream of being in the company of other castrated people is a sign that you may be angry due to a failed formality. You should not be offensive though, because there is still room for further negotiations.
3. If you dream of castrating others shows that you should be careful not to limit any options presented to you. Make use of the all available options presented to you.

CATERPILLAR

1. To dream of a caterpillar indicates that you are about to undergo some major change in your life which could be a complete metamorphosis. You must change and grow from what you are not, to a greater potential.
2. To dream of caterpillars in your own surrounding area is indicative that you need to remain flexible in your attitude to change. It may be a difficult process to change but you have to consider every possible detail.

CAVE

1. A cave represents a doorway into your inner self. To dream of a cave suggests your inclination to be spiteful of someone who has no intention to cause you any misfortune.
2. To dream of passing through a cave signifies a change of state, and a need for deeper understandings of your own negative impulses. Do not react impulsively.
3. To dream of being trapped in a cave suggests that you may be framed by a close acquaintance who may take this option as the only way out of his/her existing difficulties.

CEMETERY

1. To dream of a cemetery signifies everlasting peace and tranquillity.
2. To dream of being in the cemetery in the company of others is a sign that you may receive a surprised visit from someone dear.
3. If you are in the cemetery alone signifies an unwanted visit.

CENTAUR

1. To have a Centaur appear in a dream demonstrates the need to make a sincere judgement rather than a judgement of what others want to see or hear.
2. To dream of guiding a centaur demonstrates your ability to put things together to accomplish the end result.
3. Dreaming of having the torso or a centaur signifies your wisdom and clear visions.

CENTRE

1. To dream of being at the centre of something such as in the centre of a group of people highlights your awareness of your ability to be powerful within a situation.
2. To dream of moving away from the centre indicates that part of your life may be off balance. It is advisable to make a special effort and get those small problems behind you.
3. To dream of moving toward the centre shows your need for integrity in your day-to-day life. You need to be more professional.

CEREMONY

1. When you dream of taking part in a ceremony or religious ritual, you are conscious of a new attitude or skill that is needed or an important change which is taking place in your life.
2. To witness others taking part in a ceremony signifies that a major life change may take place on your behalf.
3. To dream of being the leader or master of a ceremony shows your capacity to accomplish most of your desires without much assistance.

CERTIFICATE

1. Certificates signify achievement. So, to dream of certificates denotes accomplishment in many ways.
2. To dream of being awarded a certificate signifies success in your given task or commitment.
3. To dream of awarding certificates to others signify success achieved through the help of somebody else. Do not hesitate to seek assistance even from someone you detest. Chances are that you will get it.

CHAIN

1. To dream of chains in any form indicates a type of restriction or dependence on others.

2. To dream of being bound by chains signifies that you will need additional strength in the form of support from others to reach a desired goal.

3. To be using a chain in your dream to bind something with the aim of securing it, suggests your confidence of winning. But you still have got to be cautious.

4. To be unlocking or removing chains from secure areas with the objective to authorise access indicates a form of needed co-operation from other people to accomplish.

CHALICE

1. To dream of a chalice is a warning that you will achieve something which may seem unattainable, through a great deal of effort.

2. To dream of using a chalice suggests that special care should be taken not to be handling occult matters without proper knowledge.

3. If you are given a chalice in your dream either as a present or otherwise, is a warning that you should be more amenable to increase your knowledge in psychic matters.

CHARIOT

1. To dream of a chariot signifies that you may be trying to get a solution for something by adopting an outdated method which is making it tedious for you. There is an easier way out.

2. To be riding in a chariot signifies that you have to break away from your reliance on others to accomplish things for you.

CHARITY

1. To dream of giving or receiving charity has a lot to do with your ability to give and receive love. A charity box in a dream usually indicates an awareness of your own needs.

2. To dream of a charitable act often alert you not to pursue your goal with disregards to other social values.

3. To be a member of a charity group is a sign that you will play a major role in contributing to accomplishments of others.

CHASE

1. Dreaming of being chased or of trying to escape is perhaps one of the commonest dreams, usually you are trying to escape responsibility, your own sense of failure and fear or emotions you cannot handle. You badly need to "shake up" and shrug off this bad patch.

76

2. To dream of being chased by a shadow warns you not to indulge in a past trauma or an undesirable past event as it can be very damaging.
3. To be chased by an animal indicates you are not yet satisfied with the outcome of something.

CHASM

1. When you dream of a chasm or large hole you are usually being made conscious of situations that contain some unknown elements which are in some way putting you in a risky position. You are going to have to make decisions one way or another.
2. If you desire to cross the chasm in your dream portends confrontation by unknown or perhaps unrecognised negative influences from others which may cause you to experience difficulty to judge your actions or reactions in the right directions.
3. To risk falling in a chasm signifies disappointment in the sense that you may be faced with severe misunderstandings of something very important.

CHEAT

1. To dream of being in the company of a cheat signifies the need for a great deal of effort to overcome what could become a major obstacle of a lifetime.
2. To be cheating someone in your dream is a sign that you may be ambitious but not doing enough to achieve your goals.
3. To be cheated by somebody else in your dream is a sign that care must be taken against too much involvement in the difficulties of others even if you pity them.

CHEMIST

1. To dream of a chemist is a sign that you may need an improvement in your academic areas to secure an advantage in various issues you may have to handle on your own.
2. To dream of being a chemist signifies good social placement and your prospects of improved professionalism.

CHESS

1. To dream of playing chess signifies a conflict of some sort shortly.
2. To be playing chess and losing, indicates that you have undertaken an activity which will not be successful.
3. If you are the winner of a game of chess in your dream is a warning that you will succeed in your forthcoming commitment but you have to be extremely careful not to lose your resources through stupidity.

CHEST

1. A chest appearing in a dream is a warning that you have important ideals and hopes, which may need to be kept secret.
2. To dream of opening a chest signifies that you have yet to show the best of yourself with regards to your home commitments or work responsibilities.
3. To be searching in a chest signifies that you have to be watchful in case you may mishandle something important.
4. If you find yourself carrying a chest in your dream signifies that you need to be aware of events happening close to you.

CHIMNEY

1. When you dream of a chimney it signifies the likeliness of your involvement of a change which may take place very shortly.
2. If you dream of smoke rising from the chimney, a surprise is on the way.
3. To dream of either constructing or witnessing the construction of a chimney signifies that the achievement of whatever endeavour you are presently undertaking is possible even if you are actually facing extreme difficulties.

CHOCOLATE

1. To dream of eating chocolates signifies the possibility of being invited to a grandiose festive activity.
2. Dreaming of either buying or being given chocolates is a sign that your participation may be needed to help to materialise something important.
3. Dreaming of serving chocolates signifies satisfaction in the way you handle an activity.

CHOKE

1. To find yourself choking in a dream is a sign that you may expect difficulty to express yourself appropriately in a given situation.
2. To attend to somebody else who is chocked in your dream signifies that there is perhaps some indecision over whether you should speak out or remain silent over a sensitive issue.
3. Chocking can also signify that you are being stifled by people or circumstances and you are not in control of either.

CHRISTMAS TREE

1. A Christmas tree, associated with festivities, will signify a big improvement you may achieve just by giving your help to someone in

78

need.
2. If you find the Christmas lights in a brilliant manner in your Christmas tree signifies an unexpected opportunity.
3. If you dream that your Christmas lights are dying out is a warning against infidelity.

CHURCH
1. To dream of a church is a fantastic dream as it portends your strong belief of attainment. You have the faith now you need the drive.
2. To dream of worshipping in a church is a sign that you should admit the truth to something you know even if it is embarrassing to do so.
3. To dream of being in a church alone is a warning that you may have to show appreciation to somebody who granted you help in some ways.

CHURN
1. Most dreams in which there is liquid being, churned, boiled or made to move in some ways indicates you may need to access your creative abilities to make use the energy and facilities which have been made available to you.
2. To dream of trying to churn out something signifies some deep-rooted grudges in you.

CIRCUMFERENCE
1. To be held within the circumference of a circle is significant that you have set limitations to yourself. Limitations which may be detrimental. You may have to identify them and get rid of them by adopting a more open mind.
2. To dream of being on the edge of a circumference signifies your luck to acquire new knowledge and information which will be very useful to your future.
3. To be out of the circumference signifies an inability for you to look at things on the bright side of life. It is a miserable fact which you should try hard to overcome.

CITY
1. To dream of a city, especially one which is known to you signifies your sense of community and your ability to feel at ease into groups of people.
2. To dream of a bustling city may show your need for social interaction. You may be too reserved and as a result you may not know what you may be missing.
3. Dreaming to be in a deserted city may portray your feelings of having been neglected by others.

4. To dream of an unknown city portrays the need for you to get involved more actively in spiritual communities.

CLAIM

1. To dream of making a claim for something which belongs to you signifies that you may be denied your right to express your reasons behind either a decision or a commitment you made.
2. If you dream of somebody else making a claim against you portends abuses of your own recourses.
3. If you dream of making a false claim from somebody else or from the authorities is a warning that you have to be cautious in case you make baseless decisions. Make absolutely sure that all your facts have been carefully evaluated first.

CLAMP

1. To dream of a clamp signifies the need for proper order and regulations within a specific area of your life.
2. If you dream of clamping something indicates that you have certain fears and you may be expressing your desire for more security.
3. If someone clamps your belongings in your dream is a warning that you must be on your guard against being involved in a quarrel.

CLIFF

1. To be on the edge of a cliff in a dream indicates that the dreamer is facing danger.
2. To dream of being on the cliff shows the need to make a decision as to how to deal with a situation which you possibly have to take a risk to get round it.
3. To be climbing a cliff signifies the need to overcome certain fears you may have in order to overcome your own limitations.
4. To be going downwards denotes a step in something new and adventurous.

CLIMB

1. To dream of climbing is the intention of getting away from something, possibly to escape. You may automatically be avoiding trouble in some ways.
2. If you dream of being involved in a tiresome climb signifies that you are trying very hard to reach new heights in your life, possibly having to make greater efforts than before to succeed.
3. If you dream of ascending through external means such as a hydrogen balloon, this dream is often perceived as an opportunity to secure a

gateway to reach enlightenment on important matters which are confusing to you.

CLINIC

1. To dream of a clinic generally means a boost in an otherwise stale relationship you may have had with someone in the past.
2. To be sick at a clinic portends a lack of interest in subjects in your daily life which are so simple, yet can be so effective to bring a change.
3. If you dream of being a staff at a clinic signifies that somebody you are well acquainted to, needs your help but is reluctant to come forward.

CLOCK

1. To dream of a clock means you may need to pay more attention to your own sense of timing or duty, or may need to recognise that there is a sense of urgency in what you are doing.
2. If the hands of a clock is pointing to specific numbers it is very important that you remember those numbers as it could be among the rare lucky numbers available to you.
3. If you dream of an alarm clock ringing, you are being warned of danger. You have to be cautious in your approach to various things within the next fortnight.
4. If the clock has stopped working in your dream signifies a dismissal of some sort.

CLOSE

1. To be close to someone in a dream can mean you are looking for intimacy, or perhaps protection.
2. To close a door acknowledges the fact that you must make a decision to put the past behind you.
3. To dream of being behind closed doors signifies that you have to be cautious against being forced into a very embarrassing situation in the company of important colleagues.

CLOTHES

1. Depending on the clothes you wear in your dream determines what action or reaction you either perceive or receive by others. In general, to be wearing your complete set of clothes in your dream portends an element of protection against being harmed.
2. Clothes can conceal or reveal. In covering up nudity they conceal your perceived imperfections and, by implication, disguise your sexuality. In revealing certain parts of you, your dreams may show in what ways you are vulnerable.

3. **Getting undressed:** can suggest the shedding of old beliefs and inhibitions.
4. **Losing one's clothes or being naked:** highlights your vulnerability and fears.
5. **Dressing inappropriately, e.g. wearing formal clothes on a casual occasion and vice versa:** When you find yourself in this position in a dream, you are conscious of your own difficulty in "fitting in" with other people.
6. It will depend on the dream scenario whether you are surprised or distressed, and it is often the emotion that you experience which gives you the correct interpretation. You may be deliberately not conforming to others' perception of you, or trying to conform too much in adopting a certain role.
7. **Clothes being worn by someone to whom they do not belong:** There is confusion in your mind as to which roles are appropriate for each character or an inability in your decision for effectiveness.
8. **A man wearing woman's clothing:** You may have to confront a nasty surprise.
9. **A uniform on a woman:** You are demonstrating the need to be aware to exercise the more disciplined side of your personality.
10. **Changing clothes:** If you consider yourself overweight, it will greatly help health wise to bring it down.
11. **Clothes that have been cut short:** You must be cautious in case you overdo something and feel stupid.
12. **Pretty clothes:** You have much to appreciate in your life. Things should be easy-going at the moment. If not it will not take a great deal to make it so.
13. **Clothes belonging to another person:** You have to pay remembrance to that person. Maybe a short mail would make the difference.
14. **Coat/cloak:** A coat or cloak can suggest warmth and love, but also protection. This protection can be either physical or emotional, and particularly in the case of a cloak, can be the spiritual protection of faith.
15. **Fear of losing the coat:** can suggest the fear of losing faith and belief.
16. **Gloves:** The meaning of gloves can be ambivalent. They can represent covering and protecting oneself, but also "showing one's hand" and challenging the status quo.
17. **Hat/Cap:** A hat is a symbol of wisdom and the intellect and also of protection. If worn back to front it warns against committing an error which might cost you your self-esteem.

82

18. **Pyjamas/Nightclothes:** Pyjamas suggest relaxation and hence openness in your character.
19. **Raincoat:** A raincoat again holds the symbolism of protection, but this time against other people's emotional onslaught.
20. **Shirt:** A shirt can suggest your ability to take appropriate actions when necessary.
21. **Shoes:** Shoes signify your ability or otherwise, to be firm in your decisions.
22. **Lacing up shoes:** in a dream is supposed to be a well-known symbol of death as are shoes on a table.
23. **Tie:** The general significance of a tie in your dream can represent correctness, good behaviour and a warm welcome by somebody unknown to you.
24. **Underclothes:** When you dream of underclothes, whether your own or other people's, it gives the impression that you are trying to hide certain undesirable attitudes either of yours or somebody else's.

CLOUDS

1. There are bright clouds and dark clouds. Dreaming of bright clouds portends an uplift from a heavy commitment.
2. Dreaming of dark clouds can be a warning of the possibility of difficulty or danger to come.
3. Clouds were previously supposed to be the vehicle for Divine Power.

CLOVER

1. Traditionally the clover plant is considered to bring luck, so to find clover in a dream denotes good fortune is on its way.
2. If found on your premises in your dream means you need to look at your ability to maintain control over something which may be considered an envy to others.

CLUB

1. To dream of being in a club such as a nightclub or sports club signifies the possibility that other people intend to rely on an advice you may not be capable of giving.
2. To dream of yourself in charge of the group or club signifies the possibility of a rise in your authority.
3. If, in your dream you find that you wish to disassociate yourself with a club, is a sign that you will be faced with an important and sensitive decision to make.

COCK

1. To dream of a cock appearing in a dream forecasts a new beginning or warning to be vigilant in one's daily work.
2. If you dream of a cock crowing you may need to be more up front and courageous in what you are doing.

COFFIN

1. If a coffin appears in your dream it signifies a financial loss. You are warned not to gamble or to engage in any financial activity within the next fortnight as it signifies failure.
2. To dream of owning the coffin shows a lack of confidence with which you approach new responsibilities in your daily life. You lack strength and courage.
3. If the coffin is damaged it signifies a possibility of a minor illness.

COIN

1. To dream of a coin is a sign of lack, as the coin always represents the lower denomination of money. You should be pushy in your objectives.
2. If you dream of picking up or acquiring coins in any way it is a sign that you have a strong desire to accomplish something but you are actually not doing enough.
3. To dream of losing or otherwise giving away your possessed coins signifies a gesture of goodwill on your part but will not be appreciated by the recipient.

COLD

1. To be conscious of cold in a dream is to be cautious against being neglected, or of being left out of things.
2. You can very often translate your inner feelings or your emotions into a physical feeling in dreams. To feel cold is one such translation.
3. To feel extreme cold in your dream signifies potential loss of friendship.

COLOURS

1. Colour is a vital part of life due to the different vibratory frequency which they possess.
2. By working with one's own colour spectrum it is possible to maintain health. Some meanings given to colours are:
3. **Black:** This colour holds within it all colour in potential. It suggests manifestation, negativity and judgment.
4. **Blue:** It is the colour of the clear blue sky. This is the prime healing colour. It suggests relaxation, sleep and peacefulness.

5. **Brown:** The colour of the earth, death and commitment.
6. **Grey:** There is probably no true grey. It means devotion and administration.
7. **Green:** This is the colour of balance and harmony. It is the colour of nature and of plant life.
8. **Magenta:** This is in some ways a colour which links both the physical and the spiritual. It signifies relinquishment, selflessness, perfection and meditative practice.
9. **Orange:** This is an essentially cheerful uplifting colour. The qualities associated are happiness and independence.
10. **Red**: Vigour, strength, energy, life, sexuality and power are all connected with this colour. A beautiful clear mid-red is the correct one for these qualities, so if there is any other red in dreams the attributes may not be totally uncontaminated.
11. **Turquoise:** The colour is clear green-blue. This is supposed in some religions to be the colour of the freed soul. It means calmness and purity.
12. **Violet:** This colour, while found by some to be too strong, means nobility, respect, and hope. Its purpose is to uplift.
13. **White:** The colour containing within it all colours. It suggests innocence, spiritual purity and wisdom.
14. **Yellow:** This colour is the one which is closest to daylight. Connected with the emotional self, the attributes are thinking, detachment and judgment.

COMB

1. To dream of a comb signifies the need to tidy up an undesired relation which may give way to seduction and illicit sexual relationships.
2. Coming your own hair is a sign of urgency on your part to put certain things straight. There are a few unsolved little issues which may be very beneficial to your lifestyle if they are handle right away.
3. To dream of coming somebody else's hair signifies your willingness to admit to something without proper understanding.

COMET

1. To dream of seeing a comet is to recognise the possibility of circumstances arising very quickly over which you have no control.
2. If the comet is in very clear sky, answer to a problem may come to you sooner than you thought.
3. If the comet is partially obscured in an overcast sky may signify the coming of calamity or danger.

COMPASS

1. Dreaming of a compass is a sign that you need to be able to pay particular attention to the differing directions which will be offered to you and to follow the one that is right for you.
2. If you are following directions on a compass in your dream it represents that justice will prevail in whatever official proceedings you may be engaged at the moment or in the near future.
3. To be losing direction even with the use of a compass in your dream can signify that you may face certain limitations and boundaries.

COMPENSATION

1. To dream of giving compensation to someone regarding a successful accomplishment indicates that the achievement or completion of one or more of your important tasks is imminent.
2. To dream of giving compensation to somebody else regarding either damage you have inflicted or as a result of a judiciary proceeding is a warning that you should be careful with lending.
3. If you dream of receiving compensation under any circumstance signifies that you may be a subject of jealousy.

COMPETITION

1. To dream of watching a competition is a sign that, at the moment, you may have to struggle a little bit to achieve.
2. If you are participating in a competition it signifies a very successful outcome in your undertakings if you win, and vice versa.

COMPRESSOR

1. To dream of a compressor (this includes various other mechanical equipments) signifies the need to take an action out of the ordinary in order to reach a successful solution.

CONVOY

2. Dreaming of a convoy signifies a position of being hampered or smothered by circumstances or people around you.
3. To dream of being in a convoy indicates uncertainty and difficulty in making decisions. Perhaps you have too many options.
4. To dream of being at the head of the convoy signifies humility and devotion.

COOKING

1. To dream of any kind of foods being cooked signifies that you have to

satisfy the need of someone in order to gain advantage over a certain issue.

2. If you are the one cooking it signifies the need to blend certain parts of your existence in new and original ways in order to succeed.

CORD

1. To dream of a cord or a tie indicates that you should be watchful for any indication of restriction within your relationship or if there is someone who is too dependent unnecessarily on you.

2. To dream of handling a cord or your neckties symbolises the need to be more appreciative of the necessity to handle whatever responsibilities sincerely.

3. To dream of being restricted in any way by the use of a cord signifies petty and annoying disadvantages which may be encountered in simple little things.

4. If you dream of trying to restrict someone else with any sort of cord symbolises your inclination to be greedy in some ways.

CORN

1. To dream of corns may represent new life; either pregnancy or new developments in other ways.

2. To be harvesting corn is to be reaping the rewards of hard work. You may be linking with some very primeval needs and requirements.

3. To be involved in a commercial activity involving corn represents a new financial dimension in your life.

CORNER

1. To turn a corner in a dream indicates that you have succeeded in moving forward into new experiences, despite what may have seemed to be obstacles in front of you.

2. Turning a right-handed corner indicates a logical course of action.

3. To turn a left-handed one indicates a more intuitive approach in your undertakings.

4. To be trapped in a corner symbolises certain elements of indecision.

CORRIDOR

1. To dream of being in a corridor signifies a state of transition; possibly moving from one state of mind to another, or perhaps between premises or even job-related issues.

2. To dream of yourself trapped in a corridor symbolises a forthcoming

unsatisfactory situation. You may have to be cautious when accepting the inevitable.

3. To dream of finding yourself in an unknown corridor signifies a spiritual emptiness.

CORROSION

1. To dream of corrosion signifies the end of an event. But it is not apparent at the moment that the end will soon come.

2. If you dream of corroded materials which normally do not corrode such as gold indicates loss of material possessions.

COSMETICS

1. To be using cosmetics in a dream indicates your desire to be at the commanding position of certain circumstance.

2. If you refuse to use cosmetics in your dream symbolises a high level of sincerity in your day-to-day activities.

3. If you use cosmetics on someone else you literally need to "make up" with whatever little disagreement you may have at present.

4. If somebody else persuades you to use cosmetics which you accept, it indicates weakness.

COUNTRYSIDE

1. When you dream of the countryside you are putting yourself in touch with your own natural spontaneous feelings. Generally it symbolises satisfaction to an accomplishment.

2. To dream of settling in a countryside signifies peace of mind and favours from others.

CRAB

1. A crab appearing in a dream can generally indicate unreliability and deception.

2. If, in your dream, the crab has a frightening appearance denotes infidelity.

3. If you are eating the crab as a delicacy, by word association, it can represent sickness, or something eating away at you.

CRACK

1. To dream of a crack in the wall or similar buildings indicates weakness or difficulty in the way you handle your life's problems. It will help enormously if you take time to think first.

2. A crack in other materials such as porcelain may represent an irrational or unexpected event.

3. To dream of a crack for example in furnitures may indicate your inability

to maintain mental peace. You may be worrying about something.

CRADLE
1. To dream of a cradle can represent a new beginning to something.
2. As a precognitive dream a cradle can represent pregnancy, while in a man's dream a cradle can represent the need for comfort.
3. An empty cradle can represent a woman's fear of childlessness or her fears of motherhood.

CRANE
1. If you dream of a building crane you are very often being told of the need to raise your level of awareness in some matters. You may be missing very important details of circumstances.
2. If you are the operator of the crane in your dream, it symbolises the sense of gaining control or status within a situation in which you can build to your advantage.

CROOKED
1. To dream of something crooked is a little embarrassing in the sense that you may have some insincerity in your dealings with others.
2. If somebody presents you with anything which you find crooked is a warning that you have to exercise your responsibility to maintain truth and honesty.
3. To dream of a crooked line or having drawn one is an indication that you have to be extremely cautious of being persuaded into fraudulent activities.

CROSS
(See Religion)

CROSSING
1. To dream of crossing a road signifies the need to recognise the possibility of danger, fear or uncertainty in your environment.
2. If you crossed the road with some difficulties or had to avoid obstacles, indicates that perhaps you may be measuring yourself against something that is non-realistic.
3. To cross several roads signifies that you have to watch out in case you may encounter something you cannot control, and which may control you.
4. To be crossing a field in your dream signifies a false sense of security, or you may need to bring your feelings out into the open.
5. Crossing a river or chasm often depicts death, not necessarily a physical death but a possible spiritual change.

CROSSROADS

1. Dreaming of crossroads indicates that you are going to have to make choices often to do with career or life changes.
2. To dream of being at a crossroad indicates the need to be aware of where you come from, in order to make intelligent decisions.
3. Often to turn left at crossroads can indicate taking the wrong decision in your responsibilities or romance, though it can indicate the more intuitive path.
4. To turn right can obviously mean taking the correct path, but can also mean making logical decisions.
5. A crossroad is generally a magical but dangerous place, since it provides you with the option to go in any direction which may or may not seem appropriate.

CROW

(see Birds)

CROWD

1. Dreaming of being in a crowd could be indicative of your wish to camouflage your feelings from others, to get out of sight or even to hide your opinions.
2. If you dream of not being part of a crowd signifies your desire to retain your anonymity while creating a façade for yourself and also the desire to frequent like-minded people for more knowledge.
3. To dream of a crowd in spiritual terms, i.e. a congregation suggests popular belief and you have to be cautious in case someone hurts your religious beliefs.

CROWN

1. To dream of a crown is to acknowledge one's own success, and to recognise that you have opportunities that will expand your knowledge and awareness. You may be about to receive an honour or reward of some sort.
2. The crown can represent victory, and dedication, particularly to duty. You may have striven for something and your greatest victory has been against your own inertia.
3. A crown signifies victory over death and attainment.

CRUCIBLE

1. The crucible in a dream links in with receptivity, intuition and the creative side of the dreamer. As a container which is capable of withstanding great heat it signifies the aspect of you which can contain

change and make it happen.

2. To own one crucible in your dream signifies great power, which when released, enables you to take responsibility for others as well as yourself.
3. To dream of a damaged or abandoned crucible indicates manifestation of spiritual or psychic energy which can be used as a source of inspiration for what you consider to be most valuable at the moment.

CRUCIFIX
See religion

CRUTCH
1. To dream of crutches suggests that you are experiencing the need for support, although it may also be that you need to support others as well. You may have to analyse carefully if you need support regarding something and make a careful approach.
2. If you dream of helping somebody else with his/her crutches signifies that you may disapprove of other people's shortcomings or weakness.
3. To own crutches in a dream, even if you are not using them is a warning not to be dependent on undesirable habits such as smoking and alcohol.

CRYSTAL
See Jewels

CUBE
See shapes

CUCKOO
See Birds

CUL-DE-SAC
1. To dream of being trapped in a cul-de-sac symbolises futile action. It is better to put off any plans you might have at the moment.
2. If you dream of going out of a cul-de-sac it symbolises the freedom from a circumstance which may be preventing a forward movement, and it may be necessary to retrace one's steps in order to succeed.
3. If you dream of the need to go in a cul-de-sac, for whatever reason, is a warning that you may be stuck in old patterns of behaviour, and may be being threatened by past mistakes.

CUP

1. The cup has much of the symbolism of the chalice, indicating a receptive state which accepts intuitive information. An offering is being made which the dreamer would do well to identify.
2. To be drinking from a cup in your dream signifies a willingness on your part to give assistance to somebody unknown to you.
3. A broken cup signifies that you will be refused a request.

CUPBOARD

1. To dream of a cupboard signifies abundance.
2. If the cupboard is damaged it signifies that you have to make special efforts to overcome a social setback.
3. If the cupboard is empty and you had the impression that it contained stocks, signifies the need for additional information before proceeding with official matters.

CYMBALS

1. Cymbals are connected with rhythm and sound, so for them to appear in a dream is an indication of the need for and return to a basic vibration. Often there is a connection with sex and sexuality since with the drum and tambourine they are used to induce an ecstatic state.
2. To be playing the cymbals yourself denotes an inclination to reconciling passion and desire.
3. To be following music with includes cymbals as one of the musical instruments indicates that you should ensure completeness in any task before finalising.

D

DAGGER

1. When a dagger appears in a dream, the meaning can either be aggressive or defensive. If you are using the dagger to attack someone then you may have to be alert in case you make hasty decisions which may cost you dearly.
2. If you dream of being stabbed indicates that you are vulnerable in some ways. It is strongly advisable for you to assess either your security or your facilities.
3. To dream of being penetrated by any sharp instrument is usually to do with one's masculine side and often refers to one's sexuality.
4. If you dream of the dagger, if turned on oneself indicates that you have to make a sacrifice of some sort in order to achieve your ambitions.

DAISY

1. Because of its connection with childhood, to dream of daisies usually represents innocence and purity.
2. To dream of planting and taking care of daisies signifies jealousy from others.

DAM

1. To dream of a dam may signify the inclination for you to conceal your own emotions and drive, or conversely you could be trying to stop somebody else's emotional outburst from happening.
2. To be building a dam in your dreams indicates you are likely to be putting up defenses against physical or emotional setbacks.
3. If the dam bursts, you may feel you have no control over emotional situations around you. This is only your feeling. Actually you can manage it with perseverance.
4. To dream of an overflowing dam indicates difficulties or frustrations ahead.
5. To dream of an empty dam signifies a serious lack and your subconscious mind has no option but to portray this image to you.

DANCE

1. To be dancing in a dream portrays happiness, feeling at ease in your surroundings and possibly getting closer or more intimate with a partner.
2. To dream of being in the audience at a dance signifies a reinforcement

of freedom of movement, strength and emotion.
3. If you dream of dancing for commercial purposes, signifies that you will have to face a transformation at some stages of your life or career very soon.

DANGER

1 When you find yourself in dangerous circumstances in dreams, you are often reflecting the anxieties and dilemmas of everyday life. You may be conscious that your activities may be harmful to you if you carry on in the same way.

2 Dreams can often point to a danger in symbolic form, such as conflict, fire or flood. You may need to have pitfalls represented in such a way in order to recognise them on a conscious level.

3 Dreaming of oneself in a dangerous or precarious position can also indicate a warning of financial insecurity.

DARK

1. To dream of being in the dark represents a state of confusion and you have to be cautious not to face unknown and difficult situations.

2. To dream of being able to see in the dark signifies that you will learn something which may be a secret which involves yourself.

3. If you dream of being disorientated in the dark denotes your inclination to depression. You may have to avoid the bad habit of giving up to something without even trying.

DATE (On Calendar)

1. If a particular date is highlighted in a dream, you are being reminded of the symbolism of the numbers contained in the date. These could be useful numbers.

2. Very often the psyche gives you information in dreams which is precognitive and it is possible to be alerted to particularly important events in dream form.

3. A certain date or day could point to a forthcoming, or maybe a past spiritual event that the dreamer has subconsciously retained.

DATE (FRUIT)

1. Because dates are an exotic fruit, when you dream of dates you are becoming conscious of the need for the rare or exotic in your life.

2. To be eating the dates signifies the need to be cared for and looked after in a way that is different from normal. You may be feeling insecure at the moment.

94

3. Fruit, and particularly the date, is often associated with fertility and fertility rites. In Roman times, dates, because of there luscious taste and spiritual connections, were often used as an aphrodisiac during prenuptial activities.

DAWN

1. To dream of dawn or a new day represents a new beginning or a new awareness in circumstances around you.
2. If you dream of walking out at dawn signifies the need for you to look for different ways of dealing with old situations. Refrain from adopting the primitive ways.
3. Also, to be involved in any event at dawn in your dream signifies the awareness of the passage of time, and perhaps the need to take action on pending issues is a necessity at the moment.
4. To dream of a new dawn signifies a great sense of hope. As the new dawn fades that sense of hope grows stronger.

DAY

1. To dream of a day passing, or register that time has passed, you are alerting yourself to the fact that action needs to be taken first before the second thing can happen.
2. Time has no real meaning in dreams, so to note that time is measurable suggests that you are actually harbouring worries about your life.
3. To dream of both day and night indicates changes that will inevitably take place.

DEAD

1. Dead people you have known appearing in dreams usually refer back to strong emotions you have had about those people, whether they are negative or positive. For instance there may be unresolved anger or guilt you still hold, and the only way you can deal with it is within a dream sequence.
2. Memories can remain buried for years, and often when people who have died appear in dreams you are being reminded of different times, places or relationships which will help you to deal with present situations.
3. To dream of being dead yourself signifies a restriction for you to voice your own feelings of frustration. You may have to let them out somehow.

DEATH

1. To dream of death indicates the possibility of a birth or a change in circumstances in one's own life or that of people around you.
2. If you fear death represents calamity, in the sense that nothing would ever be the same again.
3. To witness death in any way signifies a new beginning if you have enough courage and determination.
4. On an intellectual level you are becoming conscious of potentials you may have missed and because of this you are no longer able to make use of them. To seek new opportunities is the best approach at present.

DEBATE

1. To dream of being involved in a debate signifies the need for you to straighten things out in your present life.
2. To witness a debate in process signifies your hidden bad feelings about a new proposal from someone you do not trust.
3. To dream of being the subject of any sort of debate indicates that you should refrain involvement in situations which have legal implications.

DEBT

1. To dream of debt signifies a need to accommodate certain situations in order to bring it under your control.
2. To dream of being in debt denotes your tendency to be casual in whatever things you handle.
3. To dream of debt owed to you signifies that you should oversee that others comply to certain things before you can be fully assured of your end result.

DEEP

1. When you dream of something deep you are usually considering past family influences of which you may not be consciously mindful.
2. To dream of being deep into a physical object or environment suggests that you may be trying to understand something totally new.
3. If you dream of reaching deep into a receptacle for something, signifies that there are information available to you which you can only understand through being able to appreciate your own emotions.

DEMOLITION

1. To dream of demolition highlights the coming of major changes in the dreamer's life.
2. If you are the one carrying out the demolition signifies the need to be

in control of a certain situation under your responsibility.
3. If someone else is carrying out the demolition denotes the possibility of being powerless in handling any change within your responsibility.
4. To dream of being against the demolition of any structure signifies a sense of urgency on your part to either establish or restore order to a particular situation.

DEMON
1. To dream of a demon indicates a general sense of underlying fear in your psyche.
2. If you dream of being possessed by, and being terrified of the demon portends weaknesses in your career.
3. To dream of being the demon yourself signifies an inclination for you to be tolerant of undesirable practices you know should not be tolerated.

DEMOTION
1. To dream of a demotion, which involves somebody else, suggests the need to provide your support to someone in need.
2. If you dream of a letter of demotion or being demoted indicates an imminent change is about to take place in your life.

DENIAL
1. To dream of a denial can suggest that you are about to learn something new about somebody you have known for a long time.
2. If you dream of denying either an allegation or any other statement signifies a need for you to be alert against either mental or physical setbacks such as fatigue or sickness.
3. To dream of others denying your statement or allegation suggests that you may be persuaded into sharing something against your will.

DEPART
1. To be departing from a known location such as home indicates a breaking away from old or habitual patterns of behaviour. You may need to give yourself the freedom to be independent.
2. To dream of seeing others depart familiar places signifies a strong desire to get away from responsibility or difficulties, but you must be careful how you handle it.
3. If you dream of departing an unknown place portends rejection.

DESCEND

1. When you dream of a descent, such as the stairs or down a slope suggests that you are searching for an answer to a particular problem and need to be conscious of past trauma or something you have left behind.
2. If you are descending from anything with fear, indicates a loss of status, and yet you are aware of the positive aspects of such loss.
3. To dream of going down into the underworld, portrays your desire for the quest for mystic wisdom, rebirth and immortality.

DESERT

1. To dream of being alone in a desert signifies a lack of emotional satisfaction, loneliness or perhaps isolation.
2. Dreaming of being in a desert with someone else may show that particular relationship is sterile, or going nowhere.
3. If you dream of having to cross a desert to get to your destination suggests that you may need to consider a course of action very carefully if you are to "survive" in your present circumstance.

DESK

1. If the desk you are dreaming about is an old one, such as your old school desk or an antique one you should perhaps have to revert to certain events of the past in order to handle an existing situation.
2. If it is a work or office desk you may need to consider the way in which you are carrying out your everyday life.
3. To dream of being at someone else's desk could indicate a lack of confidence in your own abilities.
4. Daily ritual and discipline can be relevant spiritual practices in your everyday life.

DESPATCH

1. To dream of despatches signifies a surprise at home.
2. To dream of despatching letters or parcels suggest your desire to move into new ventures.
3. If you receive despatches in your dream indicates your participation in a pleasant gathering.

DESTINATION

1. It is fairly common to dream of trying to get to a particular destination, and this would normally indicate your existing conscious ambition and desire to succeed.

2. If the destination is not known to you, you may be moving into unknown territory, or be attempting something new and different.
3. Destinations such as exotic and faraway places could signify your need for stimulation, or hopes you may have for the future.
4. A Spiritual goal or aspiration is signified in dreams by knowing what your destination is.

DESTROY

1. To dream of destroying something which belongs to you signifies luck if it is obsolete. If it is still usable it signifies bad luck.
2. If somebody else is destroying your property in your dream signifies a quarrel.
3. To dream of destroying other peoples' property signifies double-crossing.

DEVIL
See Demon

DEW

1. Dew or gentle rain falling in a dream can represent a sense of newness and refreshment you have perhaps not been able to obtain, except from an external source.
2. You may need to accept that gentle emotion can clean you of whatever is troubling you.
3. Spiritual refreshment; benediction and blessing are all symbols connected to dew.

DICE

1. To be playing with dice in a dream emphasises the fact that you are playing with fate or taking chances in life which you really ought to be considering more carefully.
2. If someone else is rolling the dice, you are leaving your fate in the hands of other people and must therefore run your life according to their rules.
3. A dice, through the play on words, is a way of taking chances which in the spiritual sense, may be irrevocable.

DIG

1. To dream of digging up an object or a hole signifies your prospect of beginning the process of learning about new things which will play a vital role in your career.
2. If someone else is digging up something indicates that you may have valuable knowledge which need to be put to use.

DINOSAUR

1. When you dream of monsters or prehistoric animals such as dinosaurs indicates power.
2. To dream of being frightened by the dinosaur signifies that something can be achieved even if it seems impossible at the moment.
3. If you dream of dinosaurs in a zoo or a park denotes the uncovering of knowledge regarding a past issue.

DIRTY

1. You will dream of being dirty when you are not operating within your own principles or when someone else's action has put you in a situation which you find compromises you.
2. To be dirty in a dream may indicate that you are not at ease with your own bodily functions.
3. If someone you know has made you dirty it is an indication not to trust that person.
4. Evil or negative impulses are often shown in dreams as things or people being dirty.

DISK

1. A disk in a dream could suggest that you are about to access a great deal of valuable knowledge.
2. To dream of a musical disk could indicate that in waking life, you need to be aware of your need for relaxation. You may have to take a break.
3. To personally own a disk in a dream is significant of perfection and the renewal of life.
4. To dream of trading in disks signifies divinity and power.

DIVING

1. To dream of diving can represent the need for freedom within your life although you may associate freedom with taking risks.
2. You need to be extremely focused and attentive to dive successfully and must bring these qualities into play in a situation you are in.
3. Diving suggests the taking of spiritual risk.

DIVORCE

1. Dreaming of divorce may actually refer to your feelings about that person in the dream, and perhaps your need to be free of responsibilities.
2. It may also indicate the necessity to clarify your relationship between the various facets of your personality.
3. To dream of being divorced means that you are becoming conscious

100

of the need to express your emotion if you are to maintain your own integrity.
4. If you are obliged to grant a divorce in your dream signifies that you are moving into a new way of life, perhaps for the worse.
5. To dream of filing for a divorce would suggest a potential difficulty in understanding a loss of integration in your personality

DOCTOR

1. When you dream of a doctor, you are aware that you need to give way to a higher authority in health matters.
2. It will depend what sort of doctor appears in your dream as to the correct interpretation. A surgeon would suggest the need to eliminate something out of your life. This means that you will have to assess undesirable habits and eradicate them.
3. A physician would indicate that careful consideration should be given to your general state.
4. A psychiatrist signifies the need to look at your mental health or your mental enthusiasm.
5. The personality of a doctor in dreams suggests the appearance of the healing within.

DOG

1. Dreaming of a dog depends on whether it is one known to you, when it then may represent happy memories.
2. If unknown it may signify the qualities of loyalty and unconditional love.
3. To dream of a group of wild dogs portrays emotions and feelings of which you are afraid.
4. To dream of being chased by an enraged dog signifies the need for assistance in settling emotional issues.

DOLL

1. To dream of a doll signifies some undeveloped part of your personality.
2. To be playing with a doll in your dream signifies the need to recall some childhood memories in order to maximise your creative ability to a success.
3. To have lost, or to be searching for a doll in your dream may signify the need to be protected spiritually.

DOLPHIN

1. Dolphins are perceived by sailors as saviours and guides, as having special knowledge and awareness, and this is the image which surfaces in dreams.
2. To be in the company of friendly dolphins may signify that more attention may be needed regarding safety aspects at home.
3. Dreaming of swimming with friendly dolphins suggest putting yourself in touch with, and appreciating, your own basic nature.
4. In general the dolphin stands for spiritual sensitivity and safety.

DOOR

1. A door in a dream signifies a movement between two states of being. It can represent entry into a new phase of life, such as puberty or middle age.
2. Opening the door in your dream indicates opportunities available to you about which you must make deliberate decisions.
3. If the door in the dream is shut or difficult to open, indicates that you are creating obstacles for yourself.
4. If open it signifies you can have the confidence to move forward.

DOVE
See Birds

DRAGON

1. To dream of dragons signifies that you are entertaining chaotic belief. It will greatly help your progress if you could come to terms with images free from hatred.
2. To dream of being frightened by a dragon denotes that you may face a dangerous conflict in order to overcome certain disagreements regarding your resources.
3. If you dream of conquering a dragon means that you have a strong desire for safeguarding your power and authority.

DRAGONFLY

1. To dream of a dragonfly is to appreciate the need for freedom, but equally to recognise that freedom can be short-lived.
2. If the dragonfly is trapped in any sort of objects or obstacles, signifies that you may be pursuing an objective, but without any real focus as to what you actually want out of life. Your reactions are instinctive rather than logical.

102

3. Though the dragonfly's physical existence is short, it symbolises immortality and regeneration.

DRAFT
1. To feel a draft in a dream indicates the need to be watchful for an external force, which may come your way, which could be your only opportunity to capitalise on a situation you are in.
2. To attempt to create a draft in your dream is a warning to try not to be too far-fetched in your goal.
3. To dream of a cold draft indicates receipt of communications from a hidden channel.

DRAINAGE
1. To dream of an empty drainage indicates that you have outstanding tasks which are not being attended to.
2. If the draining is in the process of discharging, it signifies success in solving a complicated matter.
3. To dream of a blocked drainage is a warning to be cautious of what you say in the presence of people of authority.
4. To be cleaning a drainage in a dream is a sign that you may have to do a lot of persuading before you eventually get others to conform with a good approach you may have to accomplish something.

DRINK
1. In general, drinking in a dream portends good luck so much so that you are drinking pleasant drinks. For example drinking fresh, clear water or fruit juice would indicate your sense of purity or cleanliness not only on a physical plane but also on a mental plane where you will have to ability to make good and justified judgements.
2. To dream of drinking, or being forced to drink some unpleasant dreams symbolises limitations to something important to you.
3. To dream of spilled drinks represents legal proceedings.

DRIVE
1. To dream of driving will depend on the circumstances of the drive. In general to be driving your own car will signify satisfaction on a completed task.
2. To be driving a vehicle which does not belong to you will signify setbacks in trying to establish a consistent process for accomplishment.
3. To be driving on an unfamiliar stretch is a warning that you have to be careful against malicious elements.

DROWN

1. When you are drowning in a dream, this usually indicates you are in danger of being overwhelmed by emotions you cannot handle.
2. Drowning may also indicate a perceived inability to handle a stressful situation around you at the time of the dream.
3. To dream of a search for a drowned person signifies that you have allowed yourself to be put in a situation over which you have no control. You may be struggling, with no chance of being able to escape from a difficulty you are in.

DRUGS *(medical)*

1. When drugs appear in a dream, whether self-administered or not, this suggests that you may need external help to enable you to change your inner perceptions.
2. To be taking drugs suggests you feel you have relinquished control of a situation in your waking life and are having to rely on external stimuli.
3. To have an adverse drug reaction could mean that you fear madness.
4. To be given drugs against your will indicates that you are being forced to accept an unpalatable truth.
5. To be given drugs by a qualified person signifies that you have accepted someone else's greater knowledge.
6. To be selling drugs illegally indicates that you are prepared to take unnecessary risks.

DRUM

1. To hear a drum in your dream indicates that you need to be more in touch with your natural rhythms and basic urges to make progress.
2. To be playing a drum means taking responsibility for the actions and decisions you are presently taking regarding the present course of your life.
3. You may be seeking a more natural form of expression than the normal, everyday methods you use.

DRUNK

1. To be drunk in a dream means that you may have the tendency of abandoning certain responsibilities which may prove costly to you in the future.
2. To make someone else drunk is to be forcing your irresponsibility onto someone else.
3. To be in the company of drunken people in your dream indicates a need to be watchful from being too submissive.

DUCK

1. To dream of feeding ducks may signify the importance of some kind of therapeutic or calming activity.
2. To be eating duck suggests a treat or celebration is forthcoming.
3. You may need to allow the current of life to let you move rather than taking action yourself.
4. To dream of rearing ducks denotes your elements of superficiality.

DWARF

1. In a dream a dwarf denotes a part of you which needs to be rid of painful childhood trauma. You may have to avoid deep-rooted resentments.
2. To dream of being a dwarf signifies an inclination for you to conceal certain information maliciously due to awareness that it is vital to others.
3. To dream of being in the company of dwarfs signifies that you lack authoritative elements, which are crucial for your survival.

E

EAGLE
1. An eagle appearing in a dream signifies inspiration and strength.
2. To dream of feeding the eagle signifies you have the ability to use your intellect in order to succeed. You may need to become objective and to take a wider viewpoint than you have done previously.
3. The eagle also represents a form of Spiritual victory.

EARTH
1. To dream of planet earth signifies your search for some kind of an organised living pattern or social order.
2. To dream of being trapped by a pile of earth shows that you need to be more aware of, and understand, your unconscious drives and habits. You may be indulging in malpractices which are having repercussions.
3. If you dream of working with earth for the accomplishment of other products such as pottery signifies a prolonged residual benefit.

EARTHQUAKE
1. Dreaming of an earthquake alerts you to an inner insecurity that you must deal with before it overwhelms you.
2. There is great inner change and growth taking place which could cause upheaval.
3. To dream of surviving an earthquake signifies that old opinions, attitudes and relationships may be breaking up and causing concern.

EASTER EGG
1. To dream of Easter eggs may alert you to the passage of time since the mind will often produce symbols of times and seasons rather than actual dates.
2. Dreaming of eating an Easter egg indicates there is a great deal of potential available to you on a mental level that needs releasing.
3. To be giving Easter eggs away as presents signify the recovery of something important to you.

EATING
1. To be eating in a dream shows that one is attempting to satisfy ones needs. It is an indication that you have to stick to your ideals to achieve.

2. To dream of lack of appetite indicates an avoidance of growth and change. You may be in a conflict and are attempting to isolate yourself from others. This is not the right course for self-fulfilment.
3. To dream of being eaten in a dream signifies you are aware of being attacked by your own, or possibly other people's motions and you need to safeguard yourself.

ECLIPSE

1. Dreaming of an eclipse signifies your fears and doubts about your own success.
2. If you dream of having difficulties to see an eclipse signifies that others around you seem to be more important or able than you are, and as a result, do not allow you to show your full potential.
3. To dream of seeing the darker side of the eclipse signifies that you are about to go through a period of difficulty.

EDUCATION

1. To dream of a place of education, such as a school or college indicates that you should be considering your own need to safeguard discipline or disciplined action.
2. To dream of attending an educational academy denotes that you are perhaps inadequately prepared for a task you are to perform, and need more knowledge.
3. To dream of being a lecturer at an Educational Institution means that you have to be better prepared to handle a particular situation.

EGG

1. To dream of eggs signifies unrealised potential and of possibilities yet to come.
2. To dream of cooking or boiling eggs indicates that you have not made full use of your natural abilities.
3. To be eating an egg shows the need to take in certain aspects of newness before you can fully explore a different way of life.
4. To dream of cracked or broken eggs signify that you may have to withdraw and contemplate before you can undertake a new learning experience.

ELECTRICITY

1. To dream of electrical connections is to be aware of the your capability and power to accomplish things.

2. If you dream of switches signifies that you are unaware that you possess an ability to control.
3. If, in a dream you receive an electric shock, it is a warning that you are vulnerable to physical mishaps which could be averted by scaling down on daily activities which involve certain risks such as travelling on the motorway or certain tough sporting events such as rugby.

ELOPE

1. Dreaming of eloping, particularly with someone you know, is trying to escape from a situation that could ultimately be painful. You must maintain a balance between the need for emotional and material security.
2. In a dream, planning an elopement is creating circumstances where others do not understand the motives behind your actions. You are aware of your own need for some sort of integration within your personality but cannot do this without people misunderstanding.
3. Elopement can also portray your bravery for taking risks.

EMERALD
See Jewels

EMIGRANT

1. To dream of emigrants portrays your inner desire for radical changes to your life patterns.
2. If you dream of emigrating to other areas or countries indicates the possibility of having to put up with a new situation either at home or work.

EMOTIONS

1. Within the framework of a dream, your emotions can be very different to those you have in everyday life. They may be more extreme, for instance, almost as though you have given yourself freedom of expression, or you may be able to notice that there are strange swings of mood.
2. Occasionally in order to understand a dream it is easier to ignore the symbols and simply work with the moods, feelings and emotions that have surfaced. Doing this will often give you a clearer interpretation of what is going on inside you, rather than confusing yourself by trying to interpret the symbols.
3. Your emotional requirement, particularly responsiveness, to something

which is a more subtle energy, permit you to begin the process of development.

EMPLOYMENT

1. To dream of employment can suggest that you have important unrealised ambitions.
2. To dream of being in a new employment suggests that you should assess your own worth. It could be that you are worth, and are capable of much more than you have ever thought.
3. To dream of being an employer can suggest that you need to focus your attention on work that creates satisfaction, and gives you the lifestyle that you want.
4. Spiritual employment suggests using your talents and gifts effectively for the greater good.

EMPTINESS

1. To experience emptiness in a dream indicates there is a lack of pleasure and enthusiasm in certain ways of your life.
2. If you dream of handling empty containers indicates that you could be suffering from a sense of isolation, or perhaps of not having anything to hold on to. You may have had expectations which cannot be realised.
3. To dream of frequenting isolated places, or empty buildings may indicate that you may need new living patterns in order to come to terms with what is occurring in your life.

ENCLOSURE

1. In dreams, the defence mechanisms you put in place to prevent yourself from deeply feeling the impact of such things as relationships, love, anxiety or pain can often manifest as an enclosed space. Restraints and constraints can appear as actual walls and barriers.
2. To dream of being in an enclosed area can suggest your fear to approach someone in authority to demand a request which is justified for you.
3. To dream of constructing an enclosure may signify your need to re-evaluate certain aspects of your safety and that of your loved ones.

ENCROACH

1. To dream of encroachment generally signifies legal trouble ahead.
2. If you have encroached onto other people's property in your dream signifies that you may have to be cautious not to make agreements or accept things which you do not fully understand.
3. To dream of having somebody else encroached onto your property

suggests that you may have to be watchful of hypocritical acquaintances.

END

1. To dream of reaching an end or an ending to something signifies the accomplishment of a goal, or a point at which things must inevitably change.
2. If you dream of ending a piece of work or a session indicates that you need to decide what you can leave behind, and what must be taken forward. You must decide what you value most.
3. If you have reached the end of a road or stretch in your dream is indicative that a situation which may have given you problems is coming to a successful conclusion.
4. To dream of attending a Sunday service when it is just approaching an end signifies that you may shoulder the troubles of a close friend.

ENEMY

1. To dream of somebody you consider to be your enemy signifies an unconscious desire for you to make peace if the person is willing to be friendly.
2. If you dream to be at loggerheads with a person you consider your enemy signifies that a difficult settlement may be reached regarding an unpleasant official disagreement.
3. To dream of destroying your enemies indicates a need for you to be aware of frustration or impatience.

ENGINE

1. To dream of any sort of functional engine is significant of the motivating drive or energy that you need within a situation to gain control.
2. If, in your dream you seem to concentrate on the mechanical action of the engine you may need to be looking at the different dynamic ways of dealing with various present circumstances in order to emerge victorious.
3. To be dismantling the engine could indicate a serious health problem.
4. To perceive a railway engine may be putting you in touch with your own inner power or principles. All you need to do is to put them into practice.

ENGINEERING

1. To dream of engineering is to link with your ability to construct. This is your ability to create a structure which will allow you either to move forward or will make life easier for you.

110

2. To dream of engineering works as in roadwork, is to recognise the need for some fair adjustments in certain areas of your life.
3. Engineering suggests being able to use forces which are not normally available to you through techniques and mechanical means. To dream of engineering in this way highlights your ability to take control of power which is external to you. You must be able to manipulate in order to achieve.

ENGRAVE
1. To dream of engravings signify exotic tastes which can only be fulfilled by vigorous pursuit of your ambitions.
2. To dream of your name engraved on what you consider a hard, precious surface indicates that whatever your objective, it is achievable but with hard work.
3. To dream of engraving something signifies your ability to reap a big reward by trying something out of the ordinary.

ENTERTAINMENT
1. To dream of entertainment is a good sign that your mental state is at peak performance. This is the right time to tackle the most challenging task you may have.
2. If you dream of entertaining an audience is a sign of power and mobility. You may have to travel to certain places solely to accomplish your dream goal.
3. To find yourself being entertained in a dream signifies that you may be at an exhausted point in your life and the need to take a break may be very important at the moment.

ENTRANCE
1. An entrance in a dream has the same significance as a door representing a new area of experience, or to gain a new experience itself.
2. To be going through an entrance often signifies the need for you to make changes, to create new opportunities and perhaps to explore the unknown.
3. To dream of a secret entrance will signify the need for you to develop the hidden talents you have.
4. To be forced through an entrance in your dream signifies the possibility that you may be under pressure at the moment and it is important for you to contain it without frustration, or else you may end up spoiling important things.

ENVELOPE

1. To dream of envelopes signify that you may entertain unexpected visitors.
2. If you dream of different sizes of envelopes which need sorting according to size indicates a certain level of difficulties you may encounter in an interview or of an application you made or about to make.
3. To dream of writing on envelopes means that you will be promoted in certain areas of your life or an improvement will be achieved to your satisfaction.

ESCAPE

1. When you dream of an escape, you are trying to move beyond, or to avoid, difficult feelings. You may be trying to run away from responsibility or from duty.
2. It is possible that anxiety or past trauma puts you in a position where you are unable to do anything other than try to escape from the situation itself.
3. Escape also represents your own need for spiritual freedom. It may be a good idea if you could be more enthusiastic at home.

ESCORT

1. To dream of an escort is an indication of the need to look or evaluate your security needs as circumstances have now changed.
2. If you dream of escorting somebody portends a forthcoming meeting with an important person.
3. To dream of being escorted is a sign that you may have to be discreet when making the necessary contacts over very sensitive matters.

EVAPORATION

1. To be aware of evaporated water in a dream is to recognise the transformation which can take place once your emotion is dealt with properly. It is best to adopt a calm attitude.
2. To watch other liquids evaporate means that you have to adopt a strict approach to spending.
3. To dream of having to work with evaporated materials in order to gain an end-product indicates that you may have to adopt a more "back-end" role for your achievement rather than be the "front-office" operator. You have the capacity to handle more complicated matters.

EVERGREENS

1. Dreaming of evergreen trees can represent the need for vitality and freshness, for youth and vigour and sometimes for cleansing.
2. To be in woods of evergreen trees indicates a need for peace and tranquillity.
3. Evergreens, because of their ability to survive any conditions, signify everlasting life.

EVIL

1. To experience evil in a dream is usually to be conscious of your own urges, which you have judged to be wrong.
2. Other aspects of evil, such as inappropriate action by others, may be experienced as dread and disgust.
3. To dream of witnessing others performing evil doings signify the need to review a recent decision. It could be better.

EXAMS

1. Dreaming of examinations (particularly educational ones) is usually connected with self-criticism and the need for high achievement. You may be allowing others to set your standards of morality and success for you.
2. Being examined by a doctor indicates you may have concerns over your own health.
3. To dream of examining pieces of evidence indicates the possibility of having to handle a series of disadvantages.

EXCREMENT

1. To dream of faeces or excrement signifies the possibility of a change or a process which you will have to go through in order to attain a level of satisfaction with your ambitions.
2. To dream of cleaning excrements signifies the power to strike luck in gambling.
3. To dream of leaving your excrements in inappropriate places is a warning that you have to be watchful of your temper.

EXPLOSION

1. To dream of an explosion is a warning that you may be impatient with a situation and that you should not try to attain the solution in a forceful way.
2. If you dream of orchestrating an explosion maliciously, signifies negativity in your psyche which badly needs attention before you resort

to drastic and meaningless actions.

3.   To dream of having survived an explosion signifies your ability to withstand criticisms for tough and justified decisions which you feel you have a duty to make.

4.   On the other hand, to dream of being a victim of a malicious explosion signifies a warning that you will definitely achieve whatever objective you have but you may need to be patient when faced with complicated delays.

F

FACE

1. To dream of the appearance of somebody else's face signifies the necessity to understand the personality of someone you are likely to meet regarding commercial or business activities.
2. To be looking at your own face in your dream means that you may be trying to come to terms with the way you express yourself in the ordinary, everyday world.
3. If your face is hidden in your dream indicates that you are hiding your own power, or refusing to acknowledge your own abilities.
4. To have difficulties to recognise somebody's face in your dream denotes the necessity to seek knowledge or information, which are vital to you but not available at the moment.

FAILURE

1. To dream of a personal failure in the academic field denotes a strong degree of perseverance which needs to be exercised in order to succeed.
2. To dream of the fear of failure is a normal fear and it is a type of dream which will urge you to face whatever your obstacles with bravery.
3. To dream of failing to achieve a specific physical accomplishment signifies a change is necessary in your course of action regarding a new development.

FAIR

1. To dream of being in a fairground may represent a necessity to be in the public eye to facilitate ease regarding certain responsibilities you may assume shortly.
2. To be participating in a fun procession means you can drop whatever constraints or restraints you may have on yourself.
3. If you dream of playing a role in the organisation of a fair, indicates that a well-placed person in authority may give approval to your request.

FAIRY

1. To dream of fairies signify that you have facilities to make use of external forces which you do not know are available to you in order to meet your goals.

2. If you dream of being in the company of fairies it would seem that you may be trying to accomplish unrealistic objectives. It will be wise to re-evaluate certain objectives.
3. To dream of being a fairy yourself signifies certain powers or authority which you may need to assume before you can proceed with ideas you have in mind at the moment.

FALCON

1. To dream of a falcon or any trained bird can represent energy focused on a particular project with freedom to act. Such a dream may allow you to concentrate on your aspirations, hopes and desires.
2. The power that you have to succeed must be used in a contained way. A falcon, as a trained bird, can depict this.
3. If you dream of owning a pet falcon is a sign that caution needs to be taken when voicing certain dissatisfactions without having to make accusations.

FALL

1. To dream of falling objects outline the need to be careful within a known situation. Be warned about being too complacent with sensitive issues.
2. If you dream of falling from a high building indicates a lack of certainty of who you are or where you are going. You need to make a clearer objective.
3. To dream of averting a fall signifies the need to clear an imbalance between what you consider to be your priorities at the moment.

FALL-OFF

1. To dream of a fall-off shows a lack of confidence in your own ability. You may feel threatened by a lack of security, whether real or imagined.
2. To feel of being a fall-off has come to be interpreted as surrender (particularly sexual) and with moral failure, of not being as one should.
3. You may also feel you are slipping away from a situation, essentially you are losing your place. This can be because of others negative influence.

FAME

1. Dreaming of being famous or of achieving fame within a chosen field signifies that you need to recognise and give yourself credit for your own abilities.

2. To dream of being in the company of famous people denotes that even though you may be relatively shy, but in dreams you can often achieve things of which you would not believe you are capable of.

3. If you dream of working your way towards fame signifies that you are trying to make decisions as to how to move forward within your life. You have to recognise your potential to stand out in a crowd.

4. If you dream of failing to achieve fame signifies that there is the need to accept your own integrity as it is.

FAMILY

1. To dream of a healthy and happy family signifies the feeling of security and of abundance. You should not be having any feeling of lack for the moment.

2. If you dream of being a member of a harmonious family outlines the ability for you to work through your difficulties without harming anyone else.

3. Almost all of the problems you encounter in life are reflected within the family, so in times of stress you will dream of previous problems and difficulties that the family has experienced.

4. **Confusion of family members** e.g. mother's face on father's body suggests that you may be having problems in deciding which parent is most important to you.

5. **Family members suffering from injury or trauma** or appearing to be distorted in some way may reflect the dreamer's fear for, or about, that person.

6. **A family member continually appearing in dreams or, conversely, not appearing when expected** means that the relationship with that person (or the dreamer's concept of that person) needs to be better understood.

7. **Dreaming of an incestuous relationship** may indicate that the dreamer has become obsessed in some ways with the other person.

8. **Dreamer's parents crushing the dreamer** and thus forcing rebellion. This suggests that the dreamer needs to break away from learned childhood behaviour and develop as an individual. **Dreaming of a parent's death** can also have the same significance.

9. **When a parent appears in your own environment** you will have learned to change roles within the parent/child relationship and perhaps will accept your parents as friends.

10. **parents behaving inappropriately** can indicate your need to recognise that they are only humans, and not as perfect as you had first perceived.

11. **Dreaming of rivalry with one parent:** When a child is first born, it moves through extreme self involvement to an exclusive relationship, usually with the mother. Only later does he or she become aware of the need for a different relationship with a third person. Often this relationship causes the child to question his or her own validity as a person. When this question is not resolved successfully it may persist in the dream image of conflict with a parent.

12. **Dreaming of conflict between a loved one and a member of one's family:** The dreamer has not fully differentiated between his needs and desire for each person. Learning how to love outside the family is a sign of maturity.

13. **The figure of a family member intruding in dreams** suggests that family loyalties can get in the way within the dreamer's everyday life.

14. **Rivalry between siblings in dreams** usually harks back to a feeling of insecurity and doubt, possibly as to whether you are loved enough within the family framework. Thus father can represent the masculine principle and that of authority, whereas mother represents the nurturing, protective principle.

15. **Brother:** As already stated, a brother can represent both feelings of kinship and of rivalry.

16. **In a man's dream an older brother** can represent experience and authority,

17. While a younger brother suggests vulnerability and possibly lack of maturity.

18. **In a woman's dream a younger brother** can represent a sense of rivalry, but also of vulnerability, whether her own or her brother's.

19. **An older brother** can signify her extrovert self.

20. **Daughter:** When the relationship with a daughter is highlighted in dreams, it often represents the outcome of the relationship between husband and wife.

21. **In a woman's dream,** the relationship with the daughter usually suggests a mutually supportive one, although rivalry and jealousy can arise and needs to be dealt with. Sometimes this can safely be done in dreams.

22. **In a man's dream** his daughter may represent his fears and doubts about his own ability to handle his vulnerability.

118

23. **Extended family (such as cousins, aunts, uncles, nephews & nieces):** Members of the extended family usually appear in dreams either as themselves, or as typifying various parts of yourself which are recognisable.

24. **Father:** If the relationship with father has been successful in waking life, the image of father in dreams will be a positive one. Father represents authority and the conventional forms of law and order.

25. **In a man's life** father becomes a role model, whether appropriate or not. It is often only when the individual realises that he is not being true to his own nature that dreams can point the way to a more successful life.

26. **In a woman's life,** father is the "pattern" on whom she bases all later relationships. When she appreciates that she no longer needs to use this pattern, she is often able to work out in dreams a more appropriate way to have a mature relationship.

27. **Grandparents:** Grandparents appearing in dreams can highlight your attitude toward them, but also to the traditions and beliefs handed down by them. It could be said that grandparents do not know whether they have done a good job of raising their children until their sons and daughters have children of their own.

28. **Husband/Live-in partner:** Crucial within the husband/wife relationship are the wife's feelings about her own sexuality and intimacy of body, mind and spirit. Her view of herself will have been formed by her connection with her father, and any subsequent partnering will be coloured by that attachment. If her doubts and fears about validity are not properly expressed, they will surface in dreams about the loss, or death, of her husband. They may also be projected onto other women's husbands.

29. **Mother:** A child's relationship with mother is pivotal in its development. Largely it is the first relationship which the child develops, and should be perceived by the child as a nurturing, caring one. If this does not happen, fears and doubts may arise.

30. **In a man's life** this may result in continually developing dependent relationships with older women, or denying his right to a relationship completely.

31. **In a woman's life,** her relationship with her mother will colour all other relationships. She may find herself pushed into nurturing the needy male, or in forming relationships with both men and women who do not satisfy her basic needs.

32. **Sister:** The sister in dreams usually represents the feeling side of yourself.
33. **In a man's dream if she is older,** the sister can represent the potential for persecution, but also of caring.
34. If she is **younger** then she can epitomize the more vulnerable side of him.
35. **In a woman's dream if the sister is younger,** she can represent rivalry.
36. If older she stands for capability.
37. **Son:** The son in dreams can signify the dreamer's need for self-expression and for extroversion. He can also signify parental responsibility.
38. **In a mother's dream** he may represent one's ambitions, hope and potential.
39. **In a father's dream** he can highlight unfulfilled hopes and dreams.
40. **Wife/Live-in partner:** The wife/husband relationship is based on how the man perceives himself to be. If he has previously formed a good, if not successful relationship with his mother, he will attempt to prove himself a good husband through his dreams.

FAN
1. Dreaming of a fan symbolises the awareness of one's nature and the intuitive forces. Particularly in a woman's dream a fan can represent sensuality and sexuality.
2. The fan can be used as a symbol for openness to new experience and creativity. Waving a fan is reputed to clear away evil forces.
3. If, in your dream the fan is damaged or malfunctioning, portends unsuspected illness.

FARE
1. To be paying a fare in a dream is acknowledging the price that is paid in order to succeed.
2. If you dream of collecting fares of any kind from others indicates that demands may be made on you and you have to decide on their validity.
3. A fare-paying dream often occurs when one feels that past actions have not been paid for, and that you have a need to come to terms with them.

FARM
1. To be on a farm in your dream means being in touch with the inner urges in you. There are many facets of behaviour which can be interpreted and applied to your benefit.

2. To dream of being the owner of a farm suggests your need for physical comfort and to get things done in a more orderly and consistent manner.
3. If you dream to be on an unknown farmyard signifies that you lack certain security aspects regarding confidentiality.

FASTING

1. To be fasting in a dream may be an attempt to come to terms with some emotional trauma, or to draw attention to the need for cleansing in some ways.
2. To be fasting in your dream may also signify that you have a grievance which is causing you a level of discomfort.
3. If you dream of others fasting indicates your inclination to make a move toward realising a project but you have to be wary of external distractions.

FAT

1. To dream of being fat is an alert that the dreamer may have to the defences used against certain inadequacies.
2. To dream of fat people signifies a need to be conscious of the sensuality and humorous side of yourself which you have not used before.

FATHER

See Family

FATIGUE

1. To dream of feeling fatigue may indicate that you should be looking at health matters, or else it signifies that you are not using your energies in an appropriate way.
2. If you dream of others who appear fatigued denotes that you may need to recognise your ability to drive people too hard.
3. To be assisting to fatigued persons in your dream symbolises a guilty conscience. In case you have abused other individuals, an apology may contribute to mend the rift.

FEATHER

1. To dream of feathers could denote softness and lightness, perhaps a more gentle approach to a situation to enable you gain control.
2. If you dream of playing or having any sort of entertainment using feathers signifies that you may need to look at the truth within a particular situation and not to draw conclusions beforehand. You need to be calmer in what you are doing.

3. If you dream of handling feathers as a precious item means that you have to complete an action before allowing yourself to rest.

FEET

1. If, in your dream you perceive human beings with more than two feet, signifies an unexpected forthcoming confusion.
2. To dream of a particular attention to your clean, dry feet indicates a forthcoming voyage to distant land.
3. If you dream of special attention to your feet which may either be dirty or painful means that there will be delays in acquiring something already promised to you.
4. If you dream of having no feet at all indicates that you may be the target of malicious intentions.

FENCE

1. When you dream of fences you are dreaming of social or class barriers or perhaps your own need for privacy.
2. To be outside any particular fence suggests that you may be aware of boundaries in relationships which can prevent you from achieving the proper type of connection you need.
3. To be located inside a fence denotes that you may have difficulty in expressing yourself in certain ways.
4. If you dream of coming up suddenly against a fence or a barrier across your path means that there is extra effort which is needed in order for you to overcome either existing or forthcoming difficulties.
5. If you dream of trying to destroy a fence to facilitate passage signifies that you needs a careful assessment of whatever restrictions you are facing at the moment. What you consider to be harmless may be the most restrictive element.

FERMENT

1. To dream of the process of fermentation indicates that events are occurring in the background of which you are aware but must wait to take appropriate actions.
2. To dream of ensuring a process of fermentation indicates the possibility of allowing you to transform and transmute ordinary aspects of your personality into new and wonderful characteristics.
3. To dream of fermented materials is a sign that the dreamer should welcome this symbol and be prepared to move forward.

FERRY

1. To dream of being on a ferry indicates that you are making some movement towards change. Because the ferry carries large numbers of people it may also represent a group to which you belong, needing to make changes, needing to change its way of working and take responsibility for moving as a group rather than as individuals.
2. The ferry is one of the oldest symbols that are associated with death. The old idea of being ferried across a River, the boundary between life and death, gives an image of making major change.
3. If you dream that the only way of having to reach your destination is by ferry means that the dreamer needs to be aware that he may, spiritually, be moving on from his present knowledge.

FESTIVAL

1. To dream of a festival means a basic warning from your subconscious mind alerting you to take a break from whatever you may be engaged in at the moment.
2. To dream of participating in a festival activity portends a pleasant surprise.
3. If the festival was not an impressive one signifies that you have to be careful in case someone you trust may let you down.

FIELD

1. To dream of being in a particular field of work of your choice signifies freedom from social pressure.
2. To dream of being on a playing field denotes the wider spaces in which you can operate and to be aware of what is more natural to you, and perhaps to get back to basics.
3. The dreamer should make use of what is available to him on a practical level to further himself spiritually.

FIEND

1. To dream of a fiend or devil usually means that you have got to come to terms with certain fears which are frightening you. You need to confront these fears and make it work for you rather than against you.
2. To dream of a fiend can also signify that you may be afraid of your own passions, anger and fear.
3. It is said that there is sometimes little difference between "friend" and "fiend." The dreamer may find it worthwhile to look close to home if examining some kind of evil or wrongdoing for the answers.

FIGS

1. Often because of its shape, the fig is associated with sexuality, fertility, masculinity and prosperity. To dream of eating figs may well be a recognition that some kind of celebration is necessary although equally that a situation holds more potential than at first thought.
2. To dream of fig trees usually suggest that you may be trying to attempt something new which involves knowledge which you do not yet have.
3. Harvesting figs suggests that you have a lack of sexual desire or interest. It is an alarm bell which is warning you not to be negligent towards your sex life.

FIGHT

1. If you dream that you are in a fight, it usually indicates that you are confronting your need for independence. You may also need to express your anger and frustration to gain relief.
2. If you dream of others fighting suggests that you may wish to hurt someone else, although this would be unacceptable in the waking state.
3. To dream of fighting back to something is a natural defence mechanism, so when you are feeling threatened in your everyday life you will often dream of taking that situation one step further and fighting it out.
4. If you dream of trying to settle a fight between other people signifies that you may have to be cautious not to be involved too much in personal matters of others.

FILE

1. To dream of office stationeries such as files or putting them in order suggests that you need new arrangements for accomplishing things. You have to consider abandoning the primitive ways.
2. To be filing things away would perhaps indicate that you no longer need to be aware of a particular situation, but need to retain the knowledge that an experience has given you.
3. Dreaming of an abrasive file such as a metal file would indicate that you need to be aware that you can make mistakes in being too harsh with other people.
4. Dreaming of completing a file order is symbolic that a particular situation can now be dealt with in an orderly manner.

FILL

1. To dream of filling up a receptacle signifies a need for completeness in your present undertaking.

2. If you dream of filling a receptacle which appears never to get full is a warning that you must try your best and to make the necessary adjustments to things which you find are slow-moving.
3. To dream of filling up a container which is draining at the same time means that you may be working against yourself on certain commitments. Just ensure that you do not do or say things which will be disadvantageous to you.

FILM
1. To dream of being at a film, as in the cinema, indicates you are viewing an aspect of your own past or character which needs to be acknowledged in a different way.
2. To be viewing a film in a dream symbolises the desire for the creation of a different reality from the one you presently have. This usually applies to the waking self, rather than to the sleeping self.
3. If you are making a film in a dream whether or not it is your normal occupation, you may need to question the reality you are creating, but may also be warned not to try to create too many possibilities for your objectives.

FILM STAR
1. In dreams a film star or a glamorous public figure will represent the target point of your vision. This signifies that you have identified clearly what your goals are and what remains is to work towards them.
2. If you are a young person dreaming of a film star may signify that you are not ready for the responsibility of a real relationship.
3. Famous people, pop or film stars may also serve in dreams as a projection of the type of person you would like to be. You may, for instance, in real life be shy and withdrawn, but need to be admired and loved.
4. To dream of being a film star yourself signifies a need for you to reach for perfection. You need to work through various aspects of your personality.

FIND
1. If you dream of finding something, such as a precious object, you are becoming aware of some part of yourself which is or will be of use to you. You are making a discovery or a realisation, which, depending on the rest of the dream scenario may be about you or about others.
2. The mind has an uncanny knack of drawing your attention to what needs to be done to enable you to achieve your aims. It will use hiding, searching and finding as metaphors for efforts you must make in the waking state. So to find something without having to make too much

effort would show that events will take place which will reveal what you need to know.
3. To find long-lost objects suggest that you may be close to finding something within your spiritual search which will enable you to move forward.

FINGER

1. To dream of your fingers being prominent is symbolic that work needs to be accelerated to realise an end-result successfully.
2. To dream of having bruised fingers symbolises setbacks in career prospects.
3. To dream of having fingers which are not normally yours indicates a difficulty you may encounter when trying to resolve a problem in your working environment.
4. To dream of being short by one or more fingers means that you may be the victim of malicious intents.

FIRE

1. Fire in a dream can suggest passion and desire in its more positive sense, and frustration, anger, resentment and destructiveness in its more negative sense. It will depend on whether the fire is controlled or not. To be more conscious of the flame of the fire is to be aware of the energy and strength which is created. Being aware of the heat of a fire is to be aware of someone else's strong feelings.
2. To dream of being burned is an indication of your fears of a new relationship or phase of life. You may also be aware of the fact that there are consequences for your beliefs.
3. To be extinguishing a fire in your dream signifies a new awareness of spiritual power and transformation.
4. To dream of witnessing a dying fire symbolises a loss of energy or drive to accomplish an objective. A break is crucial at the moment.

FIRE BUCKET

1. To dream of a fire bucket indicates that you may have a situation around you which is out of control. The best approach at the moment is to retain your composure.
2. If the bucket is empty it signifies that certain barriers will need to be cleared to obtain a satisfactory end-result.
3. If the bucket is full indicates the accomplishment of something with external help.

FIRE ALARM

1. To dream of a fire alarm as an object signifies the need to be more alert and attentive when handling formal issues.
2. To hear a fire alarm in your dream signifies laziness. You may need to get more active towards completion of simple slow-moving tasks.
3. If you are activating a fire alarm in your dream signifies impatience. You may be impatient with certain situations and you may also need to face these situations with calmness.

FIREWORKS

1. Largely associated to celebration, dreaming of fireworks denotes that you are hoping to be able to celebrate your own or someone else's good fortune, though there may be a secondary emotion associated with that celebration.
2. If you dream of launching fireworks symbolises a strong release of energy or emotion which can have a spectacular effect on you, or on people around you.
3. To dream of getting burned, or other similar accidents while being involved with fireworks denotes an excess of spiritual emotion which needs to be channelled properly, in order to prevent it shooting off in all directions.

FISH

1. To dream of live fish is a warning to use more of your ability to be wise without being strategic. You can often simply respond instinctively to what is going on, without needing to analyse it.
2. Dreaming of a shoal of friendly fish is a good sign of abundance.
3. To dream of an extraordinarily large fish signifies the need for you to safeguard what you consider to be valuable properties without arousing suspicions.
4. To dream of dead fish signifies a drop or declination in financial activities.

FISHERMAN

1. To dream of a fisherman represents a possibility of earning a better income or an increase in some sort of facilities.
2. To dream of being a fisherman signifies that you may be contemplating various decisions regarding your career which is not appropriate at the moment.
3. If you dream of being in the company of a well-known fisherman signifies that you may need advice regarding certain imminent decisions you are about to take regarding your present life.

FISHHOOK

1. To dream of fishhooks generally signify that you may soon be faced with an atmosphere of hypocrisy and deception.
2. If you dream of using a fishhook for purposes other than fishing signifies a loss of direction or you do not fully understand the objective of something you are trying to accomplish.
3. To dream of being trapped or caught with a fish-hook thus restricting your free movement indicates a warning that you have to make urgent changes in your personal or business budgets as this may be a signal to either bankruptcy or a loss of some kind.

FLAG

1. A flag will always signify victory over something which you will have to achieve through an element of competition.
2. To dream of a national flag will signify a degree of patriotism or possibly the need to be more loyal to either a specific person or to an important duty.
3. To dream of waving a flag in a victorious manner signifies that the time is right to make demands for requests which you thought would be difficult to obtain approval.

FLAME
See Fire

FLEAS

1. There may be people or situations in your life which are causing you difficulties, or that you feel that these people are burdens and you definitely need to free yourself from them.
2. You may be aware that you are not being treated properly and that people who should be your friend are not being fair.
3. Fleas are symbolic of the type of evil which is likely to hurt, rather than destroy, such as gossip. The dreamer should be aware that he has the ability to deal with it.

FLEECE

1. To dream of the fleece of a sheep represents security, warmth and comfort.
2. To dream of covering yourself with a fleece signifies fear that what you are about to do is impossible and you lack a certain level of self-confidence.

3. If, in your dream you are either repairing or cleaning a fleece denotes that you may be in line for a spiritual reward. In this case the message would be "keep up the good work." Your task will bring you success.

FLIES

1. Flies are considered to be an annoyance, so to dream of flies is to be aware that you have certain negative aspects of your life which need dealing with. To identify these aspects will depend entirely on whether you will be sincere to accept that you approve of certain undesirable practices.
2. To dream of a swarm of flies signifies the need for an adjustment in your behaviour which may be contributing towards disadvantages you may be facing.
3. If you dream of dead flies signify that you may have limited defences with regards to clear yourself from obstacles which you are facing, out of no fault of yours.
4. If you dream of keeping or breeding flies, signify that care should be taken to avoid contacts with persons whom you suspect are involved in fraudulent activities.

FLY

1. In general to dream of flying signifies a lack of freedom. You have to release yourself from limitations which you may have imposed on you.
2. To dream of flying with suddenly-acquired wings signifies that you have a desire to gain authority over certain things which may only be possible through gaining additional knowledge.
3. To dream of being in full flight without wings is a sign of forthcoming success.

FLOAT

1. To dream of floating in mid air signifies that you may lose control over a certain situation.
2. To dream of floating on water without the aid of other facilities denotes your inclination of being indecisive and perhaps you may need to think more carefully about your actions and involvements regarding personal matters with other people.

FLOCK

1. To dream of a flock of sheep or any other animals signifies the need for you to seek the assistance of other people in order to complete something you may be attempting at present.

2. To dream of owning a flock of animals signifies materialistic gains.

FLOG

1. To dream of being flogged indicates that you are aware that someone is driving you beyond your limits, often in an inappropriate manner.
2. Flogging yourself indicates that you may be hesitant to present yourself on a professional level regarding promotion due to limitations of certain characteristics in your personality.
3. To dream of flogging somebody else means you have to be careful that you are not attempting to restrict your will while trying to pursue your objectives.

FLOOD

1. To dream of flood will usually indicate a contact through positive energy. It may be wise to pursue outstanding goals at the moment.
2. To be caught in a flood indicates your feeling of being too much under the control of others for things you can manage.
3. If you dream of a flood destroying or damaging properties is a warning that you have to watch out against being depressed regarding petty issues.
4. To dream of being unaffected by a flood indicates your ability to be able to handle an unforeseen and unexpected difficult matter.

FLOWERS

1. To dream of flowers would generally indicate a new beginning to something.
2. If you dream of being given a bouquet would indicate that you may receive a reward for a good gesture.
3. Each individual flower has a meaning as follows:
4. **Anemone:** Your present partner is untrustworthy.
5. **Arum Lily:** An unhappy marriage or the death of a relationship.
6. **Bluebell:** Your partner will become argumentative.
7. **Buttercup:** Your business will increase.
8. **Carnation:** A passionate love affair.
9. **Clover:** Someone who is in need of finance will try to get in touch.
10. **Crocus:** A dark man around you is not to be trusted.
11. **Daffodil:** You have been unfair to a friend, look for reconciliation.
12. **Forget-me-not:** Your chosen partner cannot give you what you need.
13. **Forsythia:** You are glad to be alive.
14. **Geranium:** A recent quarrel is not as serious as you thought.
15. **Honeysuckle:** You will be upset by domestic quarrels.

16. **Iris:** Hopefully, you will receive good news.
17. **Lime/Linden:** This suggests feminine grace.
18. **Marigold:** There may be business difficulties.
19. **Mistletoe:** Be constant to your lover.
20. **Myrtle:** This gives joy, peace, tranquillity, happiness and constancy.
21. **Narcissus:** Take care not to mistake shadow for substance.
22. **Peony:** Excessive self-restraint may cause you distress.
23. **Poppy:** A message will bring great disappointment.
24. **Primrose:** You will find happiness in a new friendship.
25. **Rose:** Indicates love and perhaps a wedding, within a year.
26. **Snow-drop:** Confide in someone and do not hide your problems.
27. **Violet:** You will marry someone younger than yourself.

FOG
1. To dream of fog suggests your confusion and inability to confront, or often even to see, the real issues at stake in your life.
2. To be walking in fog is often a warning that matters you consider important can be clouded by other people's mis-judgment and it may be better to adopt a 'wait-and-see' attitude for the moment.
3. To dream of being trapped in fog symbolises a need for a review of a procedure affecting your life which you are not happy about, otherwise there will be a constant struggle.

FOLDER
1. To dream of a folder signifies your contact with someone in an office to help you handle specific matters as should be.
2. If you dream of an open folder containing nothing, signifies that you may have to face an abrupt change of situation.
3. A closed folder containing documents will signify stability and security.

FOLLOW
1. To dream of following someone or something would indicate that you are looking for leadership or are aware that you can be influenced by other people.
2. It also indicates that, particularly in a work situation, you are perhaps more comfortable in a secondary position rather than out in front.
3. If you dream of being followed, is an indication that you need to deal with past fears, doubts or memories.

FOOD

1. To dream about eating suggests that you long for something which is not yet in your possession.
2. If you dream of eating different types of foods may suggest different meanings according to the needs in your life as follows:
3. **Bread:** If you dream of bread may signify that you will be satisfied with a basic need.
4. **Cake:** This signifies sensual enjoyment.
5. **Fruits:** To dream of fruits in general will signify satisfaction.
6. **Ham:** This represents your need for preservation.
7. **Meals:** This represents a lack of social activities or participation.
8. **Meat:** You have a physical need orientated towards sex.
9. **Milk:** Milk represents strength.
10. **Onion:** This will represent some kind of investigation.
11. **Sweets:** These tend to represent sensual pleasure.
12. **Vegetables:** Vegetables represent your basic needs and material satisfaction.

FOOTPRINTS

1. To dream of footprints indicate that you may need to be more creative and to avoid the tendency to do copy work.
2. If you dream of footprints stretching in front of you, there is help available in the future, but if they are behind you then perhaps you need to look at the way you have done things in the past.
3. If you see footprints going in opposite directions you need to consider past events to help you with future events.

FOREST

1. A forest is often a deserted place. To dream of being alone in a forest is symbolic of an unpleasant hard work which you will have to handle.
2. If you dream of being lost in a forest will signify forthcoming difficulties which will not last.
3. To dream of trying to locate something or someone in an area considered to be a forest will signify a meeting with a newcomer if you can recall success in locating him/her and will signify annoyance if you fail to do so.

FORGERY

1. To dream of handling forged currency signifies a loss of material possessions.

132

2. If you dream of being involved in any form of forgery suggests that you should avoid trying to make short-cuts towards accomplishments. It may cost you dearly.

FORK

1. To dream of a three-pronged fork generally signifies that you may be subjected to evil and trickery.
2. To dream of the ordinary table fork symbolises your present difficulty to make an important decision.
3. If you dream of using any sort of fork for a purpose other than what it was meant to be, is a warning that you may commit an error which will have a long-standing consequence.

FOUNTAIN

1. To dream of a fountain signifies that you will need to be patient while going through a proper sequence which needs to be completed before your next step towards accomplishment.
2. If you dream of being in fountain water represents a level of difficulties to express your emotions. You should cultivate the ability to do it without restraints.
3. To dream of owning a model of a fountain signifies that either a relationship or an accomplishment will be long lasting.

FRAUD

1. When fraud appears in a dream, particularly if the dreamer is being defrauded, there is the potential to be too trusting of people.
2. If the dreamer is the one committing a fraud, he or she runs the risk of losing a good friend.
3. If you accept that the various figures appearing in a dream are parts of your personality, you should guard against being dishonest with yourself.

FRIEND

1. To dream of well-known friends will signify that you will receive general support for whatever you need to complete.
2. To be quarrelling with your friend or friends in a dream signifies a certain recovery.

FROG

1. To see a frog appear in your dream is a good sign that you have an ability to move forward in leaps and bounds.
2. To dream of being frightened by a frog signifies a forthcoming disappointment.

3. If you dream of killing a frog means that you may inadvertently deny yourself something which you are in real need.

FUNERAL

1. To be attending a funeral signifies a longing need for peace. It is a signal from your dream that you are at your best to accomplish this very important essence of life.
2. To dream of your own funeral indicates the possibility of giving up to something you do not really understand.
3. If you dream of either your parents' or any of your close relatives' funeral signify that you may be faced with a painful transition.

FUNNEL

1. To dream of a funnel will generally signal a warning that you may need to either show or be more accurate in whatever responsibility you have to deliver.
2. If you dream of filtering a liquid in a funnel means that you may encounter unpredicted restrictions regarding a few proposals you may have.
3. If you dream of a blocked funnel signifies that you may be a victim of blasphemous statements.

FURNITURE

1. Furnitures will usually represent comfort. But there will be different meanings depending on the nature of the furniture.
2. For example, dark and heavy material would suggest the possibility of depression, whereas brightly painted objects would indicate a happy mood.
3. To dream of old furnitures will indicate that you may need to review past considerations in order to shed light on a present unsolved situation.
4. To dream of damaged furnitures may signify unexpected bad news.

G

GALE

1. To dream of being caught in a gale is a warning that you are about to face circumstances that you feel are beyond your control.
2. If the gale is blowing against you, it is an indication that you may allow those outside circumstances to create problems for you when actually you should be concentrating more on aspects of how to get rid of this situation.
3. If the wind is blowing in the same direction as yours, this may be a warning not to be complacent towards social issues. You may be held liable for abuses.
4. To dream of witnessing the destructions caused by a gale symbolises a certain level of weakness for you to face personal challenges.

GALL

1. To dream of being galled means to connect with feelings of bitterness that you may have about something that is happening in your life. Bringing that feeling to the surface and allowing it to come through in dreams gives you the opportunity to express it and to work it through.
2. To dream of a gall bladder, or of a gall bladder operation, often represents the need to give up some activity that is not doing you any good at all.
3. If you dream of a gall, like a sore on the skin, signifies that you are assimilating the wrong information, which is causing you problems and as a result you need to get rid of bitterness, difficulty and guilt.

GALLON

1. To dream of a gallon signifies the need for you to pay attention to your own welfare and to take notice of your own needs before those of others.
2. If you dream of handling a full and heavy gallon signifies that you may be regarded as the "Saviour" by others and thus be subjected to heavy demands.
3. To dream of an empty or damaged gallon is a signal that you have to take serious considerations when administering issues concerning finances.

GAMBLE

1. To dream of gambling indicates that you may need to take risks but you also have to ensure that the risks are very well calculated.
2. To dream of losing or having lost money in gambling signifies that you may need to take care against elements of exaggeration.
3. If you dream of winning money in gambling activities signifies unawareness of your under-utilised potentials.

GAMES

1. To dream of playing a high-performance game is a sign that you are making a good job in handling present circumstances.
2. To dream of playing a low-level casual game signifies that you may need to reassess your abilities and to identify which skill you need to improve in order to do things better.
3. To dream of winning a game symbolises that you may need to be more prepared to handle responsibilities towards your own financial resources.

GANG

1. To dream of being in a gang of people with criminal objectives is a warning that you may give away sensitive and confidential information through impatience.
2. If you dream that you are the target of gang crimes signifies that you are a bit lethargic to take advantages of facilities you have, and may soon live to regret it.
3. If you dream of gangs or destructions caused as a result of vandalism is a warning that you may soon face an embarrassing situation.

GARAGE

1. For a garage to appear in your dream signifies that certain details are required in order to complete something officially important.
2. To dream of being in a car repair garage is a signal that you may be too negligent with regards to personal health. You may have to ensure that you take careful considerations towards bodily maintenance.

GARBAGE

1. To dream of garbage in indicative of whether you are able to handle certain parts of your feelings which may be low at the moment and need to be sorted in order to decide what is the best course of action you need to take regarding a present situation.

136

2. To dream of collecting garbage indicates that you have to be cautious against making wrong assumptions.
3. To dream of being a garbage worker symbolises a need to restore order in certain areas of your present life hence avoiding unpleasant consequences.
4. If you dream of being trapped in garbage signifies that you may have to be cautious of attitudes which may not be appreciated by others.

GARDEN

1. To dream of a garden may indicate a need for growth in certain areas of your life. This may be either in the field of knowledge or vocational attainment.
2. To dream of being in a nice flowery garden signifies satisfaction regarding a feat soon to be accomplished.
3. If you dream of being in a closed and unattractive garden may signify that you have to stand firm against undesirable proposals even if they come from people you respect.
4. If you dream of being in an unknown garden is a warning against leaving an uncompleted job before starting the next.

GARDENER

1. To dream of a gardener can represent a need for a certain level of wisdom before you attempt your next long-term plan.
2. To dream of being a gardener indicates that you have to approach whatever present task with confidence to ensure success.
3. Sometimes you will dream of people you know are not gardeners employed in gardening jobs. To dream of such will signify a need to change or re-establish certain procedures in order to make considerable progress.

GARLAND

1. To dream of wearing garland is symbolic that you may need to look at various ways of making you happy. Mind you, these ways are right under the tip of your nose.
2. To dream of preparing and arranging garlands for a specific event signifies a move towards being more dedicated to change a situation into a favourable one.
3. If you dream of placing a garland round the neck of an important person signifies forthcoming honour and recognition for things you have accomplished.

4. If you dream of a broken garland is a signal that someone in authority is watching your movements and behaviour without your knowledge.

GARLIC

1. To dream of garlic signifies that you may have to see that you have an active sexual relationship and that your sexual needs are fulfilled.
2. To dream of eating garlic meal symbolises the importance to be protected in whatever ways against evil doings.
3. If you dream of harvesting garlic demonstrates that you have an inner need to attain abundance which is possible through determination.

GAS

1. To dream of gas, for example a leak, may indicate that you may face difficulties in controlling your own thoughts, feelings and abilities at the moment.
2. To dream of using gas as a working tool to facilitate your job symbolises mental strength which may be necessary to talk your way in your favour at the moment.
3. To dream of a gas accident is a warning of the possibility that you may have to confront unwanted strangers.

GASOLINE

1. If you dream of refuelling a vehicle with gasoline indicates that perhaps you may have to identify a certain basic need in order to make your present life complete.
2. If you dream of mishandling or using gasoline dangerously indicates that you have to watch out against being exposed to potential problems which may arise as a result of your own negligence.
3. To dream of swimming in gasoline signifies that you possess a lot more energy than you think.

GATE

1. To dream of a gate usually signifies that you may soon go through some kinds of changes in your present life.
2. To dream of passing through a gate signifies that you may have to try something in different ways in order to achieve optimum results.
3. If you dream of trying to go through a creaky, heavy iron gate which is difficult to open indicates that a pleasurable reward is guaranteed through hard work.

138

4. If you dream of being locked out of somewhere by the use of a gate may indicate a refusal to a request you consider important to you. You may have to adjust your approach accordingly.

GENITALS
1. To see your own genitals as the principal subjects in your dream signifies an urge to fulfil your sexual needs.
2. If you dream of someone else's genitals will indicate a need for you to be prudent not to disclose confidential information.
3. If you dream of mutilating your genitals is a sign that you have to be cautious not to be the subject of abuses.

GHOST
1. To dream of ghost is very often your subconscious expression that in real life you fear things which may be either non-existent or not really serious.
2. To dream of confronting a ghost indicates that bravery will prevail when it is time to take urgent action regarding matters involving your daily life.
3. To dream of being frightened by a ghost warns you to be extra cautious not to be outclassed by others weaker than you are.

GIANT
1. To dream of a giant signifies that you are able to display exceptional strength against opponents in countless ways at present.
2. If you dream of wrestling or attempting to destroy a giant is a warning that you have to be watchful of your temper.
3. If you dream of being capable of defeating a giant signifies nurtured power and you may have to develop a strong sense of charisma to attain good leadership qualities.

GIFT
1. To dream of receiving a gift signifies something to do with your talents. You may have hidden talents. You must identify it be assessing what is your greatest need at the moment and be creative to make a move in that direction.
2. To dream of presenting a gift to somebody else is a sign that you may receive precious knowledge regarding the way to handle and manage a specific situation and be honoured as a result.

3.   If you dream of a worthless gift signifies a disappointment of either being let down by somebody, or something turning out the opposite of what you expected.

GIRDLE

1.   In a woman's dream the girdle may depict her sense of her own femininity, for instance when she feels bound or constricted by it. In a man's dream it is more likely to show his understanding of his power over his own life.
2.   To dream of wearing a girdle represents wisdom, strength and power. No doubt you are progressing in the right direction in your present life.
3.   To dream of either a defected girdle or one which does not fit, signifies an interrogation.

GIRL/ GIRLFRIEND

See People

GIVE

1.   To dream of giving away something in a dream indicates the need to give more cooperation in an environment which will give room to increase your benefits.
2.   If you dream of giving away everything you possess signifies that you may be subject to abuses. It might be better if you could assess the validity of demands made to you.
3.   If you dream of giving away objects belonging to others indicates that you may have the inclination to cheat in handling financial transactions. Watch out!!!

GLASS

1.   To dream of glasses indicate the tendency to raise the level of protection with regards to relationships with other people.
2.   If you dream of broken glasses signify the opposite. Others may be inclined to protect themselves through the means of barriers in order to build a level of defence from what they consider threats from you. Threats which may or may not be apparent.
3.   If you dream of breaking or smashing glasses signify that you may very soon be faced with what is considered to be barriers and you will possess an extreme determination to overcome it.
4.   To dream of refrigerated glasses can indicate your desire for privacy so as to be effective.

GLASSES/SPECTACLES

1. If you dream of glasses or spectacles as prime subjects indicate that you have very good ability to understand new challenges.
2. If you dream of someone wearing glasses for the first time signifies that you may be short of the level of understanding required of you, or you are not sure of what direction you need to take to accomplish an objective. You may have to seek further explanation as the best approach from here.
3. If you dream of unexpectedly wearing glasses indicates that you should adopt an open, rather than a closed attitude in your quest for solving a present problem.

GLOBE

1. To dream of a world globe such as those on the world atlas indicates non-satisfaction on an explanation you will be given.
2. If you dream of an extraordinarily over-sized globe signifies that you are about to embark on a suitable but conserved lifestyle.
3. If you dream of handling a globe signifies that you have a dream to possess power and dignity. You have adequate powers within you that will enable you to create a sustainable future.
4. To dream of a damaged globe is a warning that something in your present life in incomplete. You should act upon it to prevent an escalation.

GLOOM

1. To dream of being in the dark can indicate difficulty and confusion. You may encounter difficulties to understand things outside your field of knowledge.
2. If you dream of activities taking place in enclosed gloomy areas signify negativity around which you have to be aware of, in order to be able to repel it.
3. To dream of yourself in the dark compared to others indicates a warning of the possibility of a depression which may affect you but not them.
4. Conversely if you dream to be in the light compared to others in the darkness signifies that you may have valuable information and knowledge which will be very handy to those in need of your help at present.

GLOVE

1. To dream of seeing gloves represent your inclination to hide your abilities from people around you due to selfishness.
2. If you dream of removing your gloves signify respect and an act of sincerity.

3. To dream of boxing gloves indicate that you are trying too hard to succeed in a situation where there is aggression.
4. If you dream of possessing only one glove is a warning that you may have to make extra efforts to complete a task.

GOAD
1. If you dream of goading somebody is a warning that you have to be careful how to handle a situation so as not to create circumstances which could turn around and control you.
2. If you dream of using or handling a goad signifies that you may be trying to force people to take action to move forward but as a result you have to be aware that you remain in command while doing so.
3. If you dream of somebody goading you signifies that somebody in your present life may be deliberately trying to make things difficult for you. It requires more observation to identify who.

GOAL
1. If you dream of scoring a goal may indicate that you have set yourself physical targets and that there is an actual urge to pursue that goal.
2. To dream of others scoring a goal signifies that you have unfulfilled objectives and that the only way to achieve them is to make certain adjustments in your strategy.
3. If you dream of missing a goal signifies that you have not taken all the details in a situation into account and need, perhaps, to reassess your abilities to achieve.
4. To dream of setting your life goal is a sign that you are in touch with your own internal self-determination with regards to your ability to achieve.

GOAT
See Animals

GOBLET
1. To dream of seeing a goblet represents your good mental state and enthusiasm and the ability to be able to turn something ordinary into something attractive or precious.
2. If you dream of drinking from a goblet indicates that you are pursuing whatever means to allow yourself the freedom to enjoy life to the full.
3. To dream of a set of goblets indicate that you can pursue different options available to gain improvement and recognition in whatever your present endeavours may be.

142

GOD

1. To dream of God signifies that you will be accepting commands from somebody who is considered less ranked than you are but you accept his/her power.
2. If you dream of exchanging a conversation with God signifies the need for you to ask for things which you assume will be granted to you automatically.
3. If you dream of being a God yourself, signifies greed or a hunger to rule others.
4. If you dream that people you know have turned gods signifies that you may soon submit an official request for some sort of approval.
5. Different Gods portend different meanings to different people according to different cultures and beliefs such as **Adonis:** signifies health, beauty and self-adoration.
6. **Apollo:** signifies the Sun.
7. **Chiron:** the art of healing.
8. **Jehovah:** in the sense of a vengeful god, alerts you to the negative side of power.
9. **Mars:** as the god of war symbolises the drive you require to succeed.
10. **Mercury:** suggests communication, often of a sensitive sort.
11. **Zeus:** is the king of the gods, and signifies fathering in both its positive and negative forms.

GODDESS

1. To dream about goddesses signify that you may have to form a group in order to achieve your objective if you are a woman.
2. If you are a man, dreaming of goddesses signify that you are fearful of a certain characteristic which falls within the power of a woman you frequent.
3. As with Gods, there are different goddess figures in different cultures such as **Aphrodite:** goddess of love and beauty. She governs a woman's enjoyment of love and beauty.
4. **Artemis:** who is the goddess of the moon, personifies the independent feminine spirit whose ultimate goal is achievement.
5. **Athena:** is goddess of wisdom and strategy. She is logical and self-assured and is ruled by her mental faculties rather than her emotions.
6. **Demeter:** the maternal goddess of fertility, highlights a woman's drive to provide physical and spiritual support for her children.
7. **Hera:** the goddess of marriage, denotes the woman who has her essential goal of finding a husband and being married as paramount and any other role as secondary.

8. **Hestia:** goddess of the heart, manifests the patient woman who finds steadiness in seclusion.
9. **Persephone:** who is ultimately queen of the underworld but only through having rejected her status as Demeter's daughter, gives expression to woman's tendency towards a need to please and be needed by others.

GOGGLES

1. Goggles, which represent protection, is often believed, in dreams, to be a signal that you may be moving too slow towards accomplishment. Your attitude may be a little too easy-going.
2. If you dream of wearing goggles under inappropriate circumstances signify that someone within your inner circle is not to be trusted.
3. If you dream of one-eyed goggles represent either someone is spying on you or leaked confidential information regarding you.

GOLD

1. To dream of gold indicates that you have yet to discover marvellous characteristics you possess through demands which are placed on you.
2. If you dream of buying gold signifies that you are trying to hide something, perhaps information or knowledge that you have.
3. To dream of an excess of golden materials in your usual surroundings suggest your incorruptibility and wisdom, love, patience and care.
4. If you dream of selling gold as a living signifies the necessity to make exceptional progress in either your studies or career to considered competent.

GOLF

1. A game of golf in a dream can represent your own individual achievement. To be playing such a game indicates that you need freedom of movement and clarity of vision.
2. To dream of playing golf can often represent your need to show your prowess, to be able literally to drive as far as you can, and often is used within the context of business acumen.

GONG

1. To hear the sound of a gong in a dream is to be aware that some limitation has been reached, or conversely that some permission has been granted for further action.
2. To dream of striking the gong may represent the need for strength and the need to be able to achieve a particular level of performance in your waking life.

3. If you dream of a damaged gong, or a gong which sounds awkward represents unnecessary delays that you may be causing to others which, as a result, may affect you adversely.

GOOSE
See Birds

GOSSIP
1. To dream to be gossiping means that you may be attempting your present objective the wrong way.
2. If you dream of entertaining "gossipers" mean that you may need to be extremely careful as to whom you seek support to accomplish your task. Chances are that you may select persons who may turn out to be more a burden than a help.
3. If you dream to be aware of gossips about you is a good sign that you may be too strong to be the victim of malicious intents from others.

GOURD
1. For a gourd to appear in your dream signifies that you are on the right track to pursue your present goal. You may need additional knowledge though.
2. If you dream of an empty gourd may signify that you are being denied important secret information.
3. If you dream of either filling or handling filled gourds is a good sign that success is guaranteed for whatever you may be handling at present.

GRAIL
1. To dream of the Holy Grail signifies that happiness may be the end result of a forthcoming important social event.
2. If you dream of a congregation at a holy grail would indicate that you can expect some form of satisfaction and change to occur within your life.
3. You are searching for something which you may feel at this particular moment is unattainable, but that by putting yourself through various tests you may eventually achieve.

GRAIN
1. To dream of different types of grains such as rice, corn etc. indicate that you will soon have an abundance of what you have been looking forward to.

2. If you dream of harvesting any type of consumable grains signifies that you may have unexpected opportunities.
3. To dream of a field where grains are grown indicates that you are on the point of success, that you have tended your life sufficiently to be able to achieve growth.

GRAMMAR

1. To dream of having anything to do with grammar signifies your awareness of either your own or others' difficulties with regards to communications. To eventually solve this problem is simply to gain more knowledge even if it may take a while.
2. If you dream of either teaching or learning grammar may signify your lack of knowledge. This is a signal that you may have to make a move towards improving yourself in preparation to an un-serfaced opportunity.

GRANDPARENTS
See Family

GRAPES

1. To see grapes in a dream generally indicates that a celebration is forthcoming.
2. If you dream of buying grapes signifies that you may entertain pleasant events ahead.
3. If you dream of rotten or decayed grapes indicates that you may have to make a major sacrifice to reap the required rewards.
4. If you dream of eating grapes signifies that you may need to give something up in order to achieve what you are pursuing.

GRASS

1. If you dream of fresh grass represents either a pregnancy or you are likely to obtain new ideas which may turn out to be a boost in your present goal.
2. If you dream of either cutting or trimming grass indicates that you may have to be aware not to surrender to somebody else's idea before making a proper evaluation.
3. If you dream of dead or dried grass signifies that you may be about to embark on a challenge which may turn out to be more than you can handle.

GRASSHOPPER

1. To dream of a grasshopper often indicates freedom. You may be free either from present troubles or from an unwanted colleague or neighbour.
2. If you dream of being frightened by a grasshopper is an indication that you may have to settle anything you owe sooner rather than later.
3. If you dream of killing a grasshopper is a warning that you may have to be more attentive to the way you pursue official documents.
4. If you dream of breeding grasshoppers signifies that you will receive a letter.

GRAVE

1. To see a grave as the principal subject in your dream is a sign that you may have been entertaining feelings of loss or disappointment for a while. This is reflected on the subconscious plane. Even so it is not harmful but still it is not desirable to live with the feeling of loss.
2. If you dream of digging a grave for any reason signifies that you may not be able to put up with a certain situation which is about to surface in your life. You may have to change a few approaches to enable you cope.
3. If you dream to find yourself unexpectedly in a grave signifies material loss.

GRAVELS

1. To dream of small particles such as gravel is significant that you are steering you present life directions towards a happy accomplishment, but it will take some time.
2. If you dream of skidding on gravels signifies that you should avoid taking risks in everyday life.
3. To dream of transporting gravels for whatever purpose signifies that you have objectives which you wish to accomplish but in fact you are actually making no move towards them.

GREASE

1. To dream of grease is a warning that you may have to exercise caution in handling situations which are considered sensitive or diplomatic.
2. If you dream of cleaning or removing unwanted grease signifies that you may have created circumstances which do not give you an advantage and could be "slippery" or uncomfortable. It could be wise to avoid any circumstance which you consider there may be a "catch" in it.

3. If you dream of having difficulties to handle objects because they are greasy indicate that you should use better judgment before putting yourself at risk.

GROWTH

1. If you dream of noting a difference in growth in a plant signifies that, at last, progress will be made in any of your desired objectives.
2. To dream of growth within either the stock market or other financial sectors indicate a need for you to tackle your responsibilities with more vigour to make a real change for the better.
3. If you dream of growth from the perspective of a child rate of growth, signifies that a definite positive result will be attained within any of your vision and may be achieved only over a prolonged period of time.

GUILLOTINE

1. To dream of a guillotine signifies that you may be emotionally unstable at the moment. You may be apprehensive of a situation which may surface at any moment and for this reason it causes anxieties.
2. If you dream of using a guillotine signifies that care should be taken to avoid physical injury when handling physical materials and also you may have to take care not to engage in activities which will put your dignity into question.
3. If you dream of a malfunctioning guillotine signifies that you may encounter brief but unpleasant hiccups in your love life.

GUITAR

1. If you dream of hearing pleasant guitar music can signify the possibility of a new romance for a single person or a turn for the better for already engaged persons.
2. If you dream of playing the guitar is a good sign that you may be making an attempt to be more creative in your present quest. You should pursue your present goals with determination.
3. If you dream of either hearing unpleasant sounds, or an out-of-tune guitar signifies that extreme care should be taken to prevent a suitable situation in your present life from turning sour.

GULLS
See seagull in Birds

GUN

1. A gun in your dream may signify insecurity in your present life. If you are firing a gun in your dream may signify the possibility of facing aggression from others.
2. If you dream of being shot at, is a sign that you may have to recognise and take note of your valuable pieces of work which are going unnoticed.
3. If you dream of shooting at other people, signifies that you may be vulnerable to do things which will open the way to criticisms.

GURU

1. To dream of a guru signifies that you may be gaining wisdom to handle your present directions in your life.
2. If you dream of being a guru signifies that you have abilities to lead, but not using them fully.
3. To dream of being part of an association of gurus signifies a thirst for knowledge. This may be very beneficial to you in the sense that the more you learn about something which directly relates to the accomplishment of your present goal, the more light will be shed on the correct approach which you should adopt.

H

HAILSTONES

1. If you see hailstones in your dream may signify emotions which you may find difficulties to express. These emotions may be a result of too much exposure to external influences.
2. If you dream of being trapped in falling hailstones signifies that you may have to face a difficult situation whereby you may be humiliated.
3. If you dream of handling hailstone for fun signifies your strong character which will enable you to stand against humiliations and destructive criticisms without hurting your emotions.

HAIR

1. To see your hair prominent in your dreams indicates that you will be subject to illusionary matters or even deceit.
2. If you dream of doing your hair signifies that certain area of your life needs some tidy-up or certain apprehensions need to be put straight.
3. To dream of doing somebody else's hair is a warning that you may have to pay more attention to your personal feelings before attending to others.
4. If you dream of having a haircut signifies that you have to go through some sort of a puzzle or sorting out in order to accomplish something.

HAIRDRESSER

1. To dream of being at a hairdresser indicates that you may not be totally satisfied with certain aspects of your present life. You may have to adopt a firm attitude to sort out an outstanding issue.
2. To dream of being a hairdresser indicates that you may soon forge a valuable relationship with someone in authority.
3. To dream of someone you know, unexpectedly turned hairdresser is a warning not to trust strangers where financial transactions are concerned.

HALF

1. Sometimes you may be surprised to see half of everything in your dreams. To see almost half of anything signifies incapability for you to make decisions and also you may have an inclination to handle your everyday commitments by bits and pieces.

2. To dream of being given half of something indicates incompleteness in you, being a sort of in-between state which means that you have to make decisions. Often it is about either going forward into the future or back into the past.
3. If you dream of handling jobs which are only half completed or if you dream of giving half-completed jobs signify that you will be dissatisfied with the outcome of a situation or circumstance.
4. To dream of having only half of what you feel you should have, indicates that in real life you are giving yourself limitations. You may be either too embarrassed or apprehensive to ask or get more for you.
5. To dream of being only half way to your intended destination indicates that there is some indecision. You are not as motivated as you should or could be to continue with the task you have in hand. You have made an initial effort but greater effort is needed in order to be where you want to be.

HALL
See Building

HALTER
1. To dream of a halter signifies that you are making an unconscious mistake of doing things which will eventually work against you. You have to be more attentive of the results of things you create in order to get a clue of where to start tackling the problem.
2. To dream of using a halter against somebody else means the possibility of facing restrictions which will prevent you from performing to the best of your ability.
3. If you dream of using a halter against an animal signifies that a breakthrough will surface in a slow-moving process.
4. If others are using a halter against you signifies that you may have to take more time to make a concrete evaluation of your objectives before proceeding a further step.

HAM
See Food

HAMMER
1. To dream of a hammer signifies that you need to review certain aspects of your personality which may need certain changes in order to improve on your effectiveness.
2. If you dream of using a hammer signifies that you may have to change certain plans in order to meet a deadline.

151

3. If you dream of using a hammer for any purpose other than what it was intended to, is symbolic of either disorientation or loss of direction.
4. To dream of someone using a hammer maliciously against you with the intention to harm signifies that you are unaware that you are being the subject of complaints.

HAND
1. For your hands to be prominent in your dream is a good sign that you will reap the full benefit or advantage of something or a reward from someone.
2. If you dream of your hands incapable of normal functions indicate that you have to take special care not to be involved in any disciplinary involvement as it may result in serious consequences.
3. To dream of having hands which do not belong to you, signify that you may be at the receiving end of a vengeful action.
4. To dream of having only one hand signifies a loss of income or restricted facilities.

HANDCUFFS
1. If you dream of being handcuffed is a warning to avoid providing advice on resolving a complicated social dispute.
2. To dream of putting handcuffs on someone else signifies that you may be too possessive at the moment.

HANGING
1. To dream of witnessing someone hanging signifies that you may participate in violent actions which might be best for you to reconsider your actions at the moment.
2. To dream of being hanged signifies a warning of forthcoming disaster.
3. To dream of something hanging over you signifies that you are being threatened by some circumstances around you.

HAREM
1. For a man to dream that he is in a harem shows that he is struggling to come to terms with the complexities of the feminine nature.
2. For a woman to have the same dream shows that she understands her own flamboyant and sensual nature.

HARNESS

1. To dream of wearing a harness signifies that you are actually being restrained by your own limitations, or that you are being controlled by external circumstances.
2. To dream of being aware of wearing a very tight harness indicates that you may face delays up to several months regarding something important.
3. To dream of harnessing something implies that you possess a level of control over something or someone.
4. To dream of harnessing energy signifies talent, strength and ability.

HARP

1. To dream of a harp signifies that you are actually in harmony and you may receive the approval for something without difficulty.
2. If you dream of playing the harp signifies that something which may have been a mental disturbance will soon be over.
3. To dream of a damaged harp is a warning that you may have to take precautions to preserve your happiness.

HARVEST

1. To dream of a harvest indicates that you are about to reap the rewards of some previous duties or sacrifices you have done.
2. To dream of taking part in a harvest indicates that you are about to celebrate something you will shortly achieve.
3. To dream of others doing a harvest indicates fruitfulness and fertility.

HASH

1. If you dream of "making a hash" of things, you are making things difficult for you, and are perhaps creating a problem where there isn't one.
2. You may be making things difficult for people around you, and not really doing and planning your actions carefully in an appropriate way.
3. To dream of hash, as in marijuana, indicates that you may need the assistance of something or someone to achieve something specific.

HAT
See clothes

HAY

1. To dream of hay demonstrates your strong character which shows your ability to manage things for you and others at the same time.
2. To dream of stacking hay represents a strong and healthy bond in your romantic relationship.
3. If you dream of a shortage of hay signifies that you may have to make a huge sacrifice to avoid an unwanted encounter with someone who may belittle you.

HEARSE

1. To dream of a hearse indicates that you are probably recognising that there is a time limit, either on yourself or on a project you are connected with and you may have to "move on".
2. If you dream of being ahead of a hearse indicates that it may be better to restart something you are attempting which goes wrong rather than trying to rectify it mid-way.
3. If you dream of trailing a hearse signifies that you may be approaching the end of something unpleasant.

HEART

1. To dream of a heart as the principal object in your dream signifies good health or an improving one if it is ailing.
2. To dream of the heart of an animal signifies that you may have to make certain substitution along the lines of your objective in order to move on successfully.
3. If you dream of nursing someone with heart trouble signifies that you may need to exercise more patience if you find that things are not in your favour at present.

HEARTH

1. To dream of a hearth or fireplace is to recognise the need for physical security. You may feel insecure at the moment and the best way to handle this is to evaluate the true potential dangers in your neighbourhood.
2. To dream of constructing a hearth signifies a need for some rest. You may be a bit exhausted from your actual daily activities.
3. To dream of the absence of a hearth where you were expecting one symbolises that you may be annoyed by unwanted remarks by others.

HEAVEN
See Religion

HEDGEHOG
See Animals

HEEL
1. To dream of your heel as the principal subject of your dream signifies your ability to rise in rank and leadership.
2. If you dream of having pains or other similar problems in the heel signifies that something you are attempting is incomplete.

HELL
See Religion

HELMET
1. To dream of wearing a helmet signifies your inclination for protection and preservation. You may have an unconscious apprehension. You may have to approach it with an open mind as it may have adverse effect on your behaviour in the long term.
2. If you dream of someone else wearing a helmet is a sign that you may be being deprived of valuable information.
3. If you dream of an unworn helmet signifies a need for you to reconsider a decision.
4. To dream of a damaged helmet signifies that there is a need to make changes to improve on some plans in your present life.

HEN
See Bird

HERMAPHRODITE
1. To dream of a hermaphrodite means that you may be having uncertainties about your ability to adjust to certain roles which you may consider inappropriate, based on your sexuality.
2. To dream of being in the company of hermaphrodites signify the need to achieve a balance in either a forthcoming decision or a judgement.
3. To dream of being a hermaphrodite signifies the need to assess either your behaviour or that of a loved one. There could be over-indulgence.

HERMIT
1. To dream of a hermit signifies a kind of loneliness which may prevent you from making personal or romantic relationships.

2. If you dream of being a hermit signifies that you may have to take care not to be too dependent on others for your material ends or else this will generate many future claims against you.

HEROINE (WOMAN)

1. For a man to dream of meeting a heroine signifies that he may temporarily have to rely on either his wife or a female counterpart to handle an important issue and that he should be attentive to what they say or do.
2. For a woman to dream of a meeting with a heroine signifies a strong determination which should be balanced with more will power.
3. To dream of being a heroine, regardless of your sex indicates a moment of indecision if you are a man or a stiff challenge if you are a woman.

HEXAGRAM

1. For a hexagram to appear in your dream represents the need for you to make a union or a "bridge" between two forces or circumstances to enable you to come up with something complete.
2. If you dream of drawing hexagrams indicate that you may be faced with either confusion of ambiguity.
3. If you dream of standing at the centre of a big hexagram is an indication that you may have to brace yourself to embark on a challenging adventure.

HIGH
See Position

HILL

1. If you dream of being on top of a hill indicates that you may be aware of your own expanded vision and this signifies that you may have to move towards it even if it seems you are not quite ready yet.
2. To dream of climbing towards the hilltop indicates that you have made an effort to achieve something and are able to survey the results of what you have accomplished.
3. If you dream of climbing down a hill indicates that you have achieved certain things that you previously thought impossible, and are able to undertake further work in the light of knowledge you have attained.
4. To be accompanied on top of a hill by others often indicate that you have a common goal that a journey you possibly thought was your sole initiative is actually connected with other people.

5. To dream that you having difficulties to get to the top of the hill would indicate that you are feeling as if circumstances may be in control of you at the moment.
6. If you dream of tumbling down a hill signifies a need for clarification before you take your next decision.

HIVE

1. To dream of a hive signifies that there is harder work ahead than what you previously perceived.
2. If you dream of handling hives signify that there should be more improvement of how your resources are being used. Certainly they are not being used to the maximum at the moment.
3. If you dream of finding yourself trapped in a hive represents the need for you to engage yourself in a specific activity that is needed to get you out of a situation

HOLE

1. If you dream of a hole, this represents a forthcoming difficult or tricky situation.
2. If you dream of falling into a hole indicates that you have to address some of your urges and fears immediately.
3. To dream of walking around a hole suggests that you may need to avoid complacency to enable you get around a tricky situation.
4. To dream of a hole in the roof or any hole which allows steam or smoke to escape signifies the need for you to forge your way to either a promotion or to move to a higher dimension.
5. Generally, a round hole represents strong mental capabilities and a square hole represents your strong physical abilities.
6. To dream of getting out or being rescued from a hole signifies that people who are against you may give themselves away.

HOLIDAY

1. To be on holiday in a dream indicates a sense of relaxation and also a warning of striking a balance between not only work and rest but also between other aspects of life as well.
2. If you dream of preparations for a holiday represents the need for you to certify completeness in important commitments before giving any approvals.
3. If you dream of the end of a holiday signifies that a phase or a situation in your present life may soon be over.

HOLLOW

1. To dream of a hollow object signifies that you have feelings of emptiness, lack of purpose and inability to find a direction in your life. You have to eliminate these negative feelings and clear your vision.
2. To dream of being in a hollow passageway would indicate that you need some kind of protection from what is going on around you in your ordinary everyday life.
3. To dream of feeling your body to be hollow can signify impatience where you feel that nothing is happening, where you do not feel in control and need to take control sooner rather than later.
4. Hollowness can also indicate a lack of motivation and interest particularly on your spiritual aspects.

HOLY COMMUNION
See Religion

HOME

1. To dream of being at home, especially a cosy home signifies forthcoming peace and tranquillity.
2. To dream of being at somebody else's home signifies that you may soon be in the company of important people thus the necessity to be prepared.
3. To dream of moving in a new home is a pleasant sign that success and achievement is almost guaranteed.
4. If you dream of moving out of your home with the objective of moving in a better one signifies your ability to handle different circumstances.
5. To dream of being forced out of your home portends forthcoming difficulties.

HOMOSEXUALITY

1. To dream of having intercourse with somebody of the same sex as oneself usually indicates a conflict or anxiety about a new role either at work or at home.
2. If you dream of accompanying homosexuals signify the need for you to give not only love but also parental affection to loved ones.
3. Very often, to dream of a homosexual affair is an attempt to come to terms with conflicting views and directions which may have thorny issues.

4.   To dream of being a homosexual signifies that you may resort to insincerity at some stages for your selfish ends.

HONEY

1.   To dream of drinking honey symbolises lack of pleasure in some areas of your life. This may be attributed to an extreme-focused goal.
2.   To drink of being offered honey signifies that you may go through a joyful and totally new experience.
3.   If you dream of sharing honey with someone else signifies that you are entering a much more actively sexual or fertile time.
4.   To dream of honey as a trading commodity symbolises that you have the power to regenerate.

HOOD

1.   To dream of a figure wearing a hood represents menace. While not necessarily being evil, there may be a part of yourself which may be threatened.
2.   To dream of trying to figure out somebody under a hood signifies that you may have to be more charismatic in order to be able to function in an acceptable fashion.
3.   For a woman to be wearing a hood suggests that she is being deceitful.
4.   If a man is wearing a hood, it suggests that he is withdrawing from a situation.
5.   To dream of the hooded figure of a monk can indicate the more reflective side of you as it begins to become more evident in your everyday life.
6.   To dream of wearing a hood may signify either death or loss of contact to a close one.

HOOK

1.   To dream of a hook signifies that you generally understand that you have the ability to draw things toward you that are either good or bad. The point to note is to ensure that you have good judgements to guard against bad things.
2.   To dream of being caught by a hook signifies that you are being restricted by someone, and thus not being allowed the freedom to which you feel you have a right.
3.   To dream of hooking an object symbolises the possibility that you allow other people to take control of certain aspects of your life. Do not accept things to which you do not totally agree.

4. If you dream of searching for a hook symbolises that you have to guard against getting "hooked" into religious beliefs and practices just for the sake of it.

HORNS

1. To dream of horns signify an unconscious desire for sexual activities.
2. To dream of suddenly growing horns can signify the desire to hurt. You may have to think carefully before making impulsive moves.
3. If you dream of either polishing or decorating horns signify that a level of protectiveness is necessary around personal properties.
4. To dream of a musical or hunting horn suggests a summoning or a warning.

HORSE

See Animals

HORSESHOE

1. To dream of the horseshoe is always taken as a lucky symbol and, traditionally, if it is turned upward it represents the moon and protection from all aspects of evil. When turned downward the power is reputed to "drain out" and therefore be unlucky.
2. The horseshoe is also connected as a lucky symbol to weddings. Customarily to dream of a horseshoe may indicate that there will shortly be a wedding in your family or peer group.
3. To dream of wearing a horseshoe signifies that you may be searching for long lasting happiness.
4. If you dream of fitting a horseshoe to the hoof of a horse signifies divine protection.

HOSPITAL

1. To dream of entering a hospital as a visitor will generally represent that you may need to evaluate the effectiveness of safety aspects at either your work or home.
2. If you dream of going to a hospital as a patient signifies that your being is threatened and you may become vulnerable.
3. To dream of reluctance to enter a hospital signifies that you have to take heed not to allow things to happen by themselves and let others take control of situations to your disadvantage.
4. Dreaming of being in a hospital may signify a mental creation of a transition period between something that has not gone well, and an improved attitude where things can get better.

5. If you dream of being a recovered person in a hospital signifies that you may integrate in a pleasant environment where things can be brought into a state of balance.

HOSTILITY

1. When you experience hostility within yourself in a dream, it is the direct expression of that feeling. It is safe to express it in a dream whereas you may not dare do this in waking life.
2. If however, someone is being hostile toward you in your dream, it very often means that you need to be aware that you are not acting appropriately, that others may feel you are putting them in danger.
3. To dream of having the ability to identify what is making you feel hostile in a dream, then you can usually tackle it directly in your waking life and deal with whatever the problem is.
4. If you dream of hostility from others signify that you need to be aware that others may not necessarily agree with your spiritual belief.

HOT

1. To dream of being hot indicates warm, or perhaps passionate feelings.
2. To be conscious of the fact that your surroundings are hot indicate that you are loved and cared for.
3. If you dream of being in a hotter-than-usual environment signifies that you may be subjected to extreme emotions.
4. To dream of experiencing hot objects indicate that you are perhaps having difficulty and experiencing confusion in sorting out your present feelings.
5. Spiritual passion is a deeply held feeling. It can be experienced in a dream as heat.

HOTEL

1. Dreaming of being in a hotel can mean that you need to escape from a situation in your life for a short time.
2. On the other hand it can also mean that a situation you are in will only last for a limited amount of time.
3. To dream of being a guest in a hotel can indicate that you are unsettled and feel you can only settle down temporarily.
4. To dream of having no other options but to live in a hotel signifies a basic restlessness and impatience which need to be put under more control.

HOURGLASS

1. To dream of seeing an hourglass signifies that you may be sticking to an old or primitive way of handling things for too long and that you may have to make reluctant changes fairly soon.
2. If you dream of measuring time with an hourglass signifies that you may be under stress and you are overly aware of the running out of time. This fact can become a deadly enemy if you are allowed to be put under pressure.
3. To dream of blood in an hourglass symbolises death.
4. If you dream of water or any other liquids in an hourglass symbolises illness.

HOUSE

To dream of a house, in effect may have several meanings depending on your personality and the part of the house you are involved. The following may bear various meanings as listed below:

1. **Attic:** Dreaming of being in an attic has to do with past experiences and old memories. Interestingly, it can also highlight family patterns of behaviour and attitudes which have been handed down.
2. **Basement/cellar:** The cellar represents things you may have suppressed through an inability to handle them. A basement can also highlight the power that is available to you provided you are willing to make use of it.
3. **Bathroom:** In dreams your attitude to personal cleanliness and your most private thoughts and actions can be shown as the bathroom or toilet.
4. **Bedroom:** The bedroom portrays a place of safety where you can relax and be as sensual as you wish.
5. **Chimney**: As a passage from one state to another and a conductor of heat, in dreams the chimney can indicate how you deal with your inner emotions and warmth.
6. **Hall:** The hallway in a dream is illustrative of how you meet and relate to other people.
7. **Library:** Your minds, and how you store the information you receive, can appear as a library.

HUNGER

1. To dream of being hungry indicates that your physical, emotional or mental needs are not being sufficiently satisfied.

2. If you dream of being able to satisfy your hunger represents an acknowledgement that you have to make important self-improvement to complete a clearly-laid plan.
3. To dream of helping others who are hungry signifies that you may have to be subject to the selfish ends of others.

HUNT

1. To dream of being hunted signifies the necessity for a change of state in your everyday life.
2. If you dream of being a hunter indicates that you may have a state of consciousness which can be destructive and vicious.

HURRICANE

1. To dream of experiencing a hurricane symbolises that you are sensing the force of an element in your life which is beyond your control. You may feel that the carpet is being swept from under your feet.
2. To dream of witnessing the destruction of a hurricane is a warning that you have to be cautious of someone's passion which you may not be able to resist.
3. If you dream of being a victim as a result of a hurricane signifies that you may face unfavourable prevailing conditions.

HUSBAND
See Family

HYENA
See Animals

I

IBIS
See Birds

ICE

1. To dream of an abundance of ice forewarns that you may be enclosing yourself in a situation from which it may be difficult to free yourself.
2. If you dream of freezing cold ice represents rigidity from you due to a lack of understanding of what is going on around you and you may create circumstances where people cannot get in touch with you.
3. To dream of melting ice indicates that you may be handling things which may not last at the moment.
4. To dream of handling cool drinking ice comfortably symbolises forthcoming mental relief.

ICE CREAM

1. To dream of ice cream signifies sensual tastes. You may shortly be exposed to a pleasurable experience.
2. To dream of eating ice cream indicates that you may be accepting pleasure into your life in a way that you have not been able to do before.
3. If you dream of selling ice cream indicates that you may serve as the path to accomplish the pleasure of other people.
4. If you dream of a melting ice cream is a warning that care should be taken to preserve existing pleasures because it may be in a fragile stage.

ICICLES

1. If you dream of icicles indicate that you may be having problems within your environment which may result in difficulties.
2. To dream of melting icicles indicates that the troubles that have been around you will literally disappear within a short space of time.
3. If you dream of clearing your way through icicles indicates that you will overcome present difficulties through external circumstances.

ICON

1. To dream of an icon indicates that you may encounter setbacks through accomplishing things by using old principles.
2. To dream of worshipping an icon may signify that you have lost confidence in somebody of importance and that you may be resorting to unstable solutions.
3. To dream of somebody you know, suddenly being an icon signifies that you may receive help assistance at a time most needed.

IGLOO

1. To dream of an igloo is a warning not to judge someone or something without concrete facts. The reality may be totally different to what you perceive at the moment.
2. If you dream of being in an igloo signifies that you have the ability to withstand stiff competition or resistance from external factors.
3. If you dream of constructing an igloo means that you have to watch out not to resort to deception.

ILLNESS

1. To dream of illness signifies that you may soon face certain situations which may result in disappointment or anger.
2. To dream of being ill signifies that you may take longer than expected to overcome present difficulties.
3. To dream of prescribing medication for somebody with a specific illness portends a forthcoming argument.

IMITATION

1. To dream of being imitated signifies that you should refrain from adopting an attitude that whatever you have done is the correct thing to do and that other people should learn from your example.
2. If you dream of any imitated object signifies that you may face a position where other people are seeing you as a leader, when you yourself do not necessarily feel that it is the correct role for you.
3. To dream of imitating someone else is indicative that you have the ability to be better positioned than you actually are.
4. If you dream of imitating other people considered being in authority is considered a very good sign in your quest for accomplishment provided you are imitating their good qualities and characteristics.

IMMERSION

1. To dream of immersing an object in water shows that you have to guard against approving any suggestions put to you by other people.
2. To dream of being totally immersed in water indicates that you should make a definite move to make changes to enable you to concentrate entirely on one particular task at a time to achieve the maximum.
3. To be immersing an object into any other liquids other than water signifies that you may have to make trial and errors to resolve something.

IMMOBILITY

1. To dream of being immobilised signifies that you are unaware of plottings against you.
2. To dream of immobilised persons usually indicate that you have created circumstances around you which are now beginning to trap you. You may need to remain absolutely still until you have decided what the appropriate action needs to be, and then you can move forward in an appropriate way.
3. To dream of immobilising something signifies that efforts need to be made to overcome what is holding you down.

IMP

1. An imp appearing in a dream usually foretells disorder and difficulty. The imp often has the same significance as the Devil in its aspect of tormenting one, of creating difficulty and harm within one's life.
2. To dream of being directly annoyed by an imp signifies an aspect of loss of control over a situation.

IMPRISONMENT

1. To dream of being imprisoned usually means that you are trapped by circumstances, often those you have created through your own fear or ignorance. The way out of this is to take positive initiatives in your approaches to anything.
2. If you dream of imprisoned colleagues indicates that you may feel that other people are creating circumstances around you which will not allow you to move forward. You may need to negotiate your freedom in specific circumstances.
3. To dream of being spiritually imprisoned can suggest that you are too introverted or self-involved. You may need to "open yourself up" to new influences.

INAUGURATION

1. To dream of attending an inauguration ceremony indicates either personal growth or authority within the work situation.
2. To dream that you are being given such an honour means you can receive public acclaim for something that you have done, for your ability to make the transition from the lesser to the greater.
3. Often a ceremony is necessary to mark the fact that you have succeeded in one thing and can now move on, putting that knowledge to the test in the outside world. To be dreaming of such a ceremony indicates that you can be pleased with yourself.

INCENSE

1. To dream of incense signifies spiritual qualities. You have to be more aware of social values which will contribute to improved personality from the point of view of others.
2. If you dream of smelling burning incense signifies that you have to become aware of the need to consider how best to improve yourself to adapt in a new environment.
3. To dream of lighting up incense signifies that you have outstanding goals and, at the moment, you may be having too many options as to which direction you have to take.

INCOME

1. To dream of an increased income shows you feel you have overcame some obstacles in your direction and can accept that you have value.
2. To dream of reduced income signifies your neediness, and perhaps your attitude to poverty. You have to stop the feeling of lack immediately.
3. If you dream of receiving an additional income indicates perhaps the need to look at your contacts and facilities to either earn more. The facility may be already be within your grasp.

INDIGESTION

1. To dream of suffering from indigestion shows that there is something in your life which is not being tolerated the way you would have liked.
2. If you dream a foodstuff likely to give you indigestion signifies some sort of mental block on your own progress. Perhaps you need to do things in a different way, or perhaps smaller steps.
3. To dream of recovering from indigestion signifies that you have to guard against over-participation in tough physical activities.

167

INFECTION

1. Dreaming of having an infection suggests that there is the possibility of you having negative attitudes towards other people.
2. If you dream of having an infection on your body may indicate that you feel you are being prevented from moving forward quickly enough in waking life.
3. If you dream of an undiagnosed infection symbolises that you are facing a level of restrictions due to external but controllable circumstances.

INITIATION
See Religion

INJECTION

1. To dream of being given an injection is to be feeling that your personal barrier against sensitive information has been penetrated.
2. To dream of self-injecting indicates that your expectation may be short of your desires.
3. To dream of giving an injection suggests that you are attempting to force yourself on other people. Obviously, this may have sexual connotations.
4. To dream of reluctantly having an injection signifies scepticism. You may face an indecisive situation.

INK (Liquid ink)

1. To dream of ink signifies that you may have to go through a more complicated process than expected, to complete something.
2. If you dream of reading anything specifically written in ink indicates an improved way of communication or a new channel of communication will be established.
3. To dream of blotted ink is a warning that you have to be cautious of signing or endorsing things without proper understanding. There may be ambiguity.

INSCRIPTION

1. Any inscription in a dream is information which will need to be understood. Reading an inscription can suggest that something is understood already, whereas not being able to read an inscription suggests that more information is required in order to complete a task.

168

2. An inscription appearing on a hard surface such as a rock would suggest a gain of wisdom.
3. An inscription appearing on soft surfaces such as soil or sand would suggest the need to gain an increased level of knowledge pertaining to your particular field and must be learned quickly, or else you may face unjustified criticisms.
4. If you dream of inscribing something on any sort of surface signifies that you may have to pass on a volume of knowledge to somebody else to enable you to move a step further.

INSECTS
1. For insects to appear in dreams reflect your feeling of irritation or eavesdropping.
2. If harmful insects appear in your dream can signify your feeling of insignificance and powerlessness.
3. If you dream of killing insects suggests your ability to handle a forthcoming difficult situation.
4. To dream of being stung by a harmful insect signifies that you have to watch out against underlying threats from other people.

INTERSECTION
1. To dream of an intersection such as a junction indicates there is a choice of two ways forward. Two opposites may be coming together in your waking life, and you are able to make changes and move forward in a more focused way.
2. If you are conscious of an intersection, perhaps in a pattern which appears in a dream means that you are being offered choices, and perhaps have to differentiate between right and wrong.
3. When you meet an intersection in dreams, you are putting yourself in a position of having to make choices which may have a greater impact on others than it does for you.

INTOXICATION
1. If you dream of being intoxicated by alcohol can indicate a loss of control or unexpected change of responsibility.
2. If you dream of being intoxicated by medical drugs indicate a forthcoming change of state. It is also a warning not to overdo or exaggerate in making your point.

3. To dream of being intoxicated by other substances such as harmful gasses may indicate that you need to make urgent changes either at home or workplace to avoid a brewing confrontation.

INTRUDER
1. For an intruder to appear in your dream indicates your feeling of threats in some ways. Often in dreams the intruder is masculine, and this generally indicates a need to defend yourself.
2. If you dream of battling against an intruder is a warning to guard against sex or threats to your sexuality.
3. If you dream of being an intruder is a warning that you may be on the brink of making a decision which may have serious adverse future consequences on your life.

INVENTOR
1. To dream of an inventor specifies the need for you to pay more attention to your everyday activities because what you perceive may be different to what you may think.
2. If you dream of having invented something signifies your ability to break away from something which you are not really in favour of, but you are putting up to it for no real reason.
3. If you dream of a newly invented object signifies that you should be more open-minded to new suggestions which may come your way. It may be worth considering.

INVISIBILITY
1. If you dream becoming invisible would indicate either that you are not ready to face a thorny situation that there is something you would rather forget than to work towards a solution.
2. If you dream of being conscious of facing something or someone invisible indicates that you will shortly be faced with an important situation whereby you may have to use your correct judgement to make a correct interpretation.
3. If you dream of having the ability to be invisible signifies that you have the ability to persevere towards accomplishment but you should consider other peoples' sentiments as you do so.

IRON
1. If you dream of the metal iron, it usually represents your strengths and determination.

170

2. When you dream of using a clothes iron you are often attempting to make yourself more presentable. You may also be trying to "smooth things over."
3. If you dream of doing or handling metal works, signify your ability to change an undesirable situation to one which will be generally accepted by the majority. A good sign for those in leadership positions.
4. If you dream of corroded metal iron signifies that you are not aware that something may be going wrong for sometime.

ISLAND

1. If you dream of an island is a warning that you have to guard against loneliness through isolation.
2. If you dream of being on a deserted island indicates that you may unexpectedly be out of touch with someone dear.
3. If you dream of being on a familiar island can represent safety in that, by isolating yourself, you are not subject to external pressures.
4. Occasionally you all need to recharge your batteries, and to dream of an island can help, or warn us to do this.
5. Dreaming of a treasure island indicates there is something to be gained by being alone and exploring your ability to cope with such a situation. You may actually function better in some ways.
6. In dreams an island can signify a spiritual retreat, somewhere that is cut off from the world which will allow you to contemplate your own spiritual self. This will be an effective boost to your moral.

IVORY

1. To dream of ivory warns you that you have to urgently preserve something important in your present life. This may be either a romantic relationship or an old family artefact.
2. If you dream of an ivory tower can signify that you have to guard against shutting yourself off from communication.
3. If you dream of poaching ivory indicates that you may be trying to accomplish something through the most difficult way. You may have to pause and think more.
4. If you dream of possessing jewellery which is composed of ivory signifies an element of greed in what you may achieve or earn in the near future.

IVY

1. For ivy to appear in your dreams signifies a celebration due to success and achievement.
2. If you dream of owning an ivy-covered property symbolises your need of love and affection. You may have to make reconciliation at some stages.
3. Spiritually, ivy symbolises immortality and eternal life.

J

JACKAL
See Animals

JAGUAR
See Animals

JAIL
See Prison

JAILER

1. To dream of a jailer will indicate that you feel you are being restricted in some ways, maybe by your own emotions or by somebody else's personality or action.
2. If you dream of being employed as a jailer means that there will be a sense of self or external criticism and of alienation which makes it difficult to carry out your everyday tasks.
3. If you dream of being in confrontation with a jailer signifies that you are in a difficult situation and you have to make every possible move to get out of it.
4. If you dream of experiencing yourself being unfairly treated by a jailer indicates that not only you have been party to an entrapment, but also, you have become a victim of your own circumstances.

JAR

1. A jar usually represents conservation. To dream of one will indicate your need to either secure a long-term agreement or something of durability to enable your survival.
2. To dream to be conscious of being jarred or being shaken in some ways indicate that you are not controlling the way you are moving forward. You are putting yourself in a position where you can be knocked around or hurt.
3. If you dream of a broken or shattered jar signifies that something, which has been agreed on a long-term basis, may unexpectedly come to an end.

JAW

1. To dream of a jaw would appear that you might have to make consultations regarding proposals which may not be entirely according to what you would have expected.
2. If you dream of experiencing a dislocated jaw signifies unexpected changes with which you may not get along at all.
3. If you dream of a skeleton jaw signifies that you should increase your present level of alertness in everything to avoid the possibility of missing a splendid opportunity.

JESUS
See Religion

JEWELLERY

1. To dream of jewellery usually indicates that you have, or can have, something valuable in your life. But you are also warned that you have to make the necessary moves.
2. To dream of being given jewellery suggests that someone else values you.
3. If you dream of giving jewellery signifies that you feel you have something to offer to other people. Those qualities you have learned to value in yourself through hard experience are those that you display easiest to other people.
4. If a woman dreams of giving a man jewellery usually indicates that she is attracted to a male counterpart in her present life and perhaps is able to offer him her own sexuality and self-respect.
5. If a man dreams of giving jewellery to a woman signifies that he has a lack of romantic relationship in his physical life and that he may need to spice up a little bit even if he may have a partner.

JEWELS

1. For jewels to appear in dreams almost invariably symbolise those things which you value. These may be personal qualities, your sense of integrity, your ability to be yourself, or even your very essential being.
   To dream of different types of jewels may have different meanings as follows:
2. **Amethyst:** Promotes healing and influences dreams.
3. **Diamond:** Signifies human greed, hardness of nature and what one values in a cosmic sense.

4. **Emerald:** Highlights personal growth.
5. **Opal:** Suggests the inner world of fantasies and dreams; psychic impressions.
6. **Pearl** Signifies inner beauty and value.
7. **Ruby:** Informs on emotions, passion and sympathies.
8. **Sapphire:** Highlights religious feelings.
9. **Agate (black):** Symbolises wealth, courage, assurance and vigour.
10. **Agate:** (red) peace, spiritual love of good; health, prosperity and longevity.
11. **Amber:** Represents crystallised light and magnetism.
12. **Amethyst:** Is the healing gem. Connecting the dreamer with the spiritual, it represents the influence of dreams. Also humility, peace of mind, faith, self-restraint and resignation.
13. **Aquamarine:** embodies the qualities of hope, youth and health.
14. **Beryl:** is believed to hold within it happiness, hope and eternal youthfulness.
15. **Bloodstone:** Holds the qualities of peace and understanding. It is also reputed to grant all wishes.
16. **Carbuncle:** Determination, success and self-assurance are retained in this stone.
17. **Carnelian:** Friendship, courage, self-confidence, health.
18. **Cat's eye:** Longevity, the ability to sustain, the waning moon.
19. **Chrysolite:** Represents wisdom, discretion, tact, and prudence.
20. **Corundum:** influences and helps create a stability of mind.
21. **Crystal:** Symbolises purity, simplicity, and various magical elements.
22. **Diamond:** The diamond has a number of influences: light, life, the sun, durability, incorruptibility, invincible constancy, sincerity, innocence.
23. **Garnet:** Devotion, loyalty, grace.
24. **Hyacinth:** Particularly fidelity and the truth within, but also the gift of second sight.
25. **Jade:** All that is supremely excellent, the power of the heavens, and all its accompanying delights.
26. **Jasper:** Holds the qualities of joy and happiness. Although usually associated with darker emotions such as grief and mourning, jasper also controls safety within a journey.
27. **Lapis Lazuli:** A favourable stone said to evoke divine favour, success, and the ability to show perseverance.
28. **Lodestone:** Holds within it the qualities of integrity and honesty; also said to influence virility.

29. **Moonstone:** The moon and its magical qualities, tenderness, and the romantic lovers.
30. **Olivine:** Influences simplicity, modesty, and happiness within a humble framework.
31. **Onyx:** Represents degrees of perspicacity, sincerity, spiritual strength, and conjugal happiness.
32. **Opal:** The opal not only represents fidelity, but also religious fervour, prayers, and assurance of spiritual beliefs.
33. **Pearl:** Symbolises the feminine principles of chastity and purity, and also the moon, and waters.
34: **Peridot:** Represents consolidation of friendships. Also, so to speak, the thunderbolt, which we may be "hit" with at unlikely times.
35. **Ruby:** Represents all that is associated with Royalty, that is, dignity, zeal, power, love, passion, beauty, longevity and invulnerability However, some people may consider these interpretations to be slightly ironic.
36. **Sapphire:** Holds within it worldly truth, heavenly virtues, celestial contemplation, and the feminine side of chastity.
37. **Sardonyx:** Represents codes of honour, renown, brightness, vivacity, and aspects of self-control.
38. **Topaz:** Holds the beauty of the divine, that is goodness, faithfulness, friendship and love.
39. **Tourmaline:** The qualities of inspiration and imagination are represented by the tourmaline. Friendship also comes under the same influence.
40. **Turquoise:** Symbolises courage, physical and spiritual-fulfilment, and also success.
41. **Zircon:** Much worldly wisdom is held within zircon, as well as the virtues of honour, and the glories of riches.

JOURNEY
1. To dream of having any sense of completing a journey, i.e., arriving home, touching down and so on, indicates the successful completion of your aims.
2. **Collisions:** Represent arguments and conflicts which are often caused by your own aggression.
3. **Completion of a difficult journey:** You have come through the difficulties and setbacks of the past.

4. **A journey with obstacles:** The dreamer is aware of the difficulties which may occur. You do need to be aware that you yourself create the problems.
5. **Turning a corner:** You have accepted the need for a change of direction. You may have made a major decision.
6. **Avoiding an accident:** In waking life this means that you are being able to control your impulses.
7. **Stopping and starting:** There is conflict between laziness and drive.
8. **At a standstill/in a traffic jam:** You are being prevented, or are preventing yourself from moving forward. This needs handling with care, since to stop may be appropriate.
9. **Departing: e.g. airports, stations etc:** Formerly all departures were interpreted as death. Nowadays the symbolism is much more of a new beginning. You are leaving the old life in order to undertake something new.
10. When someone in your life leaves you, you may dream of departures and the grief that parting causes.
11. In certain circumstances, to dream of wanting to leave but not being able to, suggests that there is still further work to be done.
12. To be conscious of the time of departure might suggest that you are aware of a time limit within some circumstances in your life.
13. **The destination:** when it becomes apparent, will give some ideas about the aims and objectives the dreamer has. Your declared hopes and ideals may not correspond with those you subconsciously have and your inner motivation may be totally different to your outer behaviour, and dreams will highlight this discrepancy.
14. **Driving:** The whole of the symbolism of driving in dreams is particularly obvious. It represents your basic urges, wants and needs. If you are driving you are in control.
15. If you are not happy when someone else is driving you may not trust that person, and may not wish to be dependent on them.
16. When someone else takes over, you are becoming passive.
17. If you are overtaking the car in front, you are achieving success, but perhaps in a competitive manner.
18. When you are overtaken, you may feel someone else has got the better of you. Once again the way you are in everyday life is reflected in the dream.
19. **Engine:** This represents the sexual impulse or instinctive drives, one's basic motivation.

20. **Passenger:** It will depend if you are a passenger in a vehicle or are carrying passengers. If the former, you may feel that you are being carried along by circumstances, and have not really thought out your own way forward.

21. If the latter, you may have knowingly or inadvertently made yourself responsible for other people.

22. **Travelling** with one other passenger suggests you may be considering a relationship with someone with high status.

23. **Road:** The road in a dream suggests your own individual way forward.

24. Any **obstacle** on the road will reflect difficulties on the chosen path.

25. **Any turns in the road:** will suggest changes of direction in your present life.

26. **Crossroads:** You will be offered choices, while a cul-de-sac (or close) would signify a dead end to something.

27. If a particular **stretch** of road is highlighted it may be a period of time, or may mean an effort. Going uphill will suggest extra effort while going downhill will suggest lack of control.

28. **Traffic accidents**: These may all have to do with sexuality or self image; perhaps you are not being careful to ensure that your conduct is good.

29. **A collision:** Might suggest a conflict with someone.

30. **Road rage:** Would signify not being in control of your emotions.

31. The vehicle which appears in your dream often conforms with the view you hold of yourself. For instance, you may be driving a very basic type of car or a Rolls Royce.

32. If the dreamer is driving he perhaps feels more in control of his own destiny.

33. If he is a passenger he may feel others are trying to control his life.

34. If he is with friends he may be aware of a group goal.

35. If he does not know the other people he may need to explore his ability to make social relationships.

36. **Airplane:** An airplane suggests a swift easy journey with some attention to detail. You may be embarking on a new sexual relationship.

37. **A pilot:** Be warned of over-anticipation.

38. **Bicycle:** This suggests youth and freedom, and perhaps the first stirrings of sexual awareness.

39. **Boats (and sea voyages):** It will depend on what kind of boat is in the dream. A small rowing boat would suggest an emotional journey.

40. A yacht might suggest a similar journey done with style.

41. A large ship would suggest creating new horizons but in the company of others. What the boat does in the dream will have relevance as a reflection of your waking life.
42. **Disembarking:** The end of the project, successful or otherwise.
43. **Missing the boat:** You have not paid enough attention to detail in a project in your waking lives.
44. **Any narrow waterway or river:** Suggests the birth experience.
45. **Ship:** A ship is usually taken as feminine because of its capriciousness.
46. **Ferry:** This symbolises the giving up of selfish desires. After this you may be "reborn" into a better life, or way of life.
47. **Bus**: A bus journey is that part of your life where you are conscious of the need to travel and to be with other people. You perhaps have a common aim with them.
48. **Trouble with timetables:** e.g. Missing the bus, arriving too early, missing a connection, you are not in control of your life and perhaps should sit down and re-plan how you wish to continue.
49. **Getting on the wrong bus, going the wrong way:** There are conflicting desires, and you need to be aware of your own intuition. This is usually a warning of a wrong action.
50. **Not being able to pay the fare:** You do not have enough resources to set out on a particular course of action. It may be that you have not paid attention to details.
51. **Car (also Van):** The car is a reflection of the dreamer and how he or she handles life. It reflects the physical body, so anything wrong with the car will alert you to a problem.
52. **If the engine is not working properly:** You are not able to get enough energy to go on.
53. **If the starting motor is not working:** This would suggest that you need help to start a project. It is for you to be able to translate the symbolism into your own life.
54. **An overcrowded car:** Would suggest that you feel overloaded by responsibility.
55. **Lorry:** A lorry in a dream will have the same significance as a car, except that the drives and ambitions will be connected more with your work and how you relate on a business basis to the world in general.
56. **Motorbike, motorcycle:** The motorbike is a symbol of masculine youth and daring. In dreams it is an image of independent behaviour, and often a symbol for the sexual act. It can also be a symbol of freedom.

57. **Trains:** A train will often highlight the dreamer's attitude to social behaviour and relationships with other people. It will also clarify his attitude to himself.

58. A steam train would suggest that you feel yourself to be outdated and obsolete, whereas an up-to-date electric turbo might suggest speed and efficiency.

59. **Catching the train:** You have successfully been able to have outside circumstances co-operate with you in achieving a particular goal.

60. **Missing the train:** You do not have the resources to enable you to succeed in an appropriate way, either because you have forgotten something, or because you have not been sufficiently careful. You fear that you will miss an opportunity.

61. Dreams of missing a train alternating with dreams of catching one show the dreamer is trying to sort out his motivation.

62. **Getting off the train before its destination:** You are afraid of succeeding at a particular project. This can also signify premature ejaculation. You do not appear to be in control.

63. **Getting off the train before it starts:** The dreamer has changed his mind about a situation in waking life. Railway lines and tracks will have significance as ways of getting you to your destination.

64. Being conscious of the way the track runs ahead may give you an inkling as to what direction you are going.

65. **Coming off the rails:** Might suggest doing something inappropriate.

66. **Not wanting to be on the train:** might indicate you feel you are being unduly influenced by outside circumstances.

67. **Arriving at the station:** by train indicates you have completed that stage of your life journey. You may be ready for a new relationship with the world in general.

68. The carriages on a train suggest the various compartments or sections of your life and the way you feel about them. For example, if a carriage is untidy or dirty, you are aware that you need to "clean up" an aspect of your life.

69. **Walk:** If in your dreams you are aware of having to walk, it usually suggests that you are capable of doing that part of your journey by yourself without any help.

70. **Going for a walk:** You can enjoy the process of recharging your batteries and clearing your minds.

JUBILEE

1. To dream of a jubilee or jubilee celebrations would indicate that the time is right to make important changes regarding your work or life plans.
2. Dreaming of a jubilee or jubilant occasion can represent the natural inclination with which you greet changes.
3. If you dream of your own jubilee signifies that you should not be apprehensive to go ahead with forthcoming present decisions. Chances are that you will get them right.

JUDGE

1. To see a judge in your dream signifies that something may not be just right in your surroundings or certain things are not being accomplished as should be.
2. If you dream of judging somebody else is a warning that you may be over confident in your present endeavour and may adopt an attitude of not paying attention to details.
3. If you dream of being tried signifies that you have to be careful in case you commit a stupid mistake and are accused either innocently or maliciously.

JUMPING

1. To dream of jumping up signifies that you have the urge to attain something better for yourself and that you should pursue your present goal vigoursly.
2. If you dream of jumping down may signify that you feel in danger when actually you are not.
3. If you are jumping to cover a distance just as in long jump can indicate joy.
4. If you dream of jumping up and down indicates that you may have been caught up in a situation without having the power to move either forward or backward.
5. If you dream of jumping for joy just as the skipping rope signifies sensual pleasure.

JUNGLE

1. To dream of the jungle often represent chaos or difficulties in general.
2. To be searching for something in a jungle symbolises an obstacle or barrier that has to be passed through in order to reach a new state of being.

3. To dream of being trapped in a jungle indicates that you are trapped by negative and frightening feelings which you have created yourself and which you have to accept that it is only virtual reality.
4. To dream of having to go through a jungle to reach your destination would indicate that you have passed through, and overcome, those aspects of your life which you have never dared approach before.

JURY

1. To dream of a jury usually signifies a forthcoming struggle to contain pressure from either working colleagues or business associates.
2. To dream of being a member of the jury signifies a moment of indecision at present and you must choose the option of open consultations before you proceed further.
3. To dream of a jury delivering a verdict, which is not in your favour, signifies that you may make a judgement which turns out to be unpopular. But as long as you are sincere you need not be apprehensive.

JUSTICE

1. If you dream of either justice or injustice can indicate a level of difficulty trying to sort out what is right from what is wrong.
2. If you dream of having difficulties to deliver justice signifies that you are attempting to balance two different states or ways to approach a task. Careful judgement is a prime factor at the moment.
3. To dream of being brought to justice can signify that you must pay attention to your actions or to your attitude to authority.

K

KALEIDOSCOPE
1. To dream of a kaleidoscope signifies that you may possess great skills of creativity, which is somewhat, trapped and is not being put to the full use.
2. As the kaleidoscope is a fascinating instrument, to dream of using one signifies that you are in search of a better self and a more distinguished life pattern.

KANGAROO
See Animals

KETTLE
1. To dream of a kettle signifies that a new practical approach is necessary to better understand a specific circumstance before you can effectively handle it.
2. To dream of using a kettle suggests that you need to accelerate a process of learning and growth.
3. If you dream of either a very old or damaged kettle symbolises either an association or a connection with magic or magical properties. You may also be trying to clarify a mystified subject.

KEY
1. To dream of a bunch of keys suggests the need to "open up" the whole of your personality to new experiences. This is the only way to enhance advancement.
2. If you dream of unlocking something smoothly with a familiar key signifies that you may soon secure something which may appear as if by magic.
3. If you dream of rusty keys signifies that you may soon find answers to your problems.
4. A key can also represent the dreamer's need for liberation from a stressful situation, and then initiation of a positive move.

KEYHOLE
1. To dream of a keyhole may signify that finally you may get a delayed opportunity.

2. To dream of peering through a keyhole signifies that you are conscious of the fact that your ability to see and understand is somehow impaired.
3. Since a key usually requires a keyhole, to dream of one without the other indicates some kind of confusion between your planning and executing your plans.
4. If you dream of inserting a key into the wrong keyhole is a warning that you may have to watch out against being a scapegoat under tight circumstances.

KICK

1. If you dream of kicking someone is a warning that you may react unacceptably to a particular situation. The best approach is to take a calm attitude to situations you consider difficult.
2. To dream of being kicked is a good warning that you should guard against being a victim.
3. To dream of kicking a ball around signifies your need for self-control, but also your control of external circumstances.

KIDNAP

1. If you find yourself kidnapped in a dream, you are conscious of the fact that your own fears and doubts can make you a victim.
2. If you dream you are trying to kidnap someone else would indicate that you are trying to influence someone else. It is important that you have valid facts to make effective points.
3. If you dream of being on a mission to rescue a kidnapped person signifies that you may soon face a very important and sensitive task.

KILL

1. To dream of being killed represents your coming under an influence, usually external which is making you, or an aspect of your personality, ineffective in everyday life.
2. To be killing someone in a dream is attempting to be rid of the influence others have over you.
3. To dream of witnessing criminal acts of killing means that you may be held accountable for something in which you have limited knowledge.
4. If you dream of a spiritual slaying means that you will need to be aware that what you consider worthy may need further nurturing, lest it be relinquished.

184

KING
See People

KINGFISHER
See Birds

KISS
1. When you dream about kissing someone, it can suggest an acceptance of that person as potentially a new relationship. Such an act can also signify that, on a subconscious level, you are seeking to develop a quality belonging to that other person in yourself.
2. If you dream of kissing someone in a welcome introduction signifies that a mutual agreement will shortly be established.
3. To dream of being kissed indicates that you will be greatly appreciated for a successful deed which will benefit others as well.

KITCHEN
1. To dream of doing light activities which involves the kitchen signifies that you may soon find yourself so busy that you may have to guard against pressure.
2. If you dream of a general cleaning in the kitchen signifies that you may soon face some sort of transformation and transmutation. This is much more to do with desired transformation, rather than one which is enforced.
3. To dream of being in an unfamiliar kitchen signifies that you may have to struggle to come to terms with rules and regulations which will affect you directly.

KITE
1. To dream of flying a kite can symbolise a trouble free life or an easy way through completing a formal subject.
2. If you dream of flying a kite in very light winds indicates that you may have to take a responsibility which you are not fully prepared.
3. To dream of flying a kite in what you may consider too strong winds symbolises jeopardy to freedom you may have been enjoying up to now.

KNAPSACK
1. To dream that you, or someone else, wearing a knapsack, you are in effect, dreaming either about the difficulties you are carrying, for

instance, anger or jealousy or about the resources you have accumulated.
2. If you dream of carrying a heavier than expected knapsack portends difficulties which may surface unexpectedly.
3. To dream of a torn or damaged knapsack signifies that you may have to learn how to handle negative attitudes of others to enable you acquire an important feat.

KNEE
1. To see your knees in your dream signify that you may soon receive either a much appreciated favour or support from somebody else.
2. If you dream of having painful knees thus restricting free movements can indicate your reluctance to experiment with new ways of tackling things due to over self conscious.

KNIFE
1. To dream of using a knife signifies that you may either be freeing yourself from an undesired acquaintance or trying to sever a relationship.
2. To dream of being attacked with a knife indicates either violent words or actions may be used against you.
3. In a woman's dream this is probably more to do with her own fear of penetration and violation, whereas in a man's dream it is highlighting his own aggression.
4. To dream of a table knife can indicate that a present conflict may soon come to an end.
5. To dream of using what you consider to be a blunt knife signifies small internal confusions.

KNIGHT
1. A knight appearing in a dream carries the obvious connotation of a romantic liaison which may soon flourish.
2. If a knight appears in your dream as a companion signifies that you may be involved in a heroic deed.
3. If you dream of being a knight signifies that you will make remarkable achievement but should be cautious against discouragement.

KNITTING
1. To dream of knitting signifies that a project or idea which is being worked on is beginning to come together.

2. To dream of unravelling knitted cloth suggests that a project that is being worked on needs reconsideration.

KNOB
1. To dream of a knob such as a doorknob can indicate some kind of turning point in one's life. A noticeable contrast between the door and the knob can present the dreamer with certain insights. If you dream of a plain knob on an ordinary door may indicate that the process of moving forward from a situation is very easy.
2. To dream of any other sort of knob may represent one's hold on a situation.
3. If you dream of turning a knob may signify that you have to make a special move towards something as it may be easier to achieve than the way it looks.

KNOCK
1. To hear a knock in a dream generally alerts you to the fact that your attention needs to be refocused. You may be paying too much attention to one part of your personality.
2. To dream of louder than normal knocks signifies that you may be too introverted when in fact you need to be paying more attention to external matters.
3. If you dream of knocking on a door, you may be wanting to become part of someone's life. You are waiting for permission before moving forward.

KNOT
1. A knot is one of the most interesting symbols to appear in dreams. Negatively, if it is seen as a tangle, it can represent an unsolvable problem or difficulty.
2. Positively, a knot can represent the ties that one has to family, friends, or work.
3. To dream of a simple knot could represent the need to take a different direction in a project.
4. A more complex knot could indicate that you are bound to a situation by a sense of duty or guilt. It may well be that, ultimately, the only way to escape from such restraint is by loosening the ties in your relationship with someone else, or with a work situation.

L

LABEL

1. To dream of labels signify that there may be difficulties regarding the way that others see you and understand you. Adjustments to your expressions are absolutely necessary.
2. To dream of having the wrong label suggests that you are aware that you are not perceiving something in the correct way.
3. To dream of re-labelling something suggests that you have rectified a misperception.
4. To dream of sticking a label on something signifies that you are striving to make a name for yourself and this will be the ultimate fact.

LABOUR

1. To dream of labouring in the sense of working hard, suggests that you have a goal you wish to achieve.
2. If you dream of under hard labour is an aspect of being conscious of guilt and you may have to avoid tasks which looks more like self-punishment.
3. If you dream of giving hard labour to other people signifies that there are outstanding tasks which you may be taking too long to complete.

LABORATORY

1. To dream of a laboratory signifies your ability to achieve new levels in your present life.
2. To dream of working in a laboratory indicates that you need to be more open-minded in your approach to life. You may have certain talents which need to be developed in an objective fashion, or you may need to develop your thinking faculty further.
3. A laboratory can suggest a very ordered existence, and it will depend on whether you are working in, or are specimens in a laboratory as to how you interpret the dream.
4. If you dream of building a laboratory indicates that you need to make an objective assessment of what is going on in your life.

LABYRINTH

1. To dream of a labyrinth signifies the need to explore the hidden side of your own personality. There may be much to learn and you may never regret.
2. If you dream of being in a labyrinth signifies that you will make definite progress amid impending difficulties.
3. If you dream of constructing a labyrinth is a clear indication that you may have malicious intentions behind bright ideas. You have to realise that you may not reap much, after much hard work. Better to consider more on a financial benefit.

LADDER

1. The ladder in dreams suggests how secure you feel in moving from one situation to another. You may need to make a considerable effort to reach a goal or take an opportunity.
2. Sometimes to dream of ladders can suggest career changes, and so has obvious connotations.
3. To dream of a ladder with broken rungs is an indication that you can expect difficulty.
4. To dream of a ladder being carried by someone else could suggest that another person, perhaps a manager or colleague, has a part to play in your progression.
5. To dream of having to go under a ladder signifies potential physical ailments.

LAGOON

1. To dream of a lagoon or lake signifies your need for more effort in your present commitment, as it may be slow moving at the moment.
2. If you dream of a clear stretch of water would indicate that you have clarified your fears and feelings about yourself.
3. To dream of being in a lake signifies that you will not fear something designed to deter you or you will eradicate existing fears, if you had any.

LAMB
See Animals

LAME

1. Dreaming of being lame warns you of a loss of confidence and strength.
2. If you dream of feeling lame signifies that there can be a fear of moving forward or a fear of the future.

3. To dream to be aware that someone else is lame signifies that you need to be aware of his or her vulnerability and uncertainty if you know the person.
4. To dream of a lame person whom you do not know personally signifies that there is a hidden talent within you that is still under-developed thus holding you back.

LAMP

1. In general to dream of a lamp can represent life or the brighter side of anything.
2. To dream of moving towards a lamp suggests clarity of perception, which may be slightly old-fashioned.
3. The lamp in dreams can also signify guidance, and wisdom. It can also represent previously held beliefs which may need to be updated.
4. To dream of lighting a lamp signifies that you can be a mighty moving force behind a proposed accomplishment but you may need guidance as the task may contain unfamiliar details.
5. If your lamp goes out in your dream is a warning that you may have to wait for a while before either changing career or choosing a long term commitment or agreement.

LANCE

1. A lance, as in a Knight's lance, in a dream suggests an aspect of masculine power, the penetrative aspect and also carries the connotation of sexuality.
2. To dream of a lance as a surgical instrument is also penetrative, but has a more healing connotation, as it is designed to release the negative. You may need to take short, sharp action in order to improve a situation.

LANDSCAPES

1. To dream of a rocky landscape would suggest problems, whereas a gloomy landscape might suggest pessimism and self-doubt.
2. If you dream of a recurring scene may reflect a feeling or difficulty with which you have not been able to come to terms.
3. If you dream of being in a desert might represent loneliness, whereas to be in a jungle might represent a very fertile imagination.
4. Emotionally, the landscape in a dream can suggest improvements which you can make in handling your own moods and attitudes.
5. To dream of landscape changes between the beginning and end of the dream, you perhaps need to make corresponding changes in everyday life.

LANGUAGE

1. To dream of hearing foreign or strange languages in dreams illustrate the need to establish a channel of communication to facilitate understanding between you and your peers.
2. If you dream of suddenly having the ability to speak, or otherwise communicate in a foreign language, signifies that you will be presented with facilities which may need careful evaluation to enable you choose the one most appropriate for you.

LARDER

1. To dream of a larder signifies that you will achieve increased courage or endurance to sustain a difficult job until completed.
2. To dream of using a larder for storing inappropriate objects signifies unexpected burdens.
3. To dream of erecting a larder signifies long-term peace.

LARK
See Birds

LATE
See Time

LAUGH

1. To dream of others laughing at you suggests you may have a fear of being ridiculed, or may have done something which you feel is not appropriate. You may find yourself embarrassing.
2. If you dream of laughing others may indicate that you may need to release tension in your everyday life patterns.
3. To hear a crowd laughing suggests a shared enjoyment.

LAUREL

1. The laurel or bay tree is less likely to appear in dreams nowadays, unless the dreamer is either a gardener or has particular knowledge of symbolism. In former times, it would have represented a particular type of success. Traditionally the laurel or bay is difficult to grow, so it would have symbolised triumph over difficulty.
2. The laurel wreath is often used to indicate triumph and victory, and therefore is an acknowledgment of success. It also suggests immortality.
3. The laurel or bay tree signifies chastity and eternity.

191

LAVA
See Volcano

LAVATORY
See Toilet

LEAD (AS METAL)
1. The conventional explanation of lead appearing in a dream generally signifies that you have a situation around you, which is a burden to you.
2. If you dream of handling a piece of lead signifies that you are not coping with life as perhaps you should be, and it is leaving you heavy-hearted.
3. Lead, as in pencil has obvious connections with the life force and masculinity.
4. Lead as a substance is less used nowadays than it used to be, but still has the connotations of a base metal. In dreams it can indicate that the time is ripe for transformation and transmutation. You need to instigate changes to give a better quality to your life.

LEAVES
1. To dream of green leaves can suggest hope and new opportunities on the way.
2. If you dream of dead leaves signify a period of sadness or barrenness.
3. If you dream of leaves falling from trees suggests you may need to assess how to go forward in order to avail yourself of the opportunities offered.
4. To dream of destroying dead leaves such as burning them signify that you may be unaware that a phase of your life is over and it is now time to make fresh moves towards achievement.

LEAK
1. Dreaming of a leak suggests you are wasting or losing energy in some ways.
2. If you dream of a slow leak you are perhaps not aware of the drain on your energies. You may have to assess your workload or studies.
3. To dream of gushing signifies that you need to look at "repairing" certain patterns, perhaps by being more responsible in your actions.
4. To dream of repairing a leakage signifies that whatever nature your next task, it will carry an easy way towards accomplishment.

5.   If you dream of causing a leak so as to relieve an overflow signifies that you may face unfair competition in one of your forthcoming objectives.

LEATHER

1.   To dream of leather signifies your desire for sophistication or perfection. You have the drive but you may lack the means.
2.   If you dream of owning a leather suit signifies that you may receive a surprised gift.
3.   To dream of selling leather as a trade means that you may create lucrative ideas.

LEFT
See Position

LEG

1.   To dream of your legs in a healthy state signifies free movement or an improved way of coping with your life goals.
2.   If you dream of differing legs signify that you may receive conflicting verdicts on a situation you desperately need to sort out.
3.   To dream of your legs incapable of supporting you indicate that you should make an assessment of your actions in case you make way for other people to use your own proposals against you.

LEMON

1.   To dream of lemons signify that you are in a position to influence either your colleagues or someone in authority to comply with your suggestions.
2.   If you dream of harvesting lemons signify that you have more power to push harder towards accomplishment than you think.
3.   If you dream of using lemons in foodstuff mean that you may need to consider the slightest details to enable you complete something effectively.

LENDING

1.   If in a dream you are lending your personal property to someone, means that you are aware of the need to invest before you can harvest.
2.   To dream of someone else lending you an object signifies that you may have a feeling of lack in your physical life which may be a result of laziness rather than restriction.
3.   To dream of lending money means that you are creating a bond of obligation within your life.

4. If you are being lent money you need to look at the way you are managing your resources.

LENS

1. To dream of lens will generally indicate that there is something which you do not perceive very clearly.
2. If you dream of a lens magnifying an object signifies that you may have to be cautious against handling a task which may be too confusing for you.
3. If you dream of a cracked lens indicates your inability to interpret certain aspects of a situation which may result in unnecessary delays.

LEOPARD

See Animals

LEPER

1. To dream of a leper suggests that you are aware of some aspects of yourself that you feel to be unclean. You may feel that you have been rejected in some ways.
2. If you dream of caring for a leper, you need to attend to those parts of yourself you consider unclean, rather than trying to dispose of them.
3. If the leper is offering you something, it may be that you have a lesson to learn about humility.
4. Spiritually, a leper in a dream can suggest that you have to deal with a moral dilemma.

LETTER

1. If you receive a letter in a dream you may be aware of existing problems which may exist with the person it is from. It is possible that the sender is known to be dead, in which case there are unresolved issues with that person or the situation connected with him or her.
2. If you are sending a letter indicates that you have information you feel may be relevant to the recipient.
3. To dream of a letter without knowing its contents suggests some information which is at present being held from you.
4. If a particular letter of the alphabet is highlighted, you may understand more if you can name someone with that initial.

LEVEL

1. Dreaming of a level road would indicate your way ahead is fairly straightforward.

2. A level crossing suggests that you are approaching a barrier which requires your attention. You may not, at this stage, have enough information to take action.
3. If you dream of levelling a stretch of ground with the help of machinery is a sign that you have much to do in keeping certain procedures in accordance to what have been previously agreed.
4. If you dream of handling a spirit level signifies that you may encounter a level of confusion in your actual daily working pattern.

LIBRARY
1. To dream of a library would suggest the ability to create order successfully.
2. If you dream of a disordered library would suggest that you have difficulty in dealing with information.
3. If you dream of working in a library suggests that you have the ability and, at the moment you are well suited for psychic developments.
4. If you dream of researching in a library indicates both the wisdom and skills that you have accumulated, but also the collected wisdom available to all humanity.

LICE
See Insects

LIFEBOAT
1. Dreaming of a lifeboat could indicate that you have the feeling that you need to be helped, possibly from your own stupidity or from circumstances beyond your control.
2. If you are at the helm of a lifeboat indicates that you are still in control of your own life, but are perhaps aware that you need to offer assistance to someone else.
3. To dream of being a passenger in a lifeboat signifies that you should be aware of the degree of skill you require to navigate your present life's difficulties.
4. If you dream of a capsized lifeboat signifies that there are always risks in undertaking a difficult task. You should adopt the positive approach always.

LIGHT
1. To dream of light usually means a relief of some sort. For instance, "light at the end of the tunnel" suggests coming to the end of a difficult project.

2. If light appears in dreams you are usually in the process of trying to improve who you are.
3. A very bright light often symbolises a rapid improvement or promotion for the better but you have to watch out for elements of other people becoming over demanding on you.
4. To dream of switching on the light in a dark area signifies leadership skills or creative skills.
5. To dream of your light going out signifies a series of shortcomings.
6. To dream of light emerging from candle flames indicate the waking state of your personality and your new initiative to take new steps ahead.

LIGHTHOUSE

1. A lighthouse is a warning system, and in dreams it tends to warn you of emotional difficulties.
2. Dreaming of a lighthouse whilst on land means that you are being warned of difficulties to come, probably from your own emotions.
3. If you are at sea you need to be careful not to create misunderstandings for yourself by ignoring problems.
4. A lighthouse can act as a beacon and can lead you into calmer waters. It can often have this significance in dreams whether emotionally or spiritually.
5. Generally a lighthouse highlights the correct course of action to help you achieve your spiritual goals.

LIGHTNING

1. Lightning in a dream denotes unexpected changes, which are taking place or are about to take place. These may come about through some type of realisation or revelation.
2. If you dream of being in open air lightning means that you may have to make changes in the way you think, while leaving your everyday structure and relationships in place.
3. Lightning can also indicate strong passion, such as love, which may strike suddenly but be devastating in its effect.
4. When you dream of lightning, you are marking a discharge of tension in some ways. There may be a situation in your everyday life which actually has to be blasted in order for something to happen which will change the circumstances.

LINE

1. A line in a dream often marks a boundary or denotes a measurement. It can also signify a link between two objects to show a connection which is not immediately obvious.
2. If you dream of drawing lines indicate that you tend to need boundaries or demarcation lines, and those lines can be demonstrated in dream symbolism, in ways which might not be feasible in everyday life.
3. If you dream of jumping over a line would suggest that you are brave enough to take risks.
4. The straight line can represent time and the ability to go both forward and back.
5. When horizontal, the line represents your active participation in the physical world. When vertical it symbolises an emotional emergence towards improved moral obligations.

LINEN

1. To dream of linen tablecloths may suggest some kind of a celebration.
2. Linen bed sheets on the other hand might signify sensuality.
3. In today's world where everything is done as quickly as possible, linen appearing in a dream would suggest a slowness of pace and caring which enables you to appreciate your life better.
4. If you dream of washed white linen will signify reverence and love.

LION

1. To dream of a lion signifies your strength but you may have to be cautious against using it for cruelty.
2. If you dream of wrestling with a lion signifies your admirable courage and determination to reach your goal or overcome something.
3. To dream of a dead lion will signify that the worst part of something, which has been bothering you, is now over even if the "bad patch" may still be hanging around.

LIQUID

1. To dream of a liquid will generally signify a need to follow a consistent pattern in either your waking life or something you are attempting to accomplish.
2. If you dream of different-coloured liquids may carry different meanings such as:
3. **Milk, which is white:** signifies that you have to ensure that the most important details of a project are handy before giving a go-ahead.

4. **Juices, which are mostly yellow or orange:** will signify that you may need more of something than predicted.
5. **Violet, like black currant juice:** may signify your spiritual aspiration.
6. **Red** represents anger.
7. If you dream of something unexpectedly turned into a liquid you need to be aware that in everyday life you are in a situation which may not remain stable.
8. If you dream of spilling liquid signifies a need for more attention at your home or close monitoring of children if you have any.

LIZARD
See Animals

LOAF
1. If you dream of a loaf of bread is a warning that something crucial may be missing in your everyday life to facilitate your progress.
2. To dream of sharing a loaf or loaves of bread with others signifies your kind-heartedness, which, at the same time, must be guarded against abuses.
3. To dream of either begging or asking for a loaf of bread signifies a determination on your part to be knocking on every available opportunity to secure something very important.

LOCK
1. For a lock to appear in a dream may alert you to the fact that you need to free up whatever you have either shut away or refrain from facing a thorny issue.
2. To dream of forcing open a lock indicates that you need to work against your own inclinations to lock things away in order to be free of inhibitions.
3. To be fixing a lock in your dream suggests that you feel your personal space has been trespassed upon and you need to repair the damage.
4. To recognise, in your dream that a part of your body has become locked, suggests that you are carrying extreme tension. It is possible that you need to release that tension in a physical way in order to be healthy.
5. To realise a door is locked suggests that somewhere, where you thought of as sanctuary, is no longer available to you. It may also be that a certain course of action is not right.

198

LOCUST

1. To dream of being plagued by locusts represents retribution, and to a certain extent, misdemeanour.
2. As a flying insect the locust can signify scattered thought, and concepts, which have not been properly thought out and marshalled. Put together they may be a very powerful tool, but should be used wisely.
3. If you dream of trying to destroy locusts signify that, at a certain stage, you may have to be watchful in case of misuse of your resources.

LORRY

See Journey

LOST

1. To have lost something in a dream may mean that you have forgotten matters which could be important at this stage of your life or progress.
2. To suffer a loss suggests that part of yourself or your life is now dead and you must learn to cope without it.
3. To experience yourself as being lost denotes confusion on whatever level is depicted in the dream. It may be emotionally or mentally as much as physically. You have lost the ability or the motivation to make clear decisions.
4. The search for a lost object means that you may be in search for enlightenment over something. In spiritual terms you do not know what you are looking for until you find it.

LOTTERY

1. A lottery suggests the idea of gaining through taking a risk. To dream of winning a lottery would suggest that you have either been lucky or clever in your waking life.
2. If you dream of losing might suggest that someone else is in control of your destiny.
3. A lottery can highlight all sorts of belief systems, some valid and some not.
4. To dream of entering a sweepstake may denote your attitude to greed and poverty, and to the principle of winning through luck rather than effort.
5. To dream of being a lottery maniac represents the ability to take chances, to rely on fate rather than good judgment.

LOW
See Position

LUGGAGE

1. To dream of packing your luggage symbolises temporary changes. There will be a temporary relief to something, which has been bothering you, but you may be disappointed to learn that it will not last.

2. To dream of having lost your luggage suggests that, in waking life, you may have to better manage a situation or else bad judgement may cause serious accountability.

3. To dream of handling several pieces of luggage signifies your inclination to be distracted. You have to be able to sort out your priorities and stick to each task completely before attempting a new one.

LYNX
See Animals

M

MACHINE

1. If you dream of a machine appearing in your dream denotes your exposure to something totally new and totally unexpected.
2. To dream of a machine breaking down, it warns you that you need to take care and that perhaps you are overstressing a particular part of your being.
3. To dream of a seemingly large and powerful machine signifies that you need to reassess any favours you are doing to yourself.
4. To dream of repairing a machine signifies that unexpected bad news are on the way.

MAD

1. To dream of being in a state of madness signifies that you are facing a part of yourself that is out of control and which, under certain circumstances, can be frightening. You need urgent attention to prevent over-stress.
2. To dream of being mad represents the uncontrollable aspects of extreme emotion. If you are conscious of being at odds with other people it will pay very dearly to steer well clear of them to prevent impulsive over-reaction.
3. To dream of facing someone in a state of madness signifies that you may have to change certain plans in your course of action towards accomplishment at the moment.

MAGGOTS

1. To dream of maggots will, in general signify strange feelings or worries you may have about the death of someone.
2. If you dream of clearing maggots is a warning that you should be careful not to be humiliated by others who may try to make fun of you.
3. To dream of tramping over maggots can represent impurities in your body and the sense of being eaten up by something. You may perhaps proceed with a medical check-up.
4. To be discarding or burying maggots in dreams may reflect your own fears about death and illness.

MAGIC

1. To dream of using magic signifies that you are using your energy to accomplish something without effort or difficulty.
2. If you dream of perceiving something appearing like magic signifies that you are capable of controlling the situation that you are in, to have things happen for you, and to create from your own needs and wants.
3. If you dream of learning to perform magic, it has to do with your ability to link with your deepest powers. They can be the powers of sexuality or the powers of control, or power over your surroundings.
4. To dream of trying to sort out a puzzled piece of magic signifies that you may shortly face something complicated which may take you longer than expected to handle it effectively.

MAGISTRATE

1. To dream of an authority figure such as a magistrate, it is very often to do with the need to be told what to do, or perhaps to have somebody who is more powerful than you are, to take control within your life.
2. To dream of being in the company of a magistrate signifies that you have unrealised aspirations.
3. If you dream of being a magistrate signifies that you may be overdoing certain courses of action which may not be appropriate at the moment.
4. To dream of arguing with a magistrate signifies a need for you to acquire knowledge before attempting to put a higher demand on your abilities.

MAGNET

1. We all have within us the ability to attract or repel others, and often a magnet appearing in a dream will highlight that ability. Since of itself the magnet is inert, it is the power it has that is important. You often need to realise that the influence you have over other people, comes not only from yourself, but also from your interaction with them.
2. The magnet has the ability to create a "field" around itself, a field of magnetic energy. Often the magnet appearing in a dream alerts you to the intrinsic power that you have, which is inert until such times as it is activated by situations around you.
3. A magnet will suggest a degree of charisma within the dreamer which can be used in various ways, depending upon the dreamer's inclinations.

202

MAGNIFYING GLASS

1. To dream of using a magnifying glass indicates that you should improve on your initiative to enable you have the power to create something out of the material that you have.
2. If you dream of a magnified object through a magnifying glass signifies growth in either your ability to handle circumstances or financially.
3. To dream of an unusable magnifying glass signifies that you should be more aware of your own actions. You may need to examine yourself minutely.

MAGPIE
See Birds

MAKEUP

1. To dream of makeup indicates that you have the ability to change the impression you make on others.
2. If you are making yourself up it can very often indicate a happy occasion. You need to put on a facade for people and you may even need to put on a facade for yourself so that you feel better about your own self image.
3. If you are making someone else up, then often you are helping them to create a false, or perhaps better impression.
4. To be dealing with makeup means that you have a choice as to the sort of person you want to be. You can choose your outward appearance and can create an impression that perhaps is different from the one you naturally make use of.
5. To dream of an undesired makeup signifies that you have to be cautious of false impressions coming your way.

MALLET

1. If a hammer or a mallet appears in your dream indicates that you may be using undue force or power to achieve a specific outcome.
2. The mallet is also the directing will, and to have such an item in a dream indicates that you may be attempting to make things happen in a way that is not necessarily appropriate for that particular situation.
3. To dream of owning a mallet signifies the need to be aware of how your power and energy is being channelled towards achievement.

MANDRAKE

1. When the mandrake root or a manikin is recognised in a dream you are linking with your own wish to harm other people, with your conflict with someone else.
2. To dream of handling mandrake roots symbolises your desire to possess destructive powers.
3. Harvesting or collecting mandrake signifies unconscious evil intent.

MANNA

1. If manna appears in a dream usually represents the ability you have to transmute something from the ordinary to the sacred.
2. When you are seeking something, perhaps to change your life in some ways, you often need external help when everything around you is going wrong and you are beset by problems. The symbolism of manna, of the miraculous bread appearing, is something which makes you realise that you can in fact carry on.
3. To dream of being given manna signifies a need for more active participation in your spiritual life, as there are wonderful lessons still to be learnt.

MANSION
See House

MANTIS

1. As with most insects, the mantis often represents something devious within your life, that trickster part of you that can create problems when things are effectively working out for you.
2. In dreams, you often translate a quality or a situation you are struggling with into an object. To be aware of the mantis may indicate that on some level you are aware of trickery around you.
3. The dreamer should look carefully at the appearance of a mantis, as it represents deviousness, particularly of an emotional kind.

MANURE

1. If you dream of manure signifies that some of the experiences, which you have to go through, can be painful or downright unwholesome.
2. To dream of using manure to fertilise land signifies that you should make specific moves to break down your problems and make positive use of them.

3. If you dream of manure found in inappropriate places, for example, at your doorstep would indicate that you have something in your life which will have to change form before it can be used properly.

MAP

1. If you dream of a map will often indicate the clarification of the direction you should be taking in life. You may feel that you are confused or face ambiguity and need support to clarify your way forward towards your ambitions.
2. To dream of a used map indicates that you are capable of taking a direction and learning from other people in your quest for success.
3. If you dream of buying a map because you have lost directions signifies that you need to be taught something on a preliminary stage before proceeding further.
4. If you dream of a torn or otherwise unusable map signifies a warning from your subconscious mind that you urgently need absolute control over present circumstances or else you risk being pushed around unnecessarily.

MARBLE

1. For marbles to appear in your dreams signify that something you will establish will last for a very long time.
2. If you dream of polishing marbles indicate your need for perfection. It is a good sign but you may have to be cautious against adopting an attitude that you can never be satisfied.
3. If you dream of either owning or buying marbles can represent your strong character or it may also signify the need for you to be firmer in your everyday activities.

MARE
See Horse in Animals

MARIGOLD
See Flowers

MARKET

1. Dreaming that you are in a market indicates your ability to cope with everyday life, of being able to relate to people, but particularly to relate to crowds.

2. A market is a bustling, happy place and to dream of one may indicate that you need to look after yourself more and to spend time with more people.
3. It could also suggest that you need to become more commercial in the work that you are doing, or perhaps to be more creatively influenced, rather than doing something purely and simply because it is commercial thus it has quite an ambivalent meaning.
4. A marketplace can be viewed as a place of spiritual exchange in dreams. You can establish a balance between your everyday reality and your spiritual or inner world.

MARRIAGE
1. To dream of a marriage symbolises a forthcoming valuable friendship.
2. If you dream of preparations for a wedding indicates your feelings of inferiority. You may succumb unnecessarily to simple things.
3. If you dream of your own wedding denotes that you may have to be selective of various prospective relationships which come your way.
4. To dream of an enforced marriage signifies emotional pressure as you may soon be faced with a tricky situation where you may have to identify treachery amongst your colleagues.

MARSH
1. To dream of a marsh signifies a feeling of being held back in something you want to do, and perhaps you lack either the self-confidence or emotional support that you need to move forward. A marsh or a swamp can also indicate that you are being swamped by circumstances, being trapped in some ways by the circumstances around you.
2. If you dream of being on swampy ground very often represents difficulty on an emotional level. Perhaps you are creating emotional difficulties for yourself which may help a great deal if you change your perception about your difficulties.
3. If you dream of being trapped in a marsh denotes the need for a careful re-assessment of your career as there is the possibility that inferiors may surpass you in rank or authority.

MARTYR
1. To dream of being a martyr highlights your tendency to do things without being sufficiently assertive to say no, and to act from a sense of duty.

206

2. If you dream of others being a martyr indicate that you may have too high expectations on a specific person.
3. To dream of a religious martyr often means you need to avoid any religious discussion, as this may turn out to be unpleasant.

MASK
1. To dream of a mask signifies that you may have to assess your activities and disregard those you consider to be having elements of risks.
2. If you dream of trying to unveil a mask from somebody else's face signifies that you may be short of vital knowledge which is being kept from you maliciously.
3. If you dream of wearing a mask is a warning not to entertain "shady" activities as you may end up having to take responsibility to a certain extent.
4. To dream of putting a mask on somebody else's face is a warning that you may have sensitive things to conceal.

MASTURBATION
See Sex

MATTRESS
1. In dreams the mattress has a somewhat similar connotation to a bed in that it can indicate a constant feeling you have about a situation you have created in your life, whether it is comfortable or not.
2. A mattress can also symbolise that you are aware of your own basic needs and are able to create relaxed feelings that allow you to express yourself fully.
3. To dream of owning a comfortable mattress can symbolise a comfortable sexual activity. If your sexuality has been erratic lately, it is now the best time to take up this issue, as there will be a high level of understanding.
4. To dream of being on an unfamiliar mattress signifies that you have to complete additional tasks or commitments to ensure everlasting comfort in any of your cherished dreams.

MAYPOLE
1. To dream of a maypole signifies a turning point in a specific activity you may be doing. You may have to push harder to see positive results.
2. If you dream of erecting a maypole may signify celebration to something which you will achieve through a group of people.

3. If you dream of a maypole with unattractive decorations may signify that the time has come to make a specific decision before it gets far too late.

MAZE
See Labyrinth

MEDAL
1. If a medal appears in your dream signifies that you are under-achieving. You have facilities and abilities which are not being utilised to their full potential.
2. If you dream of awarding a medal to somebody else signifies that you may soon find yourself in a position to make decisions on other peoples' behalf.
3. If you dream of being awarded a medal signifies success in your next endeavour.

MEDICINE
1. To dream of taking medication suggests that action needs to be taken in order to prevent something going wrong, which, possibly could be your health.
2. If you dream of prescribing medications for somebody else indicates your ability to take up higher responsibilities which will ultimately pave the way towards self-accomplishment.
3. If you dream of using inappropriate medicines or medicines which yields no improvement signifies that you may need external help to solve a confusion.

MEDITATION
1. To dream of seeing someone in a state of meditation signifies a need to either adhere to more discipline in your present life or ensure discipline in others.
2. If you dream of practicing meditation suggests a need for you to be more creative, hence enabling you to make real differences to a monotonous situation.
3. If you dream of taking meditation classes signifies that you need to search more from within yourself for a solution to an existing problem rather than externally.

MEDIUM
1. To dream of a medium very often means that you are looking for some kind of contact with your own subconscious, or with the dead.
2. To dream of being mediumistic would indicate that you are aware of greater powers than you believe you have in ordinary everyday life.

3. If you dream of visiting a medium signifies that you have a serious lack of self-confidence and that you may be searching for an effective way towards accomplishment.

MELT
1. To see something melting in a dream is an indication that your emotions may be softening. You are perhaps losing the rigidity you need to face the world. You are undergoing a change and are becoming softer.
2. To dream of feeling your own self melting signifies that you may be coming more involved in romance. You may need to sit and simply let a situation develop around you to the point where it is safe for you to decide your next course of action.
3. To dream of trying to maintain your grip on a melting substance signifies that you may face a difficult situation in the near future where you may have to make unpleasant changes involving other people.

MEMORIAL
1. To dream of seeing memorial such as a war memorial signifies that you need to be able to acquire knowledge regarding this memory to enable you to move on.
2. A memorial may simply be a recognition of a happier time which needs to be remembered.
3. A memorial is a tangible representation of homage and esteem.

MENSTRUATION
1. To dream of menstruation indicates that you can conceive new ideas and can be creative even if you may only have simple material.
2. Since menstruation is such an integral part of the feminine life, it can indicate in a woman's dream, her acceptance of her own emerging sexuality.
3. In a man's dream however, it can alert him to his fear surrounding relationships and union with the feminine. It can also indicate his own feminine side, and his need to understand his own sensitivity.

MERMAID
1. To dream of a mermaid signifies your ability to adapt to two extreme situations. You can cope with something in a difficult environment even if you are not used to it.

2. To dream of being a mermaid signifies that you may encounter difficulties to merge two things together to come out with the completed picture.
3. If you dream of having hooked a mermaid signifies criticisms regarding an inadvertent error.

METAL

1. Any metal appearing in dreams represents the restrictions of the real world but can also represent the hardness of feeling or emotional rigidity.
2. To dream of handling different metals have different symbolic meanings as follows: Gold means the Sun, hence a bright outcome.
3. Sliver means the Moon which represents a warning against using excessive power.
4. Copper means Venus which represents a romantic activity.
5. Iron means Mars which represents ambition or long-term goal.
6. Tin means Jupiter which represents influence.
7. Lead means Saturn which represents patience.

MICROSCOPE

1. To dream of a microscope is symbolical that you need to pay attention to details. Also you may need to be somewhat introspective in order to achieve a personal goal.
2. To dream of using a microscope signifies that something or a vital piece of information you consider of importance is missing and you may be hard pressed to come up with it.
3. If you dream of being unable to identify whatever details you are looking under a microscope signifies that someone is avoiding you.

MILK
See Food

MILL

1. A mill extracts what is useful from the crude material it is fed. It is this quality that is symbolised in dreams. You are able to extract from your experiences in life what is useful to you and can convert it into nourishment.
2. If you dream of driving a mill signifies that you may have to use your will and intellect in order to achieve an important transformation.
3. If you dream of an idle mill signifies that you may, at the moment, have ran out of useful ideas.

MINES

1. To dream of mines signify that you have great potential and this potential can only be most effective in the workplace.
2. If you dream of working with mines signify your ability to extract either useful material or information for use at a later stage.

MIRROR

1. Dreaming of a mirror suggests concern over one's self-image. You are worried as to what others think of you, and need self-examination in order to function correctly. There may be some anxiety over aging or health.
2. To be looking in a mirror can signify trying to look behind you without letting others know what you are doing. You may have a concern over past behaviour.
3. To dream of looking in a mirror can also signify that you need to "reflect" on something you have done or said.
4. If you perceive a distorted image in the mirror signifies that you are having a problem in understanding your actions.
5. To dream of a mirror image speaking to you signifies that you should be listening more closely to your intuition.
6. If you dream of looking in a shattered mirror so that you perceive only part of yourself signifies that you have to be on your guard against blackmailing.

MISCARRIAGE

1. Dreaming of a miscarriage, suggests that you are conscious of the fact that something is not right.
2. If a woman dreams of a miscarriage signifies that she needs an emotional break and a boost to her morale.
3. Dreaming of a miscarriage can also suggest the loss of work, a project or even a part of yourself, and you need time to adjust.
4. A miscarriage can represent aspects of early death.

MIST

1. Mist is a symbol of loss and confusion, particularly emotionally. Hence, to dream of mist symbolises that you may need to reconsider some of your actions.
2. To dream of being in actual mist will depend on how thin is the mist. It is symbolic that the worst of a difficult situation is over if you can manage your way fairly easily. If it is thick it symbolises that you may face a situation which will get worse before it gets better.

3. If you dream of mist clearing itself symbolises much needed relief.

MOAT

1. A moat is a representation of defences against aggression. To dream of one signifies apprehension. More self-determination may be necessary to cultivate confidence.
2. To dream of being on the outside of the moat signifies that you have forthcoming obstacles to overcome before you may eventually reach your final "destination".
3. To dream of being on the inside signifies comfort and peace of mind.

MOLE

See Animals

MONEY

1. Money in dreams does not necessarily represent hard currency, but more in the way in which you value yourself. This symbol appearing in dreams would suggest that you need to assess that value more carefully, and equally to be aware of what you "pay" for your actions and desires.
2. Money can also represent your own personal resources, whether material or spiritual, and your potential for success. In some circumstances a dream of money can be linked with your view of your own power.
3. If you dream of money consisting primarily of coins signify a forthcoming agreement or approval to something which involves your career.
4. If you dream of stealing stacks of paper money signifies that you may have to consider more time for completion of something very important.

MONK

See People

MONKEY

See Animals

MONSTER

1. To see a monster in a dream signifies the need to avoid unnecessary commitments. Do not commit yourself towards things you are not sure of being able to deliver.

2. When, in everyday life, events get out of proportion you often have to suppress your reactions. In dreams you cannot do this and so your mind create some ways of dealing with the problem.
3. Different aspects of the problem can be identified by the colour of the monster, for example, a red monster would indicate anger, whereas a yellow one might suggest resentment.

MOON

1. To dream of the moon indicates that you are active with the dark and mysterious side of yourself. It is very important to watch out against bad influences.
2. It has always been known that the moon has a psychological effect on the human being. In pagan times, it was suggested that she ruled men's emotions and guarded women's intuition. Even today, that symbolism still stands. In a man's dream when the moon appears, he either has to come to terms with his own intuitive side or with his fear of women.
3. In a woman's dream the moon usually indicates her interrelations with other women through their collective intuition.

MORNING
See Time

MORTUARY

1. For a mortuary to appear in your dream signifies that you have fear and bad feelings about death. If you feel perfect health at the moment you have no reason to entertain these feelings.
2. To dream of a dead body in a mortuary signifies that you may have to revise your contacts and ensure that no important relationships have broken up because you may need them dearly.
3. If you dream of being the only one present in a mortuary signifies that you may go through a peaceful change.

MOSAIC

1. Any intricate pattern appearing in dreams usually signifies the pattern of your life. You probably need to consider life as a whole, but also to understand and respect the many separate parts of it.
2. Within a mosaic, made up of many small parts, there is a deliberate act of creation. When such a symbol appears in dreams you are being alerted to your abilities as creator.

3. The Kaleidoscope of Life with its many facets is a potent spiritual symbol represented in dreams by the mosaic.

MOSES
See Religion

MOTH
1. To perceive a moth in your dream signifies the hidden side of nature. For this reason you may have to be aware of your actions which may be self-destructive.
2. To dream of a moth emerging from darkness signifies the recognition that you must achieve in order to survive.
3. To dream of killing a moth signifies that you may have to put up to deception which may cause emotional damage.

MOTHER
See Family

MOTORCYCLE
See Journey

MOUND
1. For a mound to appear in your dream signifies your lack of comfort and it is a warning that you have to take the appropriate actions to identify discomfort and act.
2. Emotionally, man's need for comfort and sustenance continues throughout his life. At the same time, he needs to come to terms with his dependence on the feminine. Often to dream of mounds helps him to understand this.
3. If you dream of piling a mound signifies that you are outstanding with urgent actions.

MOUNTAIN
1. To dream of a mountain symbolises an obstacle which needs to be overcome.
2. If you dream of climbing a mountain represents a challenge to your own inadequacies and free yourself from fear.
3. To dream of reaching the top of a mountain signifies the achievement of one's goal.

4. If you dream of falling down a mountain is a warning to watch out against carelessness.
5. You all have difficulties to face in life. Often it is how you face those difficulties that are important. The symbol of the mountain offers many alternatives and choices. This means you can work out, through dreams, your best course of action in everyday life.

MOURNING

1. The process of mourning is an important one in all sorts of ways. You not only mourn death but also the end of a relationship or a particular part of your life. Since sometimes mourning or grieving is seen as inappropriate in waking life, it will often appear in dreams as a form of relief.
2. If you dream of mourning a departed one signifies that you may have to take a break from either hard work or heavy studies. Whatever it may be, you should pause for a while.
3. To dream of others mourning over your own actions is a warning that you may have to consider other peoples' sentiments before taking certain courses of action.

MOUSE

1. If you dream of a mouse signifies that you may face treacherous circumstances.
2. To dream of being frightened by a mouse signifies reluctance to face a situation where you may have developed the perception that you may be defeated in front of others.
3. If you dream of killing a mouse signifies a tendency for you to take drastic measures to put a situation under control.

MOVEMENT

1. To dream of specific movements such as moving forward suggests an acceptance of one's abilities, while moving backward signifies withdrawal from a situation.
2. To dream of moving sideways would suggest a deliberate act of avoidance.
3. If you dream to be aware of moving quickly would suggest an easy acceptance of the necessity for change, whereas being moved, such as on some kind of moving walkway would signify being moved by outside circumstances or at the wish of other people.

MUD

1. To dream of perceiving mud ironically suggests the time is right for a move towards financial ends.
2. To dream of walking in the mud signifies that you may need to make adjustments to your original plans prior to meeting somebody who could make a lasting difference in your ambitions.
3. If you dream of cleaning mud from personal properties, for example in your house or car etc, signifies that you may have to be cautious against drawing conclusions too soon.

MURDER

1. If you dream of witnessing a murder suggests that you may be either denying or trying to control, a part of your own nature that you do not trust.
2. If you dream of being murdered signifies that a part of your life is completely out of balance and you have to act very fast to avoid being destroyed by external circumstances.
3. If you dream of killing someone in a state of anger suggests that you are still holding some kind of childhood anger, since it is quite natural for a child to wish somebody dead.
4. To dream of plotting to murder somebody else suggests that you need to understand proper analysis of something before even considering violence.

MUSEUM

1. If you dream of a museum signifies your inclination to old-fashioned thoughts, concepts and ideas which may not be adaptable to modern ways of life and which may even be an annoyance to your own self.
2. If you dream of being in a museum signifies that you have to cultivate the need for you to consider things but more objectively than subjectively.
3. To dream of working in a museum can signify the possibility of being reminded of something unpleasant which is long over.
4. To dream of being conscious of being in a museum but with the absence of the expected primitive artefacts suggests the uncovering of the truth regarding a past situation.

MUSIC

1. To hear music in a dream represents sensual experiences. You are, at the moment moving according to the rhythm of life and you should succeed in your present endeavours.

216

2. If you dream of playing music for entertainment signifies that you will nurture a new ability or harness new knowledge.
3. If you dream of participating in sacred music such as chants signifies that the time is right to handle an issue which has been disturbing your inner peace.

MUSICAL INSTRUMENTS

1. To dream of a selection of musical instruments signify your skills and abilities in effective communication.
2. To dream specifically of wind instruments suggest your peak intellect at the moment.
3. If you dream of Percussion instruments indicate that you need to make adjustments to meet with the basic patterns of life because at the moment you may be falling short.
4. If you dream of owning musical instruments denote sexual activities or peak sexual performance.

N

NAIL

1. Dreaming of nails in woodworks suggests your ability to hold things together. Finger and toe-nails usually suggest claws or the capability of holding on.
2. To dream of driving a nail into woodworks signifies the penetrative power of the dreamer and indicates that the time is ripe to handle anything which involves negotiations and bargaining.
3. If you dream of having difficulties to drive a nail to its position signifies setbacks in your masculinity or sexuality.

NAKED
See Nude

NAME

1. Your name is the awareness of your first possession. It is your sense of self, and of belonging. If you hear your name in a dream denotes that your attention is deliberately being drawn away from your full concentration.
2. To dream of others mistaking your name for somebody else's is a warning that you have to be alert in case you give different verdicts to same issues.
3. If you dream of forgetting names of people you know indicates a possible lack of something, hence a warning against having to resort to undesirable practices.
4. To dream of being conscious of the name of a deceased person signifies confusion in information obtained from different sources.
5. To dream of being specific of the name of a place signifies that you have to consider previously ignored means of achieving something.

NARROW

1. To dream of something narrow signifies that you are aware of restrictions and limitations. This is a warning that you have to stand against these setbacks to avoid the doldrums.
2. If you dream of a narrow road would suggest some kind of restriction, and a warning that you must not deviate from your path.

3. If you dream of having difficulties to go through a narrow road signifies that you should take care not to be narrow-minded and judgmental in your interactions with other people.
4. To dream of crossing a narrow bridge might suggest a difficulty in communication, perhaps in putting your ideas across.

NAUSEA
1. If you dream of feelings of nausea is a strong indication that you have to assess your present situation and get rid of something which is making you feel uncomfortable.
2. To dream of nursing somebody with nausea symbolises a reflection of your physical state, but since the stomach is the seat of the emotions, it may be a representation of an emotion that is distressing you.
3. The body often has its own way of alerting you to difficulties, and it may be that nausea in a dream indicates a problem before it manifests in the physical.
4. To dream of having nausea to the point of vomiting suggests that you may be presented with fictitious or cooked information.

NAVEL
1. To be conscious of the navel, whether your own or another's, is to be aware of your bodily image. You should cast aside your shyness and claim your right in this world. Get on with your ambitions no matter what others may think.
2. To dream of others being aware of your navel in plain view signifies your dependency on other people.
3. Often in nightmares you become conscious of something, perhaps a devil sitting on your navel, and this can be a personification of your own fears.

NECKLACE
1. To dream of a necklace suggests that some special events are forthcoming and carry with them special qualities or attributes. There is a richness to be acknowledged.
2. If you dream of a man giving a woman a necklace signifies that you would soon be proposed for marriage or if you are already married, you may be an invited guest.
3. If you dream of wearing a necklace yourself suggests a dignity or honour which has been conferred on you.
4. To dream of being given a necklace as a gift indicates forthcoming honour and power.

219

5. If you dream of a broken necklace signifies rivalry. You may have an unwanted competitor.

NEEDLE

1. In dreams needles suggest irritations, but can also signify the power to heal through penetration.
2. If you dream of using a needle for a purpose other than what it was meant to be used signifies forthcoming disillusionment.
3. To dream of being pricked mischievously with a needle suggests that you have to be on your guard against accepting things against your will.
4. To dream of pricking your own self by accident with a needle suggests that you may be hard-pressed for financial commitments.

NEIGHBOUR
See People

NEPHEW
See Family

NEST

1. To dream of a nest symbolises safety. You may be emotionally dependent on people around you and you may be reluctant or apprehensive of parting from them.
2. To dream of constructing a nest suggests that you may face either a physical or emotional situation where you may have to seek refuge for relief of a confused situation.
3. If you dream of destroying a nest suggest that you may have to give a second thought to a plea for help. You may feel good later on for your assistance.

NET

1. A net in dreams usually warns against being trapped and entangled in a scheme or situation.
2. In a woman's dream this will signify her seductive power, whereas in a man's dream he will be conscious of his fear of women.
3. To dream of being trapped in a net is a warning that you have to build up a strong emotional barrier to enable you face either confusing or very embarrassing matters.
4. If you dream of using a net to catch or trap someone or animals signifies an element of abuse in an advantage you may have at the moment.

220

NETTLE

1. If you dream of nettle suggests that there is a difficult situation which will have to be avoided.
2. To dream of possessing nettles in your home signifies that there may be irritation, particularly if you are not interacting with others, or with the environment you are in.
3. To dream of a patch of nettles could also suggest difficulty in communication if you are in the middle of it. Others round you may be using words or circumstances to hurt you. Watch out!
4. If you dream of being pricked by hairs of nettles signifies a worthless transaction. Think again.
5. If you dream of others using nettles maliciously against you is a warning not to allow yourself to be over stimulated by a display of unacceptable behaviour with sexual undertones.
6. To dream of nettle also has a spiritual meaning to aid against a specific danger.

NEW

1. Dreaming of something which is new suggests a new beginning, a new way of looking at or dealing with situations, or perhaps even a new relationship.
2. To be doing something new in a dream highlights the potential in a fresh learning situation. You are stimulated and excited initially.
3. If you dream of moving into a new situation, in real life your dreams can highlight your fears and difficulties which may surface as you proceed towards a new horizon.
4. If you dream of buying new household items suggest impatience to change a situation which may not be totally under your control but may be affecting you adversely. The best approach is to give constant reminders.

NEWSPAPER

1. Largely in dreams a newspaper will suggest knowledge which is publicly available. It may be information that you require in order to make sense of the world around you, or it may be something which is specific to you.
2. A tabloid newspaper may suggest sensational material, whereas a quality one would suggest better researched data.
3. A Sunday newspaper may suggest you have the ability to assimilate the knowledge you need in periods of rest and relaxation.
4. A local newspaper signifies that the facts you require are close at hand.

5.   To be buying newspapers in dreams signify new information available on a conscious level rather than subconsciously. It is information which you need.
6.   To dream of a blank page in a newspaper can have two meanings. Firstly, you may lack a certain volume of information which is not available to you for various reasons. Secondly, it can signify a great importance if you provide vital information to others.

NEW YEAR

1.   To dream of the New Year is to recognise the need for a fresh start. It may also signify the measurement of time in a way that is acceptable, or a time when something can happen.
2.   If you dream of participating in New Year celebrations signifies a new and successful turning point in your social life or even your career.

NICHE

1.   To dream of a niche generally means that you can proceed with activities which you previously had doubts about them. The time is safe to do so.
2.   If you dream of having a commercialised niche signifies your strong or peak ability to push for results which would otherwise stagger.
3.   If you dream to be positioned in a niche as in a wall signifies the need to make an urgent move towards self-fulfilment. You are unaware of an opportunity which is right under your nose.

NIECE
See Family

NIGHT

1.   Night signifies a period of rest and relaxation. To dream of being consciously aware of a clear night signifies that you are going through a period which allows you to create a new beginning with the dawning of the new day. You are about to make fresh growth.
2.   To dream of a cloudy night can suggest a time of chaos and possibly difficulty. You may be unaware of situations where other people may be using indirect channels to cause you unstoppable delays.
3.   To dream of a peaceful night signifies good progress in health issues.
4.   If you dream of a stormy night signifies that you may learn of serious illness or even the death of close ones.

NO

1. To be aware of saying no in a dream signifies an important part of your growth process. It signifies that you are capable of making decisions which go against the wishes of other people. You have a strong character.
2. To dream of consciously being refused a request for something signifies that you are coming to terms with rejection and are no longer fearful. You are capable of standing on your own two feet.
3. If you dream of saying no to something, which you inwardly believe to be the opposite, signifies selfish ends.
4. Saying no in spiritual terms entails your ability to push aside circumstances which are not compatible with your concept of progress.

NOOSE

1. A noose in a dream suggests that you have a fear of being trapped, perhaps by others' actions.
2. If you dream of making a noose signifies that you are aware that you can create a trap for yourself, henceforth, a warning to be on guard.
3. To dream of "putting a noose around your own neck" signifies that careful considerations need to be taken with regards to your daily activities because you may give away something which you badly need.
4. To dream of drawing a hangman's noose signifies that you have to be careful of a threat of death or evil intent.
5. A noose, like the halter, harness and other symbols of restraint, suggests the taming of something wild. So, for a young man about to be married to dream of a noose might indicate a fear of being restrained unduly.
6. For a young woman wishing to leave home, a noose might represent a fear of becoming trapped in the parental home.
7. To dream of tightening a noose signifies that you may face a situation where you may be prevented from self-expression.

NORTH
See Position

NOURISHMENT

1. In dreams, all symbols of nourishment are associated with basic needs. Firstly, you require warmth and comfort; secondly, shelter and sustenance. Any dream in which you become aware that your need

for nourishment is not met, signifies that you may experience rejection and hurt.
2. If you dream of nourishing others with a lack, signifies that you will make a decision which may bring benefits to you through other people.
3. If you dream of nourishing pets or domestic animals suggest that you will be faced with situations where there are strong elements of love or even romance.

NOVEL

1. To dream of a novel indicates that there is a different way of looking at and succeeding of sorting out something which may be confusing at the moment.
2. To dream of reading a novel suggests that you may be praised for something which has not been entirely your contribution and you should be sincere to give credit where merited.
3. If you dream of reading a novel and yet not following it coherently signifies that you have to change a course of action on which you may have doubts because it may have serious consequences.

NUDE

1. To dream of being nude signifies your self-image. To dream of walking alone naked in the streets signifies that you are alone and may simply have a wish for freedom of expression.
2. To dream of being seen naked in public places by other people signifies that there may be something about yourself which you wish to reveal.
3. If you dream of seeing other people nude, which creates embarrassing situations such as seeing your mother nude, signifies that you require a level of honesty and truth in your daily activities.
4. If you dream of seeing your lover or partner nude signifies that you should be aware to make your actions as ordinary as possible to avoid being snubbed at.
5. If you dream of appearing nude in a strip show, could suggest you have anxiety about being misunderstood. You are conscious of the fact that you are prepared to be open and honest, but others may not understand.

NUGGET

1. To dream of a nugget, which is most of the time made of gold, signifies the best part of a situation. This effectively means that you are about to make the most of an opportunity before others grab it.
2. To dream of finding either gold or silver nuggets signify that you are about to discover a new creative skill that you did not know it existed.

3. To receive nuggets in a dream signifies acquisition of knowledge, power, and psychic ability.

NUMBERS

Very often, numbers in dreams have symbolic significance. A number will occasionally appear as a personal significance such as your age or house number etc.

Personal meanings:

1. **One:** You will accomplish outstanding skill in the work you do.
2. **Two:** Business or personal relationships need handling carefully.
3. **Three:** Your ideas for stability and success will materialise.
4. **Four:** A secure and sheltered home is yours for the asking.
5. **Five:** You are about to make an important discovery which will bring about changes.
6. **Six:** A loving relationship is available to you.
7. **Seven:** With personal effort you can solve your problems.
8. **Eight:** Your life holds the potential for a wonderful offer.
9. **Nine:** Take care not to over-stretch yourself.
10. **Zero:** The cipher holds within it all potential.

Symbolic meanings:

1. **One:** Independence, self-respect, resolve, singleness of purpose. Intolerance, conceit, narrow-mindedness, degradation, stubbornness.
2. **Two:** Placidity, integrity, unselfishness, gregariousness, harmony. Indecision, indifference, lack of responsibility, bloody mindedness.
3. **Three:** Freedom, bravery, fun, enthusiasm, brilliance. Listlessness, over-confidence, impatience,
4. **Four:** Loyalty, stolidity, practicality, honesty. Clumsiness, dullness, conservatism, inadaptability.
5. **Five:** Adventurousness, vivaciousness, courage, health, susceptibility, sympathy. Rashness, irresponsibility, unreliability, thoughtlessness.
6. **Six:** Idealism, selflessness, honesty, charitableness, faithfulness, responsibility, superiority, softness, impracticality, submission.
7. **Seven:** Wisdom, discernment, philosophy, fortitude, depth, contemplation.
8. **Eight:** Practicality, power, business ability, decision, control, constancy. Unimaginativeness, bluntness, self-sufficiency, domination.
9. **Nine:** Intelligence, discretion, artistry, understanding, brilliance, lofty moral sense, genius. Dreaminess, lethargy, lack of concentration, aimlessness.

Esoteric meanings:

1. **One:** Oneself, the beginning; the first; unity.
2. **Two:** Duality; indecision; balance; male v female; two sides to an argument; opposites.
3. **Three:** The triangle; freedom.
4. **Four:** The square, strength, stability, practicality; the earth; reality; the four sides of human nature sensation, feeling, thought, intuition; earth, air, fire and water.
5. **Five:** The human body; human consciousness in the body; the five senses.
6. **Six**: Harmony or balance.
7. **Seven:** Cycles of life, magical, spiritual meaning; human wholeness.
8. **Eight:** Death and resurrection, infinity.
9. **Nine:** Pregnancy; the end of the cycle and the start of something new; spiritual awareness.
10. **Ten:** A new beginning; the male and female together.
11. **Eleven:** Eleventh hour; the master number.
12. **Twelve:** Time; a full cycle or wholeness.
13. **Zero:** The feminine; the Great Mother; the unconscious; the absolute or hidden completeness.

NUN
See People

NURSE
See People

NUT

1. To dream of a metal nut, as in nuts and bolts, is highlighting your ability to construct your life in such a way that it will hold together.
2. To dream of eating edible nuts may suggest that you are trying to depersonalise issues to do with sexuality.
3. To dream of decayed edible nuts suggest that you have the ability to develop your psychic powers to a very high level.

O

OAK
See Trees

OAR
1. The oar is a tool that enables a boat to move forward successfully, but its use requires some skill. Thus it stands for your own set of personal skills. You have certain skills which help you to "navigate" your life successfully.
2. If you dream of constructing or designing an oar indicates your tendency to interfere with other people's lives. Mind your own business.
3. If you dream of an oar gone missing indicates the loss of an ability you have formerly valued.
4. To dream of having full control over a boat when steering with an oar signifies that you are now in the right direction in pursuing your goals.
5. If you dream of being unable to steer a boat with an oar signifies that you may need to revise a recent plan of action. It may be incomplete or inconsistent.

OASIS
1. To dream of an oasis signifies relief in a situation which has no apparent solution.
2. If you dream of being lost and in dire need of an oasis signifies that some determination is needed in your quest to complete something because you are at the point of discouragement.
3. An oasis may also signify that whatever you perceive as something tedious may not actually be the case.

OATS
1. Oats in the form of porridge signify an almost "magical" food. Because they have been used since time immemorial as a staple food, they represent warmth and comfort.
2. Wild oats obviously have a connection in people's minds with sexual satisfaction and freedom. To dream of sowing grain suggests that you are expecting to reap a benefit from a situation at a later date.

3. To dream of eating a pleasant bowl of cooked oats signifies that you need to make whatever you are either planning or undertaking at the moment, simpler, as this will render it more effective.

OBEDIENCE

1. To dream of others obeying your commands is a direct interpretation that you have power and authority over others in your present life.
2. To dream of having to be obedient to others indicates that you are aware of their greater authority and knowledge, but not necessarily directly over you.
3. To dream of finding yourself in the position of being obedient to someone you know, in an unexpected situation, you can often expect to have an easier relationship with them in the future, perhaps because you are able to acknowledge them in a different way.

OBELISK

1. Any carved stone appearing in a dream suggests you are considering how you have shaped your own basic nature. The simpler it is, the more room you have for improvement; the more ornate it is, the more successful you are at using your creative energy.
2. An obelisk often represents a marker outlining a particular area, such as a sacred space. It can also represent old instinctive knowledge.
3. An obelisk is often representative of a Sacred Stone, and therefore the dreamer needs to be clear regarding his spiritual beliefs.

OBLIGATION

1. To dream of being under an obligation to somebody else signifies that you may need extra courage to stand firm and refuse a commitment which you find may not entirely benefit you.
2. To dream of being conscious of others' obligations to you indicate that you need to be certain you are not forcing your will within a situation.
3. To feel obliged in a dream may lead you to the performance of a task or duty that you may subconsciously, have been putting off.

OBSCENITY

1. To dream of obscenity is a warning that you have to deal with forthcoming situations safely and with prudence, as they will be sensitive situations.

228

2. Often obscenity is connected with your perception of yourself. If you are performing obscene acts, you need to be aware of suppressed impulses. If such acts are performed against you, you need to decide how you are being victimised in your daily life.
3. Obscenity is sometimes associated with acts of evil. If the dreamer identifies with this link, then he may need to be aware of his own interpretations of evil and evildoing.

OBSESSION

1. To dream of being obsessed with something indicates that you need to take time to work out a difficult situation.
2. If you dream of other peoples' unnecessary obsessions with something, signify anxiety about some past events, which you have not been able or allowed to deal with. You feel that you have not been able to fully express yourself. Take time and the right moment will eventually surface.
3. Obsessive or repetitive behaviour in dreams is often a sign that the dreamer has fully understood the message being conveyed by the unconscious.
4. To dream of being able to control obsession indicates that, after a long period of indecisiveness, an effective decision will eventually materialise.

OBSTACLE

1. Obstacles in dreams can take many forms like a wall, a hill, a dark forest, etc. Largely, you are aware that these obstacles need to be overcome. How you do this in a dream can often suggest how to tackle a problem in everyday life.
2. If you dream of facing an obstacle signifies that you are actually facing a situation of indecision and self-doubt. This situation can be handled effectively by acquiring more information.
3. Difficulty, indecision and doubt, are the three main blocks one will come up against in this particular spiritual "obstacle course." The dreamer will have to scale each one if he is to finally achieve his spiritual goal.

OCCULT

1. Occult actually means "hidden," so for someone to dream of the occult when they have no knowledge of the subject, usually suggests the need to face situations which they have been apprehensive to do so in the past.

2. To dream of the occult in its negative sense, as in black magic or Satanism, signifies that you may have to avoid a negative approach to something or an undesirable proposal.
3. If the dreamer has occult knowledge it may be important to apply that awareness in an everyday situation. The rule is always then "harm no one."
4. In dreams, the occult, due to its many strange facets, may well be alerting the dreamer to an as yet untapped arcane wisdom.

OCEAN
See Sea

OCTOPUS
1. To dream of octopus is a strong warning to be cautious against being drawn into something that is frightening and from which you may not be able to escape.
2. Creatures that are unusual and are not familiar to you may appear in dreams to alert you to certain qualities within yourself. The octopus is capable of moving in any direction and it is this symbolism you need to be aware of.
3. If you dream of being frightened by an octopus signifies that you may have to avoid a situation whereby you accept liability to something which is not your entire responsibility.

ODOUR
1. If there is an odour in a dream it is usually highly significant and will highlight whatever is happening. If it is a pleasant one it suggests good times; if a bad one then it is more likely to be a warning of unpleasant happenings.

OFFENCE
2. To take offence in a dream is to allow a display of emotion and feeling about your own sensitivity which may not be appropriate in waking life.
3. To give offence to someone in a dream is to recognise that you are not aware of other people's feelings as you should be.
4. To dream of committing an offence suggests that you are not, either consciously or unconsciously, following your own code of moral behaviour. Beware of degrading yourself.

5. If you dream of involvement in situations connected with offences signify that you may have to be watchful not to be in a greater demand than what you can deliver.

OFFICE

1. To dream of an office signifies that you may not be taking outstanding goals seriously or may not be pursuing something vigorously.
2. If you dream of being in a particularly a familiar one suggests some kind of order or bureaucracy is necessary in your life.
3. To be in office, in the sense of holding a post, signifies taking responsibility for what you do.
4. An office in spiritual terms suggests having taken responsibility for whom you are.
5. To dream of being in an unfamiliar office signifies that you may have to be aware not to take extra loads than you can effectively carry.

OFFICER

1. To dream of perceiving officer indicates that you may have to face a familiar situation but yet you may have to be careful not to be careless as you may end up in an embarrassing position.
2. To dream of facing an officer signifies that you may soon face a situation whereby you may have to conform to authority.
3. To dream of an army officer signifies that you need guidance, and need to be "told" what to do.
4. If you dream of being an officer signifies that you may have to be strong in repelling something you consider undesirable or disadvantageous.

OIL

1. To dream of cooking oil will often signify the removal of friction, or your ability of combining different elements together to form something new and desirable.
2. If you dream of massage oil suggests caring and a situation of comfort.
3. If you dream of engine oil will highlight your ability to keep things moving.
4. To dream of oiling something with the intention to lubricate it signifies your ability to cope with and remove stress or the ability to diffuse a situation.
5. To dream of perceiving burning oil suggests that you may be running out to time to secure something or to voice certain concern.

OINTMENT

1. Dreaming of ointment means you will face a situation which will involve healing. This may involve either your own self or you may contribute towards the benefit of others.
2. If you dream of a popular ointment signifies a non-specific type of healing, whereas an ointment that has been prepared specifically for the dreamer suggests a more focused approach.
3. To dream of buying ointments suggests that you may be asked for advice or a contribution towards participation in healing.

OLD

1. If you dream of what you consider to be old objects signify that you may need to refer to something in the past in order to enlighten a present situation.
2. To dream of old or elderly people suggest the acquisition of wisdom arising from experience.
3. To dream of old buildings can signify a past way of life which you thought you had left behind.
4. To dream of antiques will often represent elements of your past experience which might be worth keeping.

ONION

1. To dream of onions symbolise wholeness. You may be asked and be held responsible to ensure completion of something.
2. To dream of peeling an onion can suggest that you need to understand the various facets of your personality. You may have to be more conscious of your actions and see whether you have a rational reason behind each course of action.
3. To dream of chopping onions can signify an attempt to increase the energy available to you in some ways.

OPAL

See jewels

OPERA

1. To be attending an opera in a dream suggests observing the "drama" of a situation around you. It may be more appropriate to observe rather than take part in the situation.
2. To dream of taking part in an opera highlights your need for some kind of important input into your life to enhance positive changes.

3.   To dream of singing in an opera signifies that you should be able to express yourself in a more dramatic and tutored way within everyday situations.

OPERATION

1.   To dream of witnessing an operation signifies your awareness of your own fears of illness. You should be aware that over-indulgence in such fears might inflict health hazards on your own self.
2.   To dream of performing an operation signifies that you should be using a level of your skill to achieve something within a situation at present.
3.   If you dream of undergoing an operation means you are attempting to access some inner knowledge but are possibly fearful of the outcome.

OPTICIAN

1.   To be visiting an optician in a dream probably indicates that you do not feel you can see a situation clearly and that you need assistance.
2.   To dream of simply being at an optician signifies that you need to develop a new way of looking at things.
3.   The optician in a dream may suggest that you need to understand the skill of seeing. This may also signify clairvoyance.
4.   If you dream of being an optician signifies that there is much analysis to be done in order to shed light on something which is puzzling you at the moment.

ORACLE

1.   Most of us like to know what is going to happen to us and also like to be told what to do. So dreaming of an oracle signifies awareness and confidence in your next move.
2.   To dream of visiting an oracle indicates that you will soon instinctively predict something with reasonable accuracy.
3.   To dream of being an oracle signifies that you may need to be clearer in the way that you either share or submit information or the way you communicate. This is necessary to avoid situations whereby you may end up being the loser yourself.
4.   If you dream of someone you know suddenly turning into an oracle signifies that there is hidden knowledge revolving around you.

ORANGE

See Colour as well as Fruit under the heading Food.

ORCHARD

1. To dream of an orchard where the trees are showing flowers, will represent the potential you have for success.
2. If they are showing fruits, then you are being reassured as to the harvest you may gather.
3. To dream of owning an orchard signifies that you may need a more structured layout of either your life pattern or your work in order to be much more appreciated.
4. If you dream of picking fruits in an orchard signifies fertility.

ORCHESTRA

1. To dream of an orchestra represents the need for you to bring several issues together in order to make a coherent whole.
2. To dream of directing an orchestra signifies that you must take action which enables you to be heard and to have people understand you in order to gain control over a situation.
3. To dream of being a member of an orchestra indicates that you are, or should be part of a greater task to attain success.

ORE

1. To dream of ore signifies that you need to transform something crude into some sort of a preparatory stage in order to render it usable to assist you in your endeavours.
2. To dream of refining ore signifies new ideas, thoughts and concepts which have not yet been totally understood.
3. Whenever any basic material such as ore appears in a dream, there is an unconscious need to "dig for information". It may not present itself as usable material to begin with but will need working to enable you to make use of the information you have.
4. If you dream of trading in ore represents basic spiritual knowledge can be revealed.

ORGAN

1. To dream of organs of the body signify an inconsistent pattern of how you display your weaknesses and strengths.
2. To dream of a musical organ highlights the dreamer's views and feelings about religion. In slang terms, the organ suggests the penis.
3. In Chinese medicine, the different organs of the body represent different qualities. For instance, the gall bladder deals with the ability to make decisions, while the liver is the seat of irritability. In dreams, therefore, being conscious of a bodily organ would require you to be

aware of what is bothering you and dealing with it in an appropriate manner.

ORGANIST

1. To dream of an organist suggests that you are appreciative of the fact that, as with an orchestra, the various notes that you play can be brought into harmony. This, however, requires some skill in making the sounds available.
2. To dream of being an organist yourself denotes the need to express yourself successfully. This is very important if you are likely to face situations such as an interview.
3. If you dream of somebody unexpectedly turning into an organist, such as your mother, represents a need for a more disciplined and determined way to enable you to be listened to.

ORGY

1. To dream of an orgy signifies that you may need a tremendous release of energy which may be in the form of your own sexuality.
2. To dream of participating in an orgy indicates that you may have to take certain considerations in romantic relations because you have a hidden fear of losing control over a certain aspect of your love life.
3. To dream of familiar people taking part in orgies suggest that you have to find ways of unleashing energies which you may not be aware you have, for your present progress.

ORNAMENT

1. Dreaming of personal ornamentation suggests an attempt to enhance something that you have and value, but that you want to make more valuable. In dreams this can represent either your feelings, emotions or ideas.
2. To be conscious of ornaments in a dream tends to indicate that your personal space can be used more fully and therefore bring you greater success.
3. To dream of trading in ornaments signifies that you may have to create representations of your ideas in an artistic feature to provide better understandings.

ORPHAN

1. To dream of an orphan indicates that you may be feeling vulnerable and possibly abandoned and unloved.
2. If you dream of caring for an orphan suggests that you should not feel lonely or awkward if you are experiencing setbacks at the moment.

3. To dream of being yourself an orphan may indicate that you need to be more independent and self-sufficient.
4. If you dream of working in an orphanage suggests the need to grow up and to move away from being dependent on others.

OSTRICH
See Birds

OUTLAW
1. To dream of an outlaw signifies that there is the need to put up to certain rules and regulations for the time being even if they may not be popular.
2. If you dream of arresting an outlaw signifies an attempt to control your impatience.
3. To dream of being an outlaw yourself signifies an attempt to push things to the extreme for your selfish ends.
4. To dream of sheltering an outlaw from justice represents your inclination to be involved in activities which may have consequences which you will have to pay for, in various ways in the future.

OVAL
See Shapes

OVEN
1. To dream of ovens suggest your ability to transform character traits from something coarse to the more refined.
2. If you dream of using the oven for cooking or baking something suggests your ability to get situations moving, especially towards desirable changes.

OWL
See Birds
Ox
See Animals

OYSTER
1. The oyster is reputed to be an aphrodisiac food. In dreams it can therefore represent the sexual act or anything associated with sex.
2. The oyster is almost unique because of its ability to transform a grain of sand into a pearl. It is this quality which tends to be brought to

notice in dreams to demonstrate how you can change an irritant into something beautiful.

3. To dream of breeding oysters suggests your ability to work well towards identifying negative qualities in your life but having the inability to eradicate them completely.

P

PACKING

1. If you dream of packing suitcases in preparation for a journey signifies the need to prepare carefully for the next stage of your life. There is a need, or want, to get away from old ideas and difficulties.
2. If you dream of packing an object signifies the need to establish some kind of order in your life. To dream of packing commercial items signify that you may have to go through some kind of selection process in order to help you decide what is most important to you at the moment.

PADLOCK

1. To dream of locking a padlock suggests that you are attempting to hide away either an embarrassing feeling or an emotion.
2. Conversely, if you dream of opening a padlock signifies that you are about to entertain new ideas and experiences either through your own creativity or through the help of colleagues.
3. To dream of locked padlocks signifies that you have apprehensions relating to threats to your security. When you have such dreams all you have to do is to ensure that you are comfortable with whatever ways you are secured.
4. If you dream of a non-functional padlock signifies that you may face an argument relating to justice.

PAINTING

1. To dream of painting a picture is often an alert for you to search for talents which will help you realise a specific goal.
2. To dream of looking at paintings indicate that you are questioning or paying attention to ideas and concepts of which you have not been consciously aware.
3. To dream of painting as in decorating suggests you are making recognisable changes in the way you think and feel.
4. To dream of painting miniatures signify that you may need to concentrate on various details of your present life.
5. If you dream of painting large pictures indicate that you may need to adopt a wider perspective on a job or a plan you have ahead.

238

PAIRS

1. To dream of anything in pairs signify that you have some sorting to do. This will be in the sense of having to "match" things in your present life to make it effective to work for you.
2. If you dream of forming pairs to complete a set, for example, a pair of shoes, a cup and a saucer etc, signifies that you have to consider every possible detail before finalising an important task, as the risk of omitting an important element is high.
3. If you dream of having to join someone else to complete a pair for whatever reason signifies that you may have to consider team work to generate a positive result within a short time.

PALM

1. To dream of a palm tree signifies rest and relaxation. Ensure you have adequate rest and relaxation at the moment to minimise the risk of potential health hazards.
2. To dream of planting palm trees suggest blessings and prosperity in your present life.
3. If you dream of the palm of your hand being prominent symbolises generosity and sincerity.

PAN

1. In dreams a pan signifies nurturing and caring. It is also a signal that you are in the best frame of mind to take up any particular training.
2. To dream of using a pan can suggest your ability to make effective combinations of different things to transform a situation or a task to something different and effective.
3. If you dream of using a pan for purposes other than what it was meant to be, signifies the need to be alert against being distracted at the crucial moment.

PANTOMIME

1. For many people the pantomime is a happy childhood memory, and often appears in dreams as a reminder of happier times. It can also suggest the more spontaneous, humorous side of your nature.
2. Because the images associated with pantomime are often exaggerated and larger than life, the pantomime can be used in dreams as a setting to draw your attention to something of which you need to be aware.

PAPER

1. Paper is one of those images which in dreams, is dependent on the circumstances in the dreamer's life. For instance, in a student's life, paper would suggest the need to pay attention to the studies.
2. In a postman's life there may be job anxieties, whereas festive wrapping paper could indicate the need for, or the possibility of celebration.
3. To dream of blank writing paper signifies a lack of communication, or a need to communicate with someone.
4. If you dream of using blank plain papers is a sign that you are about to make a new beginning in something to do with work.
5. If you dream of disposing used papers signify that there is a potential for growth through both learning and creativity.

PARACHUTE

1. Dreaming of a parachute suggests that, whatever is happening to you in real life, you have protection that will see you through.
2. To dream of an open parachute indicates that you are able to withstand certain difficulties to the point of overcoming them.
3. To dream of yourself parachuting is a sign of freedom. You will be relieved from a situation you considered a burden.
4. To dream of watching others parachuting signify your ability to make progress to a level above everybody else.

PARADISE

1. To dream of being in a place you consider to be paradise signifies your unconscious desire to harness the ability to attain things to perfection.
2. If you dream of any situation which involves paradise signifies that you may have a desire to be a happier person but you are facing obstacles which you consider cannot be removed to enable you to eventually reach happiness. These so-called obstacles are only in the form of mental blocks. In real life they are only virtual obstacles.
3. To dream of sending someone to paradise signifies that you will be satisfied with either a proposal made to you or something you have requested.

PARALYSIS

1. When paralysis is felt in a dream you are probably experiencing great fear or suppression. You should take the necessary steps to address your real situation and face life with more dignity.

2. Sometimes when you feel paralysed in dream is simply your imagination, which is playing tricks on you due to the fact that you may have been involved in frightening, or fearful ideas lately.
3. If you dream of attending to somebody who is paralysed is a warning to be watchful for situations with hidden elements which can cause substantial restrictions on you.

PARASITES
1. To dream of parasites such as lice or fleas suggest that you may be aware that someone is attempting to live off your energy in some ways. You should take adequate care not to be too much involved.
2. To dream of having parasites on your body signify that you may have unclean ideas at the moment and you should be ashamed or uncomfortable about them.
3. To dream of destroying parasites signify that you may not be satisfied with something at present and you should be taking appropriate steps to redress the situation without being arrogant.

PARCEL
1. To dream of receiving a parcel signifies that you need to explore something in detail before making any particular commitments.
2. To dream of sending out a parcel signifies that you may need extra energy to accomplish something.
3. In general, parcels and packages can suggest future potentials or skills.

PARENTS
See Family

PARROT
See Birds

PARTY
1. To dream of being in a party alert you to either your social skills or lack of such skills. In waking life you may be shy and dislike such gatherings, but in dreams if you are coping with the groups involved, signify that you have a great potential.
2. To belong to a political party would indicate that you are prepared to stand up for your beliefs, that you have made a commitment to a particular way of life.

3. To find yourself in a party in a dream can also indicate your need for celebration, to mix with other people to create a potentially happy atmosphere.

PARSLEY

1. To dream of parsley signifies that you may have hidden powers in either the physical or psychic plane.
2. To dream of harvesting parsley signifies that you need to make a careful assessment of what actually you dislike at present, and make it a special point to get rid of it rather than putting up with it.
3. To dream of serving beverages with flavourings of parsley signifies that a determined move is necessary to make effective changes you have in mind.

PASSAGE
See Hall in Buildings

PASSPORT

1. To dream of seeing a passport signifies that you may have to take serious decisions to preserve your self-image as it is in danger of being tarnished.
2. To dream of using your passport to identify yourself signifies that you will shortly move on to new things or face new situations which are, in general, challenging.
3. To dream of losing your passport signifies that you may have to put your self-esteem aside and put up to things you hate.

PATH

1. To dream of a path signifies the direction you have decided to take in life. A smooth path will signify a good direction where as a difficult or rocky one alerts you to think again.
2. To dream of having to design or introduce a new pathway, it is often a symbol that you have the ability to "see" in the future, the outcome of a forthcoming situation.
3. If you dream of being led on an unfamiliar path signifies that there is a need for you to turn toward a spiritual direction.

PEACOCK
See Birds

PEARL
See jewels

PEDESTAL

1. To become conscious in a dream that something has been placed on a pedestal you have obviously attempted to make that thing special. You have elevated it to a position of power.
2. Most human beings have a tendency to idolise or worship certain characteristics. Dreams will often show the appropriateness, or otherwise, of such an action.
3. Putting someone or something on a pedestal suggests spiritual worship and idolatry, which can impede one's spiritual journey if that worship is misplaced.

PELICAN
See Birds

PEN/PENCIL

1. If a pen or pencil appears in a dream indicates that you are expressing or recognising the need to communicate with other people.
2. If the pen does not work, it signifies that you do not understand information you have been given. If you dream of losing your pen signifies that you do not have enough information to proceed with an aspect of your life.
3. We all have an ability to learn but need to have some ways of transmitting our learning to other people. A pen would suggest the learning would be more permanent than a pencil.
4. The powers to transcribe spiritual knowledge and to keep a record of that information are a necessary part of development. Dreaming of a pen or pencil may suggest that you could attempt automatic writing.

PENDANT
See Necklace

PENGUIN
See Birds

PENTACLE
See Shapes

PEOPLE

1. The people who appear in your dreams are those having special significance to the meanings of your everyday life. Often they appear simply as themselves, particularly if they are people you know, or

243

have a relationship with in the here and now. Special attention needs to be paid.

In order to disentangle the various types of "information" which each character brings to the dreamer, it is often necessary to decide what or whom each one makes you think of. That way you will reveal the deeper meanings and connections.

2.   **An individual from the past:** could link you with that period of your life, and with specific memories which may, or may not, be painful.

3.   **A neighbour:** or close associate usually appears in a dream to highlight a particular quality in that person.

4.   **Somebody else's mother, father, brother etc.,** may suggest your own family members or possibly jealousy. Sometimes, rather than trying to decipher the meaning of the dream it is enough to look at what bearing the dream character's actions have on the dreamer's everyday life. Similarly, there may be a marked contrast in the way the dreamer handles a situation with two of his dream characters. It is as though two options are being practiced.

5.   **Composite characters:** As with composite animals, the composite character will emphasise one characteristic or quality in order to draw the dreamer's attention to it.

6.   **Adolescent:** To dream of being an adolescent is an alert that you have to concentrate on the undeveloped side of yourself.

7.   Dreaming of an adolescent of the opposite sex usually means dealing with a suppressed part of one's development. There may be conflict over freedom.

8.   **Ancestors:** To become conscious of your ancestors in a dream signifies the need to focus on the very basic elements of your life. A need for a solid foundation is necessary.

9.   **Authority Figures:** *(such as judges, police, teachers etc),* Your concept of authority is first developed through your relationship with your parents. Depending on how you were treated as a child, your view of authority will be anything from a benign helper to an exploitative disciplinarian. Most authority figures will ultimately lead you back to what is right for you, although not necessarily what you might consider good for you.

10. **Baby:** To dream about a baby that is your own, indicates that you need to recognise those vulnerable feelings over which you have no control. You may be attempting something new.

11. If the baby is someone else's in the dream, you need to be aware of that person's ability to be hurt, or that they may be innocent of something.

12. **Boy:** To have a dream about a boy shows the potential for growth and new experience. If the boy is known he reflects recognised qualities in the dreamer. You are contacting your natural drives and ability to face difficulties.

13. **Boyfriend:** To dream of a boyfriend, whether present or former, connects with the feelings, attachments and sexuality connected with him. To dream of having as a boyfriend, someone whom you would not anticipate, indicates the need to have a greater understanding of the way the dreamer relates to men, consideration may need to be given to the loving, nurturing side of masculinity. You may still be searching for the ideal lover.

14. **Carers, such as a nurse:** This suggests the more compassionate, nurturing side of yourself. Often it is that side of you which has been called or has a vocation. Usually there is also, for men, a non-sexual relationship.

15. **Child:** *(Your own)* Dreaming of a child gives you access to your own innocent being. When you are able to get in touch with that side of yourself you give yourself permission to clarify a potential for wholeness, which you may not previously have recognised.

16. **Crowd:** Crowds in dreams can indicate how you relate to other people, particularly in a social sense. They may indicate how you can hide yourself, or indeed how you hide aspects of yourself and do not single out any one attribute. You may also be attempting to avoid responsibility.

17. **Dictators: (e.g. Hitler, Stalin etc.)** If the dreamer has had an overbearing father, a known dictator may appear in dreams as representing that relationship.

18. **Emperor or Empress:** *see authority figures*

19. **Girl:** When a girl of any age appears in your dreams you are usually attempting to make contact with the more sensitive, innocent side of yourself. Those qualities of intuition and perception may be somewhat under-developed but can be made available.

20. If the girl is known to you, you probably are aware of those qualities, but need to explore them as though you were approaching them from the girl's point of view.

21. If she is unknown, you can acknowledge that a fresh approach would be useful.

22. **Girlfriend:** When a girlfriend or ex-girlfriend appears in a man's dream there are usually issues to do with masculinity and femininity involved. There may be fears to do with sexuality.

23. If a girlfriend appears in a woman's dream, there is a matter of concern in your present life situation.

24. **Hero or any heroic figure:** In a man's dream the figure of the hero can represent all that is good in him.

25. **Hero in a woman's dream as being on a quest:** This suggests you are aware that something is wrong at the moment but you are struggling to identify it.

26. **The hero's failure:** Suggests you have a weak point through which you can be attacked. To have such a dream indicates that you are not paying attention to the details in your life.

27. **The death of the hero:** can often suggest the need to develop the more intuitive side of yourself, to be born again to something new.

28. **A conflict between the hero and any other dream character:** Suggests a basic disharmony between two facets of your own character. The hero often appears in dreams as an antidote to some hated external figure within the dreamer's everyday life.

29. **High Priest, Astrologer, or anyone with similar esoteric knowledge:** Any character within your dreams who appears to have knowledge of magical practices or similar types of knowledge usually is a first introduction to the Higher Self. It signifies that you can only acquire specific knowledge, which is essential for you at the moment, by meeting someone specific.

30. **Inadequate Person:** This signifies an aspect of yourself at your peril, and cannot afford to dismiss such an image when it appears.

31. **Intruder:** Suggests the need for a change in attitude in the dreamer in order to be able to have a meaningful relationship within his social circle.

32. **King:** A personality such as an emperor may indicate that some aspects of other peoples' attitudes are alien to the dreamer, but should perhaps be accepted.

33. **If the king is old or on the point of dying:** The dreamer will be able to reject outworn or old-fashioned family values.

34. **Ministers:** Ministers usually hold a special place in the dream hierarchy, since their authority is given to them not by man alone, but to all intents and purposes by God or an ultimate power. There is therefore an "otherness" about them.

35. **Man:** Any man appearing in a dream shows an aspect or facet of the dreamer's character in a recognisable form. Even when you are threatened by a negative character trait, you can still access room for improvement.
36. **An old man:** Can represent the innate wisdom you have.
37. **A man in a woman's dream:** Signifies the more logical side of her nature. She has, or can develop, all the aspects of the masculine which enable her to function with success in the external world.
38. If the man is one she knows or loves: Signifies that she may be trying to understand her relationship with him.
39. **An unknown man:** Suggests that part of the dreamer's personality is not recognised.
40. **Negro or any member of an ethnic minority:** Any aspect within yourself which is out of the ordinary or different can manifest in dreams as a member of another race.
41. **Old People:** In dreams, old people can represent either your ancestors or grandparents, hence wisdom accrued from experience.
42. **A group of old people:** Usually this signifies the traditions and wisdom of the past, those things which are sacred to the "tribe" or family. Older people usually stand for your parents even though the dream figures may bear no relationship to them.
43. **Pirate:** Dreaming of a pirate suggests there is an aspect of your personality which destroys your emotional connection with the soul.
44. **Prince or Princess:** To dream of such figures represent luck.
45. **Queen:** To dream of a queen signifies the possibility that you may have to handle a situation which involves a woman in authority.
46. **Stranger:** A stranger in a dream represents limited knowledge. There may be a feeling of awe or of conflict, which you need to deal with before you can progress.
47. **Twins:** Twins in a dream can suggest two sides of your personality. Identical twin represent ambiguity. You will be confused about identical options involving an important decision.
48. Non-identical twins represents a conflict between what you have planned and how will your plans be executed.
49. **Woman** *(In a woman's dream)* This will often represent an aspect of her own personality, which in most cases she has not yet fully understood.
50. **In a man's dream:** Such a figure denotes his relationship with his own feelings and with his intuitive side. It may also show how he relates to his female partner.

51. **A goddess or holy woman:** This signifies your ability to demonstrate the highest potential you may have at the moment. The time may be ripe to move according to your instinct.
52. **An old woman:** This will mostly represent the dreamer's need for support and wisdom.
53. **An unknown woman:** To dream of an old woman represents the likelihood of facing situations of uncertainty, if this is in a woman's dream.
54. **An old woman in a man's dream**: represents unreliability.

PEPPER

1. To dream of pepper signifies the need to liven up a situation you are in. It is an urge that it is not time to take an initiative.
2. If you dream of crushing pepper signifies that you are anxious to make certain changes which will affect you directly.
3. To dream of being aware of the strong smell of pepper signifies that you may be constantly reacting to something or a situation that is not to your liking.
4. To dream of adding pepper to enhance taste suggests comfort in romance.

PERFUME

1. When you dream of smelling perfume, you are often being reminded of particular memories which can be extremely evocative and you may need to recapture a certain emotion associated with that specific perfume.
2. If you dream of having your own preferred perfume, signifies your urge to make a sustainable self-impression.
3. To dream of an undesirable perfume signifies the need to disassociate yourself from people with whom you may have casual relationships.

PERSPIRATION

1. To dream of perspiration signifies that you may be unaware of an important event which may take place during your absence.
2. To dream of drying up perspiration on your own body signifies the need to handle your own emotions and fears.
3. To dream of perspiration having colours other than normal is a warning against deceit.

PET

1. To dream of a pet signifies that you are reacting to a natural drive in yourself to either give or receive love.
2. If you dream of owning a pet signifies that perhaps you need to question your ability to look after something or someone more vulnerable than yourself.
3. To dream of your pet gone missing signifies that someone else has control over your life. You can only do what is expected of you.
4. If you dream of having new pets signifies your need for unconditional love.

PHEASANT
See Birds

PHOENIX
See Birds

PHOTOGRAPH

1. To dream of looking at photographs mean that you are often looking at some aspect of yourself, perhaps an area where you feel you need urgent improvement.
2. To dream of being given a photograph of oneself indicates that you need to be taking an objective view of situations around you or perhaps of yourself within that situation. You need to stand back and look very clearly at what is going on.
3. To dream of looking at photographs of someone who belongs in the past is to be looking at that person's qualities, perhaps bringing them forward into your own life, and making use of those same qualities.

PHYSICIAN
See Doctor

PIANO

1. For a piano to appear in your dream is a symbol of your own creativity. It is a sign that you need to learn and practice using your creativity to reap benefits you never imagined.
2. To dream of playing a piano indicates that you may need to look at your workday situation in the light of making something happen in order to use your best potential.
3. If you dream of listening somebody else playing a piano is a sign that you should be aware not to use your creative powers for the benefit of

others. You may risk making all the efforts and end up not being recognised.

PICTURE

1. A picture in a dream is usually an illustration of something which is part of your life. For instance, in a dream, a picture that you have painted might have more emotional impact than a reprint of another picture.
2. To dream of painting a picture signifies dignity. You are a level-headed person and you should stand firm to preserve your self-respect.
3. To dream of receiving a printed picture signifies that you may have to explore details of things under your responsibility as there may be flaws within them.

PIER

1. Dreaming of a pier would suggest happy times and memories to most people. You may have an association with a particular town or it may simply be that a seaside pier signifies rest and relaxation.
2. To dream of a pier as a point of embarkation or arrival may suggest new opportunities or a task soon to be completed.
3. To simply be at a pier in your dream signifies both a beginning and an ending and moving to a new level of spiritual understanding.

PIG

See Animals

PIGEON

1. To dream of seeing pigeons signify that you may be in a tight or restricted situation and you desperately need to act towards freedom.
2. If you dream of keeping pigeons at your home or some other familiar places signify that you may soon be relieved of a task you considered heavy.
3. To dream of feeding pigeons signify that you may be placed in a difficult situation whereby you may need to give unbiased judgement.

PILL

1. To dream of taking a pill signifies that you may take an action which will put yourself through an experience you need in order to improve your performance or potential.
2. To dream of being given a pill suggests that you may have the power to handle things on your own rather than using external support.

250

3. If you dream of taking a pill which has an unpleasant taste denotes the need for you to avoid making hasty decisions to things which sound good.

PILGRIM

1. To dream of pilgrims signifies the spiritual side of your personality. You have a goal in life, which may require faith to achieve.
2. If you dream of being on a pilgrimage signifies a secure personality and you may not need much input from others to enable you complete whatever you desire provided you create the correct circumstances.
3. To be on a pilgrimage means to be at a holy place. Hence, to dream of a pilgrimage signifies purity and sincerity.

PILLAR

1. To see a pillar in your dream signifies the ability to create stability and to stand firm in the presence of difficulty.
2. To dream of an oversized pillar suggests that you should be taking more responsibility for your actions.
3. Pillars mostly indicate a sort of support, so to become aware of supporting pillars indicate that the structure that you have given your life may need some attention.
4. If you dream of installing pillars with the intention of supporting a structure signify your strength in negotiating your way through success.
5. To dream of a damaged or otherwise non-supportive pillar signifies that you need to do more work with regards to long-term plans. You may also need to review your achievements as they could be only partially achieved.

PILLOW

1. To be conscious of a pillow in your dream may suggest a need for comfort. Please review your situation and ensure that you face situations causing discomfort.
2. A feather pillow would suggest gentle support, whereas a stone pillow would represent a degree of rigidity.
3. If you dream of a pillow fight signifies a conflict between what you need and what you have at the moment.
4. If you dream of a burst pillow signifies that you have to be careful of how you handle things at present as you may be at risk of losing something you consider very precious.

PIMPLE

1. To be overly conscious of something like a pimple in a dream is to suggest some worry as to how one comes across to others. A pimple can also represent some kind of blemish in your character which at some time or another will have to be dealt with.

2. Since a pimple usually suggests the body's inability to throw off toxins, such a symbol in dreams indicates your inability to throw off infection or negativity. It has only come partly to the surface of your consciousness.

3. If you dream of nursing a pimple signifies a need to review a completed task. You may be able to improve it further thus increasing your self-esteem.

PIN

1. To dream of a pin holding things together indicates the emotional connections or bonds that you use. You have good connections but you are not fully using them.

2. To dream of a pin piercing an object suggests a trauma, although it may be quite small.

3. To experience a feeling of pins and needles in your dream suggests that you are not ensuring an adequate flow of energy in a situation around you.

4. If you dream of pinning things together which refuse to hold, signifies that you may need to avoid a temporary solution to whatever situation you may be in, because it may cost more to find a permanent solution at a later stage.

5. To dream of being accidentally pricked by a pin suggests that you may temporarily lose something personal which will cause great annoyance.

PIPE

1. To dream of a water pipe signifies that, despite the fact that you may have a moderately weak character, you are able to handle your emotions properly in difficult times.

2. To dream of a pierced pipe of water signifies the possibility of being upset by someone unusual.

3. If you dream of a tobacco pipe suggests that you may have to make a move to escape from an emotional trap.

4. When you are in difficulty in everyday life, a simple symbol such as a pipe or conduit will indicate how making connections between the various aspects of a situation will help resolve it.

PISTOL
See Gun

PISTON

1. A piston in a dream can be taken to mean sexual drive or activity. In this context it is more of a mechanical action than a loving act, and may show the dreamer's appetite to sex.
2. In a woman's dream a piston may reveal her fear of being hurt sexually. She may be aware that she is simply being used, and that there is no tenderness.
3. In a man's dream such an image may be indicative of his sense of identity and masculinity. If the piston is not rigid a man may fear impotence, whereas a woman will feel perhaps that she cannot trust her partner.
4. A piston may also represent a person's drive for success. The dreamer may need to assess the amount of effort that is necessary for him or her to be able to achieve his or her goals.
5. The piston, being only part of an engine, requires the rest of the components to operate successfully. Often a great deal of help can be gained by considering the way in which the piston works. In other words, when at a particular stage of development, your actions may have to be forceful and you may need additional facilities to succeed.

PIT

1. To dream of a pit signifies that you are conscious of a particular feeling. You may be in a situation which you cannot get out of, and this signifies special courage for you to get out to it.
2. To dream of digging a pit suggests that you have to be conscious of the fact that you may be creating certain situation which will be a major disadvantage to yourself.
3. To dream of others digging the pit, suggests that you may feel you have no control over your circumstances and that doom and disaster are inevitable.
4. If you dream of rescuing others from a pit, particularly if they are members of your own family, suggests that you have information which may be of use to them to enable them to overcome their problems.
5. If you dream of pushing someone into a pit indicates that you are trying to suppress some part of your personality.
6. If you dream of being conscious of a bottomless pit signifies that you do not have the resources to recover from a previous situation.

7. If you dream of being trapped in a pit signifies that you may have no choice but to go forward with a great risk.

8. To dream of facing a pit signifies that you have extreme courage.

PLACES

1. Places in dreams can reflect your inner state of mind or mood. To dream of being in a familiar place signifies that you may need to recall something to help you sort out your present situation.

2. Interpreting the symbolism of certain places gives you an insight into your own "inner landscape": For example, a place that becomes fertile or lighter in the course of the dream indicates that an aspect that the dreamer has not previously appreciated is now developing possibilities and potentials, possibly for spiritual development.

3. **Countryside:** The countryside can suggest a particular mood or feeling, especially of freedom.

4. **Composite recognised scenes:** You are usually drawing attention to particular qualities, ideals and moods which all have a bearing on your success.

5. **The dreamer's birthplace:** represents a secure space.

6. **A bright and sunny place:** suggests fun and liveliness.

7. **A dark and murky scene:** signifies despondency and gloom.

8. **Darkened places**: can represent unawareness.

9. **Jungles:** signifies a need for understanding of your sexuality.

10. **A sheltered place:** signifies peace and security.

11. **Unknown places:** Aspects of yourself of which you are not aware.

12. **A place that seems familiar and yet you do not know:** signifies a situation which is continually rerunning in your life.

13. **Wide-open spaces:** offer you freedom of movement.

14. **An unfamiliar place:** will signify new aspects of the personality which have not yet become fully conscious.

PLAIT

1. To dream of a plait using three strands indicates the interweaving of body, mind and spirit. It also represents the influences of womanhood.

2. To dream of plaiting string, rope, hair etc. highlights your ability to weave the different influences of yours, or someone else's life into a consistent pattern.

3. To dream of hair plaited into various shapes indicates spiritual attainment.

PLANETS

1. Dreaming of planets is to be linking with very subtle energies which surround you and have an effect on your life, even though you may not be consciously aware of it.
   The interpretations of the significances are as follows:
2. **Jupiter:** suggests growth and expansion, and also freedom from limitation.
3. **Mars:** indicates activity and war but also drive.
4. **Mercury:** signifies communication, intuition and mental powers.
5. **Moon:** represents your emotions and your links with someone trustworthy.
6. **Neptune:** Inspiration is necessary in your work.
7. **Pluto:** Your ability to make transformations.
8. **Saturn:** You are under the influence of restraint.
9. **Uranus**: Gives you control over sudden changes.
10. **Venus:** highlights love and beauty.

PLANK

1. To dream of a plank of wood indicates that something needs repairing, or that you feel safer carrying your own means of support.
2. If you dream of the plank being used in flooring, the symbol is one of security, but if it is to be used as a door or as decoration on a wall, it signifies defence.
3. To dream of walking the plank suggests taking an emotional risk.
4. To dream of using the plank for making something, it suggests assessing the required material you have for undertaking a project.
5. To dream of using the plank for making a box, you should take care not to become trapped within a situation.

PLANTS

1. Because of the process of growth and decay that plants go through naturally, they become a symbol for progressive change. Hence, to dream of live healthy plants signify your ability to cultivate potential.
2. To dream of dying plants suggest that you may have reached a stage where there is no more advantage within a situation.
3. If you dream of the plants growing wild, there is a part of you that needs freedom.
4. To dream of plants grown in regimented rows, you are aware of too much concern for the views of other people.

PLATE

1. A simple plate will indicate a need for simplicity within your life, whereas a more ornate one may suggest the need for celebration.
2. To dream of holding a plate, you are aware of what you have received from other people.
3. If someone else is giving you the plate, they are offering you something which belongs to them, but which you can now share.
4. To dream of an empty plate signifies that you have specific needs and appetites to complete an immediate task.
5. To dream of owning a plate suggests that you have achieved a certain level of awareness.

PLATEAU

1. To dream of reaching a plateau can represent a period of peace and tranquillity.
2. If you dream of reaching a barren plateau signifies that you may need some further stimulus to help you move on.
3. To dream of reaching a peaceful plateau signifies that you can rest on your laurels and take time out to assess your progress and still have plenty of time ahead.

PLAY

1. To be watching a play, signifies that you are trying to view your own life objectively. The content of the play may give you clues as to what your course of action should be in everyday life.
2. If people you know are in the play, you should be aware of conscious details of interactions with them.
3. To dream of participating in a play signifies that you may face unexpected situations which means that you have to seek explanation elsewhere.
4. If you dream of a non-interesting play signifies that the best opportunity is to learn your lessons through experience.

PLUMBING

1. To dream of plumbing works indicate a need to bypass obstacles in order to create security for yourself and to control the flow of emotions within.
2. To dream of doing plumbing works yourself signify that perhaps something may be wrong with you or with part of your body. You may not be in the best of health.
3. To dream of faulty plumbing works signify that you may have to participate in a specific event despite your reluctance.

256

PLUNGE

1. To dream of taking a plunge is to recognise that you are facing uncertainty.
2. If you dream of plunging from very high is a warning that you may have to reconsider the risk which you are about to take.
3. To dream of plunging, like diving in a swimming is a plunge for pleasure and hence, it signifies that you have exceptional ability to go forward.
4. To dream of a plunger, like in something that clears a blockage, usually indicates that you need to use some force to enable you to deal with difficulty.

POCKET

1. To dream of a pocket is to be dealing with your personal secrets or thoughts, those things that you have deliberately chosen to hide rather than done so on impulse.
2. If you dream of empty pockets signify that you have secret thoughts that you do not want to share with anyone else. There may also be thoughts about your own abilities and the value that you have within your own personal community.
3. If you dream of a loaded pocket indicates that you have a sense of ownership and possession.
4. To have something other than cash in your pocket means that you have to be appropriate to what sort of ownership you take.
5. To dream of having a torn pocket signifies that you have to take serious steps to avoid financial constraints.

POINT

1. To dream of something pointed signifies that you have a healthy sexual appetite.
2. To dream of sharpening something to make it pointed signifies a lack of sexual activity. You may be sexually active but may also be short of satisfaction.
3. If you dream of a point (as on paper) is a warning to be more focused in your daily activities or else you may end up being taken in.

POISON

1. To be aware of poison in a dream means that you need to avoid an attitude, emotion, or thought which may not be good for you.

2. To dream of being a victim of poison signifies that you should take steps to avoid being influenced by other people's attitudes and beliefs as these can often contaminate the way you think and feel.
3. If you dream of giving poison to others or animals signifies that you have evil intent which can delay your spiritual progress.

POKER

1. A poker in your dream suggests the tendency to take aggressive actions and also rigid attitudes and behaviour.
2. To dream of playing a game of poker suggests that you are taking a risk in everyday life. It may be important to note who you are dealing with.
3. To witness a game of poker in your dream suggests unbending discipline which is necessary for spiritual development.

POLE

1. To see a pole in your dream is an expression of the life force you possess.
2. To dream of fitting a pole in the ground signifies the need for stability as well as maintaining standards.
3. If you dream of a bended pole signifies that spiritual or heroic standards of behaviour need to be instigated.

POOL

1. Dreaming of a pool deals with your need for the understanding of your own emotions and inner feelings.
2. A pool in a wood, for instance, may suggest the ability to understand your own need for peace and tranquillity.
3. An urban swimming pool might signify your need for structure in your relationships with other people.
4. A pool in the road would suggest an emotional problem to be gotten through before carrying out your plans.
5. To dream of being in a swimming pool may suggest that you need a form of cleansing, particularly of old traumas and emotions, or past misdeeds.

POPE

1. Often to meet the Pope in a dream is to meet the side of yourself which has developed a code of behaviour based on your religious beliefs.

2. The Pope often appears in dreams as a substitute for the father, or as a personification of God.
3. To be in the company of the pope signifies that you have the desire to attain your ambitions but you may need spiritual guidance.

POPPY
1. To dream of a poppy symbolises a sacrifice.
2. To dream of wearing a poppy on your clothes signifies that, in order to move forward effectively, you need to try your best to forget past difficulties.
3. If you dream of poppy blossomed in other trees is a warning against trickery.

POSITION
1. To dream of something in the wrong position signifies that you are going about things in the wrong way.
2. To dream of something higher or above you signifies intellect, ideals and consciences are being brought to your attention.
3. To dream of the upper part of something signifies that your superiority may be being brought into question.
4. To dream of anything underneath, below, or downstairs signifies the immoral side of your personalities. There can also be negative sexual implications.
5. To dream of something appearing upside down warns against the potential for chaos and difficulty.
6. If you dream of the back of things signifies the possibility of rejection.
7. To dream of the front of things generally signifies acceptance.
8. Having the attention drawn to a backward and/or forward movement is usually indicating the potential to adopt a regressive backward-looking tendency. There is a need to retire into the past, rather than tackling fears and moving ahead.
9. **Centre:** To be conscious of the centre of any object or place in a dream is to be aware of a goal or objective.
10. **Far/Near:** In dreams, space and time can become confused. Dreaming of something, which is far away, may indicate that it is far away in time. This may be future or past, depending on the dream.
11. **A long way in front:** signifies a bright future.
12. **A long way behind:** would suggest that a situation you may be pondering over has already occurred.
13. **Near:** This generally means a recent or immediate event.
14. **Horizontal:** This usually symbolises the material world.

15. To dream of being below something can indicate a need to explore the underside or negativity of a relationship or situation.
16. **Opposite:** Anything in a dream which is opposite the dreamer may suggest some difficulty in reconciling two paradoxes (good/bad, male/female, up/down, etc.).
17. **One thing deliberately put opposite another:** There is a deliberate attempt to introduce discord.
18. **Changing the position from opposite:** Differences may be adjusted.
19. **To dream of something on your right:** The right side represents the more dominant logical side. It is the consciously expressed, confident side which perceives the exterior world in perhaps a more objective sense.
20. **Movement to the right:** indicates that something is coming into conscious awareness.
21. **Left:** The left side suggests the less dominant, more passive side. Often it is taken to represent all that is dark and sinister, and those parts of your personality which you try to suppress.
21. To dream of anything appearing on the left side can be accepted as a symbol of support.
22. To dream of feelings of being left behind suggest a sense of inadequacy, of disintegration and of having to leave the past behind.
23. **Indecision over left or right:** suggests an inability to decide whether to rely on drive or instinct.
24. **Straight:** Straight suggests a direct approach is necessary to avoid misunderstandings.
25. **Top:** Suggests success in your endeavours. To be on top is to have assumed control.
26. **Trying to reach the top:** suggests more effort is needed.
27. **Up:** You have the capability of achieving a degree of supremacy. You are capable of getting the "upper hand" in particular situations.
28. **Under:** Being underneath something suggests either taking shelter or submitting to someone else's handling of your dealings.
29. **Vertical:** The vertical in dreams tends to represent the spiritual realm.
30. **The North:** Sometimes signifies darkness.
31. **The East:** Traditionally suggests birth and mystic religions.
32. **The South:** This represents earthly passion and sensuality.
33. **The West:** This symbolises death.

POVERTY

1. To dream of experiencing poverty signifies a sense of being deprived of the ability to satisfy your basic needs. You may feel inadequate, either emotionally or materially.
2. Poverty in a dream can be conveyed by poor surroundings. It may be that you need to deal with your surroundings rather than yourself.
3. If you dream of pitying those who are poor signifies denial. You may face a situation where you may be misguided about the true facts.

PRAYER

1. To dream of prayers suggest the idea that you need to seek outside help for yourself. You may need someone else's authority to succeed in what you are doing.
2. To dream of praying denotes that you need to use your own inner sense of self to access greater powers which are virtually available to you.
3. If you dream of prayers in a congregation signifies that you may need collective agreements to pursue a specific matter successfully.

PRECIPICE

1. To dream of a precipice signifies that you have a fear of failure. Generate the courage to proceed as your feelings of fear may only be apparent.
2. If you dream of stepping off a precipice signifies taking risks, since you do not know the outcome of your action.
3. To dream of trying to climb a precipice is to be making a tremendous effort to overcome obstacles which have arisen.
4. If you dream of being trapped in a precipice is a warning that you should take the appropriate measures to protect yourself against psychic attacks.

PREGNANCY

1. Dreaming of pregnancy usually denotes a fairly protracted waiting period being necessary for something, possibly the completion of a project. A new area of your potential or personality is developing.
2. To dream of someone else being pregnant suggests that you are in a position to observe part of yourself developing new skills or characteristics. You may be unaware of what the outcome of this process will be.

3. If you dream of a man being pregnant, particularly if it is a woman's dream, is probably a projection of her own wish for the man to take responsibility within her life.

PRESENTS
1. To dream of receiving a present signifies that you are being loved, recognised and also gaining from the relationship.
2. To dream of giving a present denotes that you appreciate that you have characteristics you are able to offer other people.
3. If you dream of many presents can signify as yet unrecognised talents and skills.
4. To present something in a dream (as in presentation) is offering work that you have done for approval and recognition.

PRIEST
1. To see a priest in your dream highlights the need for spiritual enlightenment. You may have to refrain from adopting a "tit-for-tat" attitude.
2. If you dream of being a priest is a warning that you may not be doing enough to make valuable contributions in terms of intangible assets such as knowledge which you have but reluctant to share.
3. If you dream of somebody unexpectedly turned priest signifies that you may have to be very "choosy" in the contents of your next project or else you may end up doing hard work with no relevance.

PRISON
1. Prison, in dreams, stands for the traps you create for yourself. You may feel that outside circumstances are making life difficult, but in actual fact you are creating those circumstances yourself.
2. Often you create a prison for you through a sense of duty or guilt and this can often be shown in dreams. The types of locks and bolts you perceive in your prison may show you how you are imprisoning yourself. For example, a lock with a key would suggest that you know how to escape, whereas a bolt shows that you have to make a greater effort.
3. To dream of a prison with a barred window would suggest that you are being prevented from using that which is external to you.
4. If you dream of being in a prison signifies that there is a way forward in your present life but you may have to make special efforts to see it.

PRIZE
1. To dream of winning a prize is a sign that you will succeed in overcoming your own obstacles.
2. If you dream of giving away prizes suggest that you are giving public acknowledgment to efforts others have made.
3. If you dream of receiving a prize which you feel should not be rightfully yours suggests that you may be materialistic.

PROCESSION
1. In a dream, to see a group of people marching with the same purpose as in a procession signifies that it is very important at the moment to adopt a set of priorities for yourself so as to gain a measure of direction for your life.
2. A procession is often a way of marking a special occasion with pageantry and dignity. In dreams such an image can often represent the dreamer's need to have his own successes and abilities recognised.
3. Spiritually, a procession is indicative of a group of like-minded people but also of people who have great knowledge. In dreams you are recognising the importance of whatever system of belief or religion you belong to. You recognise that respect must be paid.

PROPELLER
1. To see a propeller in your dream is a warning that you have to put more drive and intent behind your progression.
2. If you dream of being the driving force behind a propeller suggests that you need to undertake a journey of discovery to "kick-start" something important in your life at the moment.
3. If you dream of a propeller which appears to have one or more blades missing is a warning not to be discouraged in whatever you may be attempting at the moment even if progress may seem slow.

PROSTITUTE
1. Dreaming of a prostitute usually suggests a sexual need. In a man's dream it may signify his need for relationship at any cost.
2. In a woman's dream it can suggest her own need for sexual freedom. Often, dreaming of a prostitute forces you to look at your own sense of guilt or uncertainty about yourself.
3. To dream of paying a prostitute may suggest that you do not trust your own sexual abilities.

4. To dream of being paid for sexual acts may suggest that you feel uncomfortable with relationships.
5. In dreaming of prostitution, you may actually be indulging with a poor self-image. You are minimising your abilities and talents. This may be in a work situation as much as in your personal life.
6. If you dream of your own family members in prostitution signify that you have to make it a point to accept other people's values.

PSYCHOLOGIST
See Analyst

PUBLIC HOUSE
1. To be in a pub in a dream and aware of your behaviour indicates how you relate to groups and what your feelings are, about society. You may feel that it is appropriate to use a public place to create new relationships, or to come to terms with your own sense of loneliness.
2. If you dream of perceiving a pub in your dream signifies that you may be longing for something but you have the wrong attitude that things will come your way without having to make an effort.
3. If you dream of your own house turned into a pub signifies that good omens prevail.

PUDDLE
1. For a puddle to appear in a dream signifies that you are becoming aware of your emotions and taking correct steps to handle them.
2. To dream of mopping up the puddle signifies that you are trying to reabsorb emotion that you may feel to be inappropriate.
3. If you dream of looking at your reflection in a puddle signifies the importance to decide what future action needs to be taken at the moment.

PULL
1. To dream of pulling something suggests that you are being alerted to do something about a situation you face at the moment.
2. To dream of being pulled suggests that you may feel that you have to give in to outside pressures. You definitely need extra efforts to avoid such a situation.
3. If you dream of pulling others against their will signify that you may feel that you have to go along with something and do not have the ability to refuse.

PUNISHMENT

1. To dream of being punished signifies that you have fears of retribution from an external source.
2. To dream of punishing someone signifies that there is conflict in your life and you are facing difficulties to resolve it. You may have to guard against rebuking others for your own shortcomings.
3. To dream of witnessing others being punished signify that you have concerns for other people but you also have reservations as well.

PUPPET

1. If a puppet appears in your dream denotes that there is perhaps a sense of being able to manipulate circumstances or people around you to your advantage
2. To dream of someone else working the puppet suggests that you may feel that you are being manipulated. It would be wise to look at how you are cooperating in everyday life in becoming a victim.
3. If you dream of the puppet manipulating you suggests that you are aware that bureaucracy is causing you difficulty. Keep a cool approach.

PUPPY

See Dog in Animals

PURSE

1. A purse is normally used to hold money, or something of value to us. In dreams it therefore becomes something of value it its own right. To find a purse would suggest that you are about to handle something of value.
2. To dream of losing a purse is a warning against being careless.
3. To dream of a cash-loaded purse signifies that you are on the correct path towards your goal. Keep pursuing.

PUS

1. To perceive pus in your dream signifies that something or a particular situation may have bad elements within it and is going bad.
2. To dream of an infected area on yourself producing pus indicates that you should guard against negative elements such as fears, self-doubts and jealousy. The tendency for you to entertain these bad elements is strong at the moment.
3. To dream of others helping you with pus suggests that you have internal negativity and you need to learn to heal yourself.

4. In a spiritual sense, pus is the result of having attempted to fight something which is "evil," and although you may have overcome it, you are left with the results to clear up.

PUSHED

1. To dream of being pushed suggests that there is an energy around you and you have to use it to enable you achieve what you want.
2. To dream of pushing something is a good sign that you are exerting your will positively.
3. If you dream of pushing something uphill, such as a car suggests that you are trying to resist natural forces.
4. To dream of being pushed from behind by someone is a warning not to endure unnecessary pressure as this may drive you to an emotional breakdown.

PYRAMID

1. To dream of a pyramid signifies that you need the element of power to realise something important. Power means knowledge. You may need to upgrade your knowledge before proceeding further or else you may end up placing the cart before the horse.
2. To dream of entering a pyramid signifies that you may have to search for the interpretation of something before you can give a proper explanation.
3. To dream of a disintegrating pyramid is a sign that you may have to guard against involvement in matters of dispute, as there may be greater complications than you think.

Q

QUAIL
See Birds

QUAKER
1. To dream of meeting a Quaker indicates that you must avoid a religious debate which comes your way.
2. To dream of being a Quaker signifies that you may have to be more independent and think for yourself without apprehension of what others may think.
3. To dream of somebody suddenly turned a Quaker denotes a nasty surprise.

QUARANTINE
1. Dreaming of having to put an animal into quarantine signifies your inability to look after a vulnerable part of yourself or the environment you frequent.
2. If you dream of being in quarantine signifies that you may face a situation of being either neglected or isolated from an event you feel you should be included.
3. To dream of others in quarantine signify that you may be placed in a situation where demand for your help may be heavy.

QUARREL
1. To dream that you are quarrelling indicates that you have an inner conflict. You may have to make careful analyses to enable you make proper judgement.
2. To dream of quarrelling with authority, e.g. police, indicates that you may face a tricky situation in deciding between what is right and wrong.
3. If you dream of somebody else quarrelling with you signifies that you may be involved in a situation where you may be obliged to do something in a way to please somebody else in particular and not you.

QUARRY
1. Dreaming of a quarry means that you have to make extensive use of the positive knowledge and perceptions you may have, to enable you reach accomplishment.

2. To dream of using the services of a quarry signifies that you have to pursue someone or something vigorously in order to meet a specific deadline.

QUARTET

1. To dream of a quartet signifies that you may need a level of collaboration to finalise an enquiry regarding a personal matter.
2. To dream of being part of a quartet signifies that you may need to make repeated attempts to achieve something. You will not succeed on the first go.

QUAY

1. To dream of being on a Quay indicates the possibility of either moving forward into a new phase of life or leaving an old one behind.

QUEEN

See People

QUEST

1. To dream that you are on a quest for something signifies that you may face several options and you have to choose the best one to maximise the chance of success.
2. To dream of having been on a successful quest signifies reliability in your everyday dealings.
3. To dream to be on what you consider to be an impossible quest signifies that you have to demonstrate more frankness in whatever discussions you may become involve, as this will ensure greater respect.

QUESTION

1. To dream of asking questions indicate a degree of self-doubt. Please ensure that your facts are properly documented to avoid humility.
2. If you dream of being questioned signifies that you are aware that you have knowledge to be shared and that others may be putting pressure on you for it.

QUESTIONNAIRE

1. To dream of filling up a questionnaire suggests that you may need to make an attempt to change your circumstances before you can be certain of what you should actually do to bring about a change.
2. A questionnaire in a dream depicts the use of your mental faculties in a focused, decision-making way.

3. If you dream of designing a questionnaire signifies that you will need explanations to things under your responsibility which may go wrong in simple circumstances.

QUEUE
See Line

QUICKSAND
1. Quicksand signifies a lack of security. In old-fashioned dream interpretations it represented business difficulties.
2. To dream of being trapped in quicksand suggests that you have been put in a difficult situation that is not necessarily of your own making.
3. If you dream of helping somebody else out of quicksand signifies that you have under-developed powers to talk your way to success.

QUIET
1. Becoming aware of how quiet it is in a dream shows that you need to cease being active for a while, perhaps in order to restore your emotional or spiritual balance.
2. If you dream of trying to quieten other people suggests that you need to listen more carefully to others in waking life.
3. To dream of a usually noisy place such as a market to be quiet, signifies your unawareness that you may be being observed.

QUINTESSENCE
1. "Quintessence" literally means "five beings," but is taken to mean "supremely perfect." To dream of this is to link with your need to create, and to create as perfectly as you can.
2. Perfection is one of those things that the more you know the more you realise how far you are from perfect. So to dream of the quintessence is to recognise your own and others' potential.

QUIP
1. To become aware of a joke or quip by someone else in a dream, you are alerted to the fact that you can allow yourself to be affected by other people's sense of humour. You have to guard against this.
2. If you yourself is the one who is communicating through wit or sarcasm, you may often be surprised by your own ability.
3. To dream of being offended by quip signifies that you have to watch out against being made a scapegoat.

QUOTATION

1. To dream of giving a quotation, as in a building estimate, can signify the value that you put on your services or talents. You may have difficulty with the accuracy, or the acceptance of the quote and therefore, in waking life, you will need to reconsider your own self image.

2. To dream of using a quote, e.g. a saying, is a warning that you may have to guard against being deceived.

R

RABBIT
See Animals

RACK
1. A rack in a dream suggests a need for you to keep order, or put in order, things or procedures. There is a need to adopt a strategy in order to be consistent in your progress.
2. To dream of being on a rack, in the sense of being tortured, would suggest you have either done something you are ashamed of, or have put yourself in the position of being someone else's victim.
3. If you dream of a damaged rack signifies the likelihood of an argument or even chaos.

RADAR
1. To dream of a radar signifies your ability to interpret messages or instructions for optimum effectiveness.
2. If you dream of operating a radar signifies that you may shortly be in search for something specific or you may have to get involved in specific enquiries to enable you to get the required information in order to make effective decisions.
3. Radar can also suggest that a degree of clairvoyance is available to the dreamer.

RADIANCE
1. When something appears as radiant in a dream it is being marked as having some kind of special quality, which you may need to explore further.
2. Radiance represents something out of the ordinary or supernatural. It also suggests purity of thought, wisdom and the transcendence of the mundane.
3. Radiance is a sign of pure spirituality. You are on the path of enlightenment.

RADIO
1. To dream of hearing a radio suggests that you have effective communication links to the proper channels which you need for progress.

2. To dream of having difficulties to follow what is being broadcast over a radio denotes that you may have proper facilities available but they are being used better by others than you.

3. To dream of a damaged radio suggests that you have a weakness of accepting things you know you shouldn't.

RAFFLE

1. In a dream to be taking part in a raffle can indicate your desire to win or come out on top.

2. If you dream of selling raffle tickets indicate your need to help others, whereas to be organising a raffle suggests that you must collaborate with a group of people to achieve collectively.

3. Although gambling may not be acceptable in the dreamer's normal code of behaviour, because a raffle is also a charitable act, it may, in dreams, be representative of soothing the dreamer's conscience at having taken a risk.

4. To dream of winning a prize in a raffle suggests your elements of authority which can only be displayed over a group of people rather than an individual.

RAFT

1. To dream of a raft signifies that you may have to deal with forthcoming emotional difficulties.

2. To dream of paddling on a raft signifies that you have the potential, ability and courage to stand against a difficult situation which may be unexpected.

3. To dream to be on a sinking raft is a warning that you have a long and arduous road ahead. But succeed, you will.

4. If you dream of successfully reaching your destination on a raft signifies that you may have justified reasons to pursue your ambition despite the displeasure of a close acquaintance.

RAILWAY

1. To dream of railway lines signify that you are actually going forward in your endeavour or you have the potential to go forward.

2. To dream of a single track indicates that you have limited options in your quest for achievement.

3. If you dream of multiple tracks suggest that you have a wider range of options to move forward but you may encounter difficulties to choose the best one.

272

4. If you dream of standing on a railway track suggests the idea of keeping to one goal and being single-minded about it.

RAIN

1. In its simplest meaning rain stands for tears and emotional release. You may have been depressed, with no way to release your feelings in everyday life. Hence to dream of rain is a warning that you should have emotional relief.
2. If you dream of being in the rain signifies fertility through the sexual act.
3. To dream of being in the rain yet not getting wet signifies that you may have the tendency to hide the misgivings of someone very close. It is a difficult situation but it is not the best of decisions.

RAINBOW

1. For a rainbow to appear in your dream is the promise of something better to come.
2. More esoterically, a rainbow is said to represent the seven steps of awareness necessary for true spirituality.
3. A rainbow symbolises the spiritual glory that is available to the dreamer through understanding and learning.

RAM
See Animals

RAPE
See Sex

RAT
See Animals

RAVEN
See Birds

RAZOR

Different razors may symbolise differently as follows:
1. **A cut-throat razor:** suggests that you may be pursuing unnecessary elements on your way forward.
2. **A safety razor:** suggests a less risky method is needed to enable you to reveal the truth about yourself.

3. **An electric razor:** suggests that you need to pay attention to the image you put across in everyday life.
4. **Using a razor on someone else:** symbolises a caring act unless your actions are deliberately violent.

REACHING OUT
1. To be reaching out for something in your dream signifies your desire for something you do not have. This may be either emotional or material. You may be trying to manipulate circumstances in such a way that others become aware of your needs.
2. You may also be attempting to grasp a concept, an idea or an opportunity, which appears to be beyond your reach or understanding at the moment. You may have to study a particular circumstance more intently.
3. You may also be trying to control others by your own emotional neediness. This is particularly relevant when you become conscious of rejection or distaste in others.
4. If you dream of reaching out for something which you fail to get hold of, suggests that you need to stand back and review your plans more carefully.

READING
1. Reading a book in a dream suggests that you are seeking information.
2. To dream of reading a letter signifies that you have a level of uncertainty in your actions.
3. Reading a list of any form indicates a need to give some order to your life.
4. Reading a Bible or other holy book signifies making an attempt to understand a spiritual belief.
5. Reading a novel is to begin to understand your own need for fantasy.
6. A psychic reading suggests a need to understand yourself on a deeper level.

REAP
1. To dream of reaping suggests that you have a need but you also need a way of gaining from your activities.
2. The saying "as ye sow, so shall ye reap" can be interpreted as if you do good deeds, then that good will be returned. When you dream of reaping a reward for something you have done, you approve of your own activities. More negatively, a harmful act will return to haunt you.

274

RED
See Colours

REFLECTION
1. To dream of perceiving a reflection has a great deal to do with the way you see yourself at that particular moment. If the reflection is in a mirror, then your image will be perhaps more "solid," whereas one seen in water will be more transient.
2. The story of Narcissus and the way he fell in love with himself (or rather his own image) is a warning to you against self-worship.
3. If you dream of perceiving an image other than yours when you look in the mirror or any other media, signifies an illusion. Be extremely cautious not to make any financial agreements or commitments to anyone, even those you trust most.

REFRIGERATOR
1. To dream of a refrigerator is a sign that you should consider certain elements of self-preservation. You may be turning cold emotionally or sexually.
2. To dream of rotten food in a refrigerator suggests that you may not be being sustained properly, hence, the need to make a move towards preventing inadequacy.
3. To dream of refrigerating leftover food indicates you are storing up resentment. This, in turn, will "cool down" your own responses to love and affection.

REINDEER
See Deer in Animals

REINS
1. In dreams, reins, as a form of restraint, indicate the need to control the power and energy that you have.
2. If you dream of being reined suggests some form of inhibition, either your own or other people's. To dream of broken reins denote freeing yourself from constraints, that which was placed on you while you grew up.
3. To dream of holding reins indicate intelligent control and will.

RELIGION

In the religious realm there is a wide variety of symbolism as follows:

1. **Angel:** In spiritual terms the angel symbolises pure being and freedom from earthly difficult matters.

2. **Dark angels:** are reputed to be those angelic beings who have not yet totally rejected the ego or earthly passions. When this image appears in a dream you are being alerted to a spiritual transgression, which often, has already happened.

3. **Warning angels:** usually symbolise what should not be done.

4. **Buddha:** The figure of Buddha appearing in dreams is highlighting the necessity to be aware of the Qualities of Being, that Buddha taught. It links you to the power of renunciation and of suffering, but in the sense that experience of suffering is valid.

5. **Ceremony/Ritual:** Denotes that you are in need of basic spiritual necessities.

6. **Christ:** appearing in dreams epitomises the recognition of the ability to reconcile the physical and the spiritual, God and Man. He personifies perfect man, a state to which we all aspire.

7. **Appearing on the cross:** he signifies redemption through suffering. You do not need to be crucified physically to suffer.

8. **The ideal Christ:** is that part of yourself which is prepared to take on your portion of the sufferings in the world, by working within the world.

9. **The anarchic Christ:** is the part of you where love and lust for life permit you to break through all known barriers.

10. **The cosmic Christ:** is the part that is prepared to take on cosmic responsibility, that is, to be connected with the Universal Truth.

11. **Church, chapel, temple:** We all are aware of our need for sanctuary from the batterings of the everyday world. Within the church we are free to form a relationship with our own personal God. In dreams we may also have the realisation that our body is our temple.

12. **Church or Religious Music:** These sounds, dedicated to the perception of God that one has, are sacred sounds and are a way of expanding the spirit.

13. **Crucifixion:** Such images in a dream link with the human being's need to sacrifice himself through passion and through pain.

14. **Devil:** represents temptation. This often arises from the repressed sexual drives which demand attention.

15. **Ghosts:** Independent forces within, which are separate from the individual's will. It will depend on the dreamer's belief as to whether

276

he accepts the appearance of ghosts as psychological or spiritual apparitions.

16. **Gods/Goddesses:** We are each given the opportunity to make real our fullest potential. In doing so, we must undertake an exploration and possibly a confrontation of our perception of gods and goddesses.

17. **Heaven:** is a state of being where the energy is of such a high frequency that there is no suffering. In dreams it appears when the individual is transmuting his awareness into dimensions other than the physical. It is reputedly a place where bliss exists.

18. **Hell:** is a state of being where nothing is ever as it seems and could be thought of as continually existing in a state of negative illusion. Reputedly it is a state of Agony where one's worst dreams are fulfilled.

19. **Holy Communion:** The belief that Christ's body was transmuted into heavenly food, symbolised by the Last Supper, appears in dreams as the intake of spiritual food. Holy Communion represents a sacred sharing.

20. **Icon:** An icon is a representation of a religious figure or concept. It can, through usage, become revered as a holy object in its own right.

21. **Incense:** Incense is an offering to the gods and a physical form of prayer through perfume and smoke.

22. **Initiation:** takes place when some barrier is transcended to enable you to have access to other ways of being.

23. **Mother Mary:** The symbolism of Mary, both as the maiden and as the mother, is a potent one. She epitomises all that is woman, and all that is holy.

24. **Moses:** often appears in dreams as the holy figure who will lead us out of difficulty.

25. **Old and New Testaments:** A resource and a repository for knowledge is available; in dream image this will often appear as books.

26. **Priest/Prophet:** A conflict between the present and the future.

27. **Religious Service:** is the act of worship which is used to bring people together.

28. **Third Eye:** This is the developed clairvoyant perceptiveness that comes with spiritual development. It is the Third Eye of Buddha and symbolises unity and balance

RENT

1. To dream of paying an agreed rent is to undertake a personal responsibility. You are prepared to look after yourself and to take responsibility for who you are.

2. To dream of paying high rent indicates that you have to learn how to handle money and value.
3. To dream of receiving rent suggests that you have entered into a transaction which will benefit you.

REPTILES
1. To dream of reptiles signify that you have a basic need for either food or sex.
2. If you dream of being frightened by reptiles suggest a need for control or proper management of something under your responsibility.
3. If you dream of a crocodile would suggest some fear of an aggressive nature.
4. To dream of feeding a lizard or stroking a snake signifies bravery.

RESCUE
1. To dream of being rescued is a powerful image, since it leaves you indebted to your rescuer.
2. To dream of rescuing someone else often suggests that you wish to have a relationship with that person.
3. If you dream of having to rescue others from danger, out of your own fault, signifies that you need a degree of nobility and courage.

RESIGN
1. To dream of resigning from work means you are aware of major changes in your life.
2. To dream of being resigned suggests that you have accepted the status quo in your life.
3. If you dream of being asked to resign from a particular post or responsibility signifies that you may be short of ideas to motivate yourself or others to complete something still outstanding.
4. To dream of seeing others resign from their duties is a warning that you are unaware of happenings which have been deliberately kept out of your way.

RESTAURANT
1. Dreaming of a restaurant or cafe suggests a need for company. You may be fearful of being alone, but equally be afraid of allowing someone to delve too far into your private space.

2. To dream of a restaurant may also alert you to be conscious of the need for a "relationship" with the place you are eating at, as much as with the person with whom you are eating.
3. Spiritually a restaurant symbolises your need to belong to a group of people who all have the same habits, and perhaps a diversity of beliefs.

RIBBON
See Bridle

RICE
1. Rice as an image in dreams suggests food, both for the mind and the body. It also suggests abundance.
2. Rice is supposed to be magical and symbolises spiritual nourishment.
3. Like most grains, spiritually, rice symbolises immortality.

RING
1. For a ring to appear in a dream usually signifies a relationship of some sort.
2. A wedding ring suggests that you are about to make a union and a promise.
3. A ring belonging to the family would represent old traditions and values.
4. An engagement ring suggests a more tentative promise of devotion.
5. An eternity ring would be a long-term promise.
6. A signet ring would indicate setting the seal on something.
7. A bull ring suggests an element of cruelty.

RITUAL
1. To dream of witnessing a ritual signifies that you may have to practice certain actions or drills over and over again, in order to achieve a specific result.
2. Religious rituals have taken a life of their own and help concentrate the power of the many. Magical rituals have become "power centres" in their own right.

RIVER
See Water

ROAD
See Journey

ROBE

1. Dreaming of a robe, such as a bathrobe symbolises the state of being relaxed and at ease.
2. To be dressing someone else in a robe signifies the desire to protect him or her.
3. A robe can suggest your attitude to sex and relationships. If it is clean, then you have a good self-image. If dirty, it symbolises the opposite.
4. In spiritual terms the white robe symbolises innocence, and the seamless robe represents holiness.

ROCK

1. To dream of rock suggests that you have a degree of stability in the real world.
2. If you are on firm, "rock-like" ground indicates that you have to be aware that you must stand and not be dissuaded from your purpose.
3. Seaside rock can signify happier, more carefree times ahead.
4. To dream of smashed rocks signify extreme confusion ahead.

ROCKET

1. To dream of a rocket is a sign that you may not be aware of the energy that is available to you.
2. To be given a rocket suggests recognising that you are not functioning the way you should.
3. To take off like a rocket means moving very fast with regards to a project you have.
4. To dream of firing a rocket signifies that explosive power and energy which is available should be carefully looked at, since you need this type of power in order to make radical changes in your life.

ROCK (AS IN ROCKING CHAIR)

1. To dream of rocking in a chair suggests the need for you to get more recreation. You may feel perfect health but the need is obvious.
2. To dream of rocking someone suggests the need to be soothing others who may need your comfort.
3. Conversely, being rocked is to guard against pressure and stress, as these elements are disastrous.

ROD
See Staff

280

ROOF

1. To dream of being aware of the roof of a building indicates that you may need shelter or protection from an emotional stress.
2. To dream of a leaking roof suggests that you are open to emotional attacks. You have to avoid this by not taking sarcasms personally.
3. To dream of being on top of the roof signifies that you may be short of protection from a facility, which may either be out of date, or being withdrawn from you purposefully.

ROOM
See Buildings

ROOT
See Tree

ROPE

1. To dream of a rope can suggest strength and power, though the power can turn against you.
2. To dream of a rope made of unusual substance, such as hair, there is some special bond or necessity which requires the qualities that that substance has.
3. To dream of being tied up with a rope denotes that something is holding you back from expressing yourself.
4. If you dream of a noose in a rope suggests despair and possibly death.

ROSARY
See Necklace

ROSE

1. The rose in dreams has a great deal of symbolism. It represents love and admiration, and in a bouquet it represents a strong bond. It can also suggest fertility and virginity.
2. As a psychological symbol rose represents perfection. It contains within it the mystery of life and its grace and happiness. It also suggests the cycle of life, through the cycle of its own growth and decay.
3. A bright red rose will suggest perfection and passion, life and death, Time and Eternity.

RUINS

1. To dream of something in ruins signifies that you either need to pull things together or look at how you are making yourself vulnerable.
2. To dream of deliberately ruining something denotes that you need to clarify a self-destructive element in you. It is of utmost importance that you take up this matter urgently to avoid a calamity.
3. To dream of somebody else ruining your property or belonging signifies that you have to take measures to protect yourself against physical harm.

RUNNING

1. To be running in a dream suggests speed and flow. To be running forward suggests confidence and ability. To be running away from something or a situation signifies fear and an inability to do something.
2. Obviously in dreams of running, time and place are significant. To dream of running something, as a business is to be taking responsibility.
3. If you dream of being on the run, perhaps for something about which you feel guilty, signifies that you may be trying to do something too fast.

RUSH

1. To be in a rush suggests that you have to contend with outside pressures. To be rushing suggests that you are putting pressure on your own self.
2. People in general, need to learn how to manage time successfully, and to be rushing suggests that you have not done so.
3. To dream of rushing, signifies that you do not see the best of your world. Conversely if you use your opportunities successfully then you will be happily rewarded.

RUST

1. Rust represents neglect and negligence. You have not looked after the quality of your life properly. Please make a move as you still have time.
2. To dream of cleaning up rust suggests that you recognise your own negligence.
3. Dreaming of rust appearing as you look at an object signifies that a project has reached the end of its useful life.
4. Spiritually, you may have to remove evidence of contamination before you can progress. Rust may signify old outdated attitudes.

S

SACK

1. To perceive a sack in your dream denotes that perhaps you have made an effort to move on but you have also created circumstances which make you feel bad about yourself at the moment.
2. A sack in a woman's dream may mean pregnancy.
3. To dream of emptying a sack signifies that you have reached a point where you will have to make an important decision in which you have to consider every aspect of things which will enable you to move forward.
4. If you dream of filling a sack is a sign that you are about to have plenty but also a warning that you have to guard against greed in the sense of refusing help to others

SACRIFICES

1. To dream of having to do a sacrifice signifies that the dreamer is prepared to give up his ego or individuality for the sake of something greater or more important than himself.
2. Doing a sacrifice in a dream often means there is usually some expectation of a forthcoming reward for some hard work.
3. If you dream of sacrificing an animal suggests that you are conscious of the fact that your lower, more basic instincts can be given up in favour of spiritual power.

SADDLE

1. A saddle appearing in a dream will indicate a need to exercise control over someone. Obviously this can suggest sexual control, particularly in a woman's dream.
2. In a man's dream it is more likely to signify his need to control his own life in some ways, perhaps the direction in which he is going or the circumstances of his own life. It will be more the sense of his own masculinity and drive which is highlighted.
3. To dream, for example, of a motorcycle saddle, will suggest a more rigid type of control than a horse's saddle, which is flexible and removable.
4. To dream of a saddle, which is slipping, signifies that you are about to lose authority in a situation in your life.

5. To dream of a saddle which does not fit in some ways, remembering that it is also designed for the comfort of the rider, denotes that you may be being made uncomfortable by external circumstances rather than by your own volition.

SADISM
1. Sadism often arises because of anger still held, but suppressed from childhood hurts. It is the wish to hurt or provoke a reaction often in someone you love. In waking life most of us are not capable of being sadistic, but in dreams we can do what we like, so sadism becomes acceptable.
2. It will obviously depend on whether you are being sadistic or if someone is being sadistic towards you as to the interpretation. You know that in dreams other people can represent parts of yourself, so you need to consider whether you are causing yourself harm deliberately or inadvertently.
3. You may feel that you wish to punish yourself for some supposed misdemeanour and, as a displacement activity, you dream of sadistic behaviour.

SAILING
1. To dream of sailing, you are highlighting how you feel you are handling your life. It is a warning not to pursue things which are considered to be against your interests at the moment.
2. If you dream of sailing in a yacht signifies that a sense of individuality is needed because it will be advantageous if others are unaware of certain plans you have at the moment.
3. If you dream of sailing on a liner signifies that you may need a group effort to accomplish something.
4. To dream of trying to sail against the wind suggests that you have created difficulties possibly by setting yourself against public opinion.
5. To dream to be sailing with the wind means you are using opportunities to the best of your abilities.
6. To dream of watching sailing boats suggests a sense of spiritual freedom and the ability to use your intellect.

SAILOR
1. To dream of a sailor represents freedom, both of movement and of spirit. You are most likely to be free from the present ordinary life difficulties.

2. If you dream of being a sailor suggests that you are totally in control of your own destiny at the moment. It is the best time to push ahead with any plans you may have.
3. If a sailor does appear in a dream, particularly in a woman's, he is usually a somewhat romanticised figure and signifies that someone around will be willing to provide the necessary help she needs, if only she cares to ask.

SAILS

1. Sails suggest the idea of making use of available power. Often the type of sail will be relevant. Old-fashioned sails would suggest out-of-date methods, whereas racing sails might suggest the use of modern technology.
2. Because a boat or ship is usually thought of as feminine, the sails in dreams can represent pregnancy and fertility.

SALAD

1. If you dream of salad is a warning that you may be short of some kind of nutrient or stimulus and the dream state has alerted you to this.
2. To dream of dressing a salad for someone else, there is perhaps part of yourself which needs attention more than the rest.
3. If you dream of eating salad signifies that you may soon take steps to address circumstances which contribute to hold you back.

SALMON

1. The salmon signifies abundance and masculinity and is phallic. In its fight to mate by swimming upstream it can also symbolise the sperm. Often a salmon can appear in a woman's dream as a symbol of her wish for pregnancy
2. In common with most fish when they appear in dreams the salmon signifies your basic urges, most often the need for survival. By being able to put in effort you reap the rewards of your actions.
3. In mythology the salmon signifies knowledge of other worlds (the lands beneath the sea) and of other worldly things. This refers principally to the subconscious.

SALT

1. In dreams, salt highlights the subtle qualities you bring to your life, those things you do to enhance your lifestyle. It has been suggested that if the water were removed from the human body there would be enough minerals and salt left to cover a quarter.

2. As a symbol of permanence and incorruptibility salt is important in dreams. As in the old days salt was paid as salary, so nowadays to be given salt is to be given one's correct worth.
3. To dream of eating something, which you consider to be salty, is a warning that you may be overdoing something in your present life.
4. But to dream of eating a tasteless food is a sign that you may be trying to pursue something which you lack pre-requisites.
5. If you dream of adding salt in foodstuffs signify that you have a sense of balance in life at the moment and you should take care to maintain it.

SAND

1. Sand in a dream suggests instability and lack of security. When sand and sea are seen together, you are demonstrating a lack of emotional security.
2. When the sands are shifting, you are probably unable to decide what you require in life.
3. To dream of being conscious of the sand in an hourglass signifies that you are conscious of time running out.
4. Sand can represent impermanence. Building sand castles is something of a fantasy occupation since they will be washed away by the tide. To dream of doing this would indicate that the structure you are trying to give to your life does not have permanence, and may be an illusion.

SAP

1. To see sap appearing in your dream means that you are perhaps ready to undertake new work or perhaps a new relationship. You are aware of your own vitality and strength and prepared to take on new challenges.
2. Sap used to be a derogatory term for a wimp or someone who had no backbone. In a negative sense you may become aware in dreams of inappropriate behaviour or ideas.
3. The life force you use can often be perceived as the sap in plants.

SATAN
See Demon

SATELLITE

1. To dream of a satellite suggests that you may soon have efficient and effective contacts with someone which will contribute to make the change you've been waiting for.

2. To dream of using a satellite indicates the dependency that you can have upon another. It is a warning that you may need to take steps towards more independence.
3. If you dream of a non-functioning satellite signifies restrictions in what could have been a splendid opportunity for you to establish important contacts.

SAVINGS

1. To dream of making a saving may represent resources, either material or emotional, which you may have to pay attention to ensure proper use of it.
2. To dream of savings you did not know you had would suggest that you are able to summon up extra energy or time perhaps by using material or information from the past.
3. To dream of making savings in the present suggests you may need to give consideration to the financial means that you have in the here and now, in order to succeed in the future.
4. If you are aware of your goal in making savings you should perhaps make long-term plans.
5. When you dream of savings, you are aware of the need for conservation. This may be on a personal level, or in a more global sense. If there is a feeling of self-denial in your making savings you may not have managed your resources properly in the past and are having to suffer for it now.
6. To dream of someone else giving you their savings suggests that you will be exposed to the required knowledge and expertise to realise your accomplishment. But you have to be on the lookout for it.
7. If you dream of giving your savings away signifies that you no longer have need of whatever those savings mean to you.

SAW
See Tools

SCAFFOLDING

1. A scaffold or scaffolding in a dream will usually indicate that there is some kind of temporary structure in your life.
2. A hang man's scaffold will suggest that an activity which is presently going on in your life must come to an end.
3. If scaffolding appears in dreams you should decide whether it is there to help you build something new or whether you must repair the old. If you are building new, that structure will support you while you

287

build, whereas if you are repairing the old it will support the previous structure while you make the necessary changes.

4. To dream of erecting scaffolding structure suggests that you should take steps to enforce something which is fragile in your life. It is more likely to be a fragile relationship.

SCALES

1. Scales in a dream suggest the necessity for balance and self-control. Without that balance you cannot make a sensible decision regarding potential courses of action.

2. To dream of unbalanced scales signify that you need to search your conscience and discover where you are not functioning properly.

3. To dream of bathroom scales would suggest a more personal assessment than a public machine, whereas a weighbridge might suggest that you need to take your whole life into consideration.

4. If you dream of a doctor's scales may suggest that you may face a potential health problem.

SCAPEGOAT

1. The word scapegoat actually comes from the sacrificing of a goat to appease the gods, and in dreams this symbol can be highly relevant. If in your dream you are the scapegoat for someone else's action then you have to be cautious against being turned into a victim.

2. If you dream of resisting against being made a scapegoat signifies that other people may be trying to make you pay for their misdemeanours.

3. If you dream of making another person a scapegoat indicates a blame shift, and that you are not taking responsibility for your own actions.

SCAR

1. A scar in a dream will generally suggest that there are old hurts, which have not been fully dealt with.

2. To dream of someone else who has been scarred, it may be necessary to discover if you have hurt others in the past. If this is so, you can use positive thinking techniques in the waking state to help you release your guilty conscience.

3. Spiritually, a scar may suggest that something negative and harmful has occurred, which is an external force, rather than internal. You may not have dealt with it as well as you might.

288

SCEPTRE

1. The sceptre is representative of royal power and sovereignty. When it appears in dreams it is usually indicative that you have given someone authority over you.
2. To dream of holding the sceptre indicates that you have the ability to harness power and authority at the present stage of your life.
3. If someone else is using the sceptre and is bestowing honour or power on you, then you can accept that you have succeeded in your particular project.
4. The sceptre can represent the magic wand and in dreams can indicate your right to use such magic. Spiritually it also signifies the transmission of divine power from above rather than below. Thus it is masculine power.

SCHOOL

1. School is an important part of everyone's life. In situations where you are learning new abilities or skills, the image of a school will often come up in dreams.
2. When you are relearning how to deal with your own personalities, the school or classroom will often appear in dreams.
3. If you dream of being at school signifies the need to get rid of old, outmoded ideas and concepts. To dream of being at a school as an educator rather than a student signifies that you need to take steps to increase your potential to earn more from a facility you may have.

SCISSORS

1. To dream of a pair of scissors signifies that you may have feelings you do not think are appropriate, emotions that you cannot handle, or mental trauma which needs to be excised.
2. To dream of surgical scissors is a warning that there is the necessity to be more precise in something you may be attempting to complete at the moment.
3. If you dream of cutting something with scissors signify that you have to be cautious not to retaliate impulsively to hurtful remarks.
4. Dreaming of sharpening scissors suggest that you need to handle your communication better with colleagues, whereas using blunt scissors suggest that you are likely to create hostility by speaking sarcastically.
5. To dream of a hairdresser using scissors signify your fears of losing strength and status.

SCREW

1. It will depend on what society you belong to when interpreting screw. To the criminal element a screw will mean a prison officer or jailer. To a younger element in society it is a slang word for the sexual act. So there could be word play, even if the object seen is a proper screw.
2. To dream of screwing two pieces of wood together would presuppose that you intend to make something which will last.
3. If you dream of tightening a screw in wood or other materials would suggest that you will soon be satisfied for a job well done.

SCROLL

1. For a scroll to appear in your dream suggests that there will be an opportunity for you to progress but you lack the proper knowledge. You have to make a move to educate yourself in a specific field or else you risk losing what should be rightfully yours.
2. A scroll can also represent hidden knowledge, and also the passing of time. Thus, under certain circumstances, dreaming of a scroll signifies having to wait until the knowledge you have gained can be used at an appropriate time.
3. To dream of being given a scroll, suggests that you are deemed responsible enough to use the information you have gained.

SCYTHE

1. The scythe is a cutting instrument, and therefore has the same significance as a knife. In dreams it usually suggests that you need to cut out nonessential actions or beliefs. You need to be fairly ruthless in order to achieve a desired end.
2. The scythe is a very old-fashioned symbol for the passage of time. Its appearance in dreams shows you are linking with very deeply held concepts and ideas.
3. The scythe, like the hourglass, is often held by the figure of death and represents the ending of physical existence.

SEA
See Water

SEAL

1. To dream of seeing an official seal generally signifies legality or correct moral action. In dreams, the possession of a seal gives you the authority to take responsibility for your own actions.

290

2. When you dream of legal documents, to become aware of the seal can indicate that a conclusion has been reached which is both binding and secret.
3. To be breaking a seal indicates that you are possibly breaking a confidence. It has also been suggested that a man breaking a seal in a woman's dream suggests that she will lose her virginity.
4. Also see *Seal* in *Animals*.

SEARCH
1. To be searching in a dream is an attempt to find an answer to a problem. If you are searching for someone signifies that you may be conscious of your loneliness.
2. If you dream of searching for something is a sign that you may be aware of an unfulfilled need.
3. Searching in a dream for something you have lost can suggest either that you need information from the past, or that you feel you have lost your identity.

SEARCHLIGHT
1. A searchlight in a dream denotes focused attention and concentration.
2. To dream of the searchlight turned on you signifies that you need to consider your actions and behaviour.
3. If you dream of using the searchlight trying to locate something signifies that you have the strength to stand against forthcoming criticisms.
4. A searchlight will allow you to comprehend spiritual matters, so that you can reject the unnecessary.

SEED
1. A seed in dreams stands for your potentiality. You may have an idea which is only just beginning, or a project which needs nurturing.
2. In a woman's dream a seed may suggest pregnancy.
3. Often in dreams a seed will suggest the validity of something you are planning. You need to know the right conditions in which to grow and mature.
4. A seed carries great potential and latent power. It is this symbolism which is relevant spiritually.

SERPENT
See snake in Animals.

SEX

1. To dream of having sex is a sign that you may be mishandling certain situations in your present life which is having repercussions as a result. Hence, the sex symbolism is a warning that you should be doing things in such a way to maximise your satisfaction.

2. If you dream of having the desire for sex and hence, making deliberate attempts towards it, signifies that you may be short of something very important in your life at the moment. You may need to make the necessary moves towards fulfilling your needs. They are within reach.

3. To dream of seeing others having sex signifies that you may be exposed to confidential information and you may have to be cautious of the way you handle it.

There are several meanings to other aspects connected to sex and these can be analysed as follows:

4. **Castration:** in a dream suggests fear of loss of masculinity and sexual power.

5. **Clothes in sexual dreams:** can have particular relevance often to do with the dreamer's perception of him or herself. Being fully clothed would suggest some feeling of guilt.

6. **Contraception:** Dreaming of contraception can indicate a fear of pregnancy and birth.

7. **Ejaculation:** The images in a dream prior to orgasm can suggest the nature of the dreamer's attitude to sex and sexuality. The conflicts which arise in the dreamer because of his sexual desire for someone can be dealt with in the dream state through dreaming of emission or orgasm.

8. **Fetish:** To be having fetishes in your dream highlights fear, immaturity and lack of capability.

9. **Hermaphrodite:** Dreaming of a hermaphrodite (someone who is both masculine and feminine) suggests either bisexuality, which is an erotic attraction to both sexes, or the perfect balance within one person of the masculine and feminine qualities.

10. **Homosexuality:** To dream of the desire to have sex with someone of the same sex as yours signifies forthcoming confusion which will be very embarrassing.

11. **Incest:** in a dream usually characterises the need for expressed love, that is, love expressed in a more tactile way. In dreams incest can highlight guilty feelings about one's parents or members of the family.

12. **Intercourse:** The wish or need to be able to communicate with someone on a very intimate level can translate itself into intercourse in a dream.
13. **If intercourse is interrupted:** the dreamer may have inhibitions of which he or she is not consciously aware.
14. **If a child is then born as a result of sexual act:** Certain integration you will attempt will be successful.
15. **Kiss:** This can indicate a mark of respect, or a desire to stimulate the dream partner. It suggests you should be aware of what arousal you need.
16. **Masturbation:** dreaming of masturbation signifies that there is a need for comfort.
17. **Perversion:** When sexual perversion appears in dreams, you are avoiding or attempting to avoid issues to do with closeness and bonding.
18. **Phallus:** Any image either of or to do with the phallus signifies everything that is creative, penetrative and masculine. It demonstrates vitality and creativity in both its simplest and most complex form.
19. **Rape:** Any image of rape appearing in a man's dream is a warning against attempting to breach regulations. In a woman's dream it signifies that she has hidden fears or apprehension.
20. **Sadism:** Sadism appearing in a dream would suggest that it is probably a counterbalance to the dreamer's conscious way of being in the world. You may have to be cautious against someone who presents himself as the nice person. He may not at all be.
21. **Semen:** Semen is the sign of masculinity and of physical maturity and is often seen in dreams as some other milky fluid.
22. **Transvestism:** This signifies confusion so far as gender is concerned in dreams.
23. **Venereal Disease:** In a dream this can suggest awareness of some kind of contamination. This need not necessarily be of a sexual nature, but could also be emotional.

SHADOW

1. To dream of your shadow being prominent signifies that you may have to take absolute steps towards psychic self-defence. You may be vulnerable to psychic attacks.
2. If you dream of having a shadow, which does not resemble yours, is a warning against being involved in trickery.

3. If you dream of having a shadow which has movements which do not follow yours, signifies that you need to have your own way in making decisions. Do not rely on the input of others at the moment.
4. If you dream of having no shadow at all signifies that you may have to be on the lookout in your health matters.

SHAPES

Shapes in dreams have different meanings as follows:
1. **The Centre:** The centre symbolises the point from which everything starts. You will be on the right footing in your next endeavour.
2. **Circle:** The circle represents unity and perfection.
3. **A circular object:** such as a ring, may have the same meaning as the circle.
4. **Crescent:** This signifies the feminine, mysterious power which is intuitive and non-rational.
5. **Cross:** the cross signifies the need to overcome the obstacles to spiritual progression.
6. **The four arms pointing in opposite directions:** signify conflict, anguish and distress, but ultimately going through these to reach perfection.
7. **The hung cross:** with the figure of Christ represents the sacrifice of self for others.
8. **The intersection:** signifies a forthcoming important decision.
9. **The three upper arms:** are said to stand for God the Father, Son and Holy Ghost, but more properly any Divine Trinity.
10. **Diamond:** A diamond in a dream indicates that you have greater and lesser options available.
11. **Hexagram:** A hexagram is a geometric figure which symbolises the harmonious development of the physical, social and spiritual elements of human life and its integration into a perfect whole.
12. **Oval:** The oval symbolises restrictions.
13. **Patterns:** In dreams the patterns which appear evenly signify a successful outcome. Complicated patterns which need figuring out is a sign of setbacks.
14. Pentagram: *See Star*
15. **Sphere:** The sphere has a similar meaning to the globe, and indicates perfection and completion of all possibilities.
16. **Spiral:** The spiral is the perfect path to evolution. The principle is that everything is continually in motion, but also continually rising or raising its vibration.

17. **If the spiral is toward the centre:** You are approaching your own success by an indirect route.
18. **A clockwise spiral:** This is a movement towards consciousness and enlightenment.
19. **If counter clockwise:** You will be taking a direction towards a possibly regressive behaviour.
20. **Square:** You will have a balanced project which will be effectively managed.
21. **A square within a circle:** Signifies speedy progress.
22. **Any figure within a square:** This is the Self or perfect Man.
23. **Star:** The star, particularly if it is a bright one, indicates the individual's hopes, aspirations and ideals. It is those things you must reach for.
24. **The five-pointed star or pentagram:** evokes personal magic, and all matter in harmony. To be correct, the star should point upward. In dreams it signifies the dreamer's ownership of his own magical qualities and aspirations. If it is pointing downward it symbolises evil and witchcraft.
25. **The six pointed star, or Star of David:** is made up of one triangle pointing upward and another pointing downward: the physical and the spiritual are joined together in harmony to create wisdom. Twelve stars signify both the Twelve Tribes of Israel and the Apostles.
26. **Swastika:** The swastika with its arms moving clockwise portrays ideal man and the power he has for good.
27. **Moving counter clockwise:** The swastika in this form signifies all that is sinister and wrong.
28. **Triangle:** The triangle represents standing man, with his three parts, body, mind and spirit. All three aspects represent perfection.

SHARK

1. To dream of a shark may indicate that you are being attacked unfairly; someone is trying to take something that is rightfully yours.
2. Being in a sea of sharks suggests that you are in a situation where you do not trust anyone.
3. To be pursued by a shark may suggest that you have put yourself in danger and created a situation by entering someone else's territory.
4. To dream of being frightened by a shark symbolises the fear of death. You need not.

SHAVE

1. For a man to dream of shaving his face, suggests that he is trying to change his image.

2. If a woman, she is likely to be shaving other parts of her body in order to create a more beautiful image. Both acts suggest removing an unwanted layer, that is, a facade which has been created.
3. To dream of having "a close shave" suggests that you have taken too many risks. You should be more aware of the difficulties you can have as well as the danger you put other people in.

SHEARS
See Scissors

SHEEP
See Animals

SHELLS
1. In dreams a shell represents the defences you use in order to prevent yourself from being hurt. To dream of a cracked shell is a warning that you may have to address ways to improve your security.
2. If you dream of being in a shell signifies that you are protected against hurtful intents but it is a warning against being too individualistic.

SHELTER
1. Any shelter signifies protection. The human is aware of the need for a safe space, and this symbolism comes across in dreams quite strongly.
2. To dream of giving shelter to someone in dreams signifies that you may be protecting a part of yourself from hurt or difficulty.
3. To dream of being given shelter is a sign that you are conscious of the fact that there is protective power in your life.

SHIELD
1. To dream of a shield is a sign that there is the need for preservation.
2. If you dream of shielding someone else, then you need to be sure your actions are appropriate and supportive.
3. To dream of being shielded, you need to be clear as to whether you are erecting the shield or whether it is being erected for you.
4. In spiritual development the shield appears as a symbol of a particular stage of growth. It is at this point that the individual needs to appreciate that he has control over his own destiny.

SHIRT
See Clothes

SHIVER

1. To be conscious of shivering in dreams can represent either a fear of conflict, or of coldness of emotion.
2. There is also a shiver of excitement. You may, in waking life, be reaching a conclusion or coming to a peak of experience.
3. When you shiver in a dream you may be getting near to releasing unconscious behaviour.

SHOE

See Clothes

SHOP

1. A shop in dreams signifies something you want or feel you need.
2. If it is a shop you know then you are probably consciously aware of what you want from life.
3. If it is an unknown shop then you may have to search your mind for information to enable you to come up with a successful idea.
4. To be shopping is to be making a fair exchange for the satisfaction of your desire. You have the energy (money), which can be exchanged for something you want. If you are shopping for food you need sustenance; if for clothes you may need protection.

SHOOT

1. To be shot in a dream is a warning to guard against injury to your feelings. It could also indicate that you may feel that you are becoming victims or targets for other people's anger.
2. If the dreamer is shooting something he may have to deal with his own fears. He could be guarding against meeting parts of his personality he does not like.
3. But if you dream of shooting somebody else warns you against having the tendency to be forceful in your demands of everyday life.
4. To dream of being on a shooting range suggests needing to produce accuracy in your life.

SHOVEL

1. To see a shovel in your dream signifies the need to uncover a past joy or trauma, or possibly even a learning experience.
2. The type of spade or shovel will be of relevance. A garden spade would suggest being totally pragmatic, whereas a fire shovel would indicate a need to take care.

3. To dream of shovelling compost, for instance, would mean considering the sum total and most fertile aspects of your life, whereas shovelling sand might suggest that you need more time to consider something important.

SHRINK

1. To dream of seeing something shrink signifies that you may be aware of losing face or of feeling small.
2. To dream to see somebody shrink can indicate that someone is losing his or her power over you.

SHROUD

1. In a dream a shroud can be a frightening image, since it is associated with death. You will learn of the death of someone you know personally.
2. A shroud can signify a covering up of something you do not fully understand. You know that it is there, but you do not wish to have a look at it.
3. In spiritual terms a shroud is a mark of respect.

SICK

1. To feel sick in a dream signifies that you should identify a bad feeling you have, which needs to be gotten rid of.
2. If you dream of assisting a sick person suggests that you should be on the lookout against being influenced with bad feelings.
3. If you dream of a sick pet signifies that you should take the necessary measures to protect yourself against verbal abuses.

SICKLE

1. To see a sickle in your dream represents mortality and death. As so often happens, this is not necessarily a physical death, but the death of a part of your activities.
2. If you dream of using a sickle to cut grass signifies that you may be short of ideas of how to accomplish something. You may need advice at present, in order to be effective.

SIEVE

1. The sieve in dreams is a symbol of the ability to make selections. This is in the sense of being able to sort out the large from the small, good from the bad etc.

2. On a psychological level the sieve represents the ability to know oneself. You are able to make conscious choices which will enable you to extract the best from life.
3. Spiritually the sieve is said to represent fertility and rain clouds in the sense that pure rain, or water, permits proper growth.

SIGNATURE
1. Your signature in a dream suggests that you have an appreciation of yourself. You are prepared to recognise who you are and to make your mark in the world.
2. At times when you are arranging legal matters or agreements, but are actually not sure if you are doing the right thing, your signature can appear in dreams as obliterated or illegible.

SILENCE
1. Silence in a dream can suggest uneasiness and expectancy. You may be waiting for something to happen, or not to happen.
2. To dream of someone else being silent when you expect him or her to speak, is a sign that you are unsure as to how you should react in a forthcoming gathering.
3. When you are silent in your dream signifies that you may have difficulties to voice your feelings or opinions. You may be either inhibited by your own self or by outside influences.

SILVER
1. On a practical level, silver appearing in a dream suggests finance or money. Silver is something of value which can be held in reserve against possible difficulty.
2. Silver on a more psychological level has been taken to represent the qualities of the moon. This is in the sense that something or someone is available, but is at the same time somewhat remote.
3. If you dream of wearing silver on your body signifies that you have the desire to have more materialistic gains. You should pursue your actual goals.

SING
1. To dream to be singing is to be expressing your joy and love of life. You should expect a wonderful outcome of something shortly.
2. If you dream of singing alone signifies that you have learned to be skilled in your own right.

3. To dream of singing in a choir suggests your ability to worship or express yourself in a peer group. Obviously, if the dreamer is a singer in waking life, the interpretation will vary.
4. To hear singing as chants in dreams is to be in touch with a high vibration. Your psychic intuitions may be at peak level at the moment.

SINKING

1. To dream to be sinking suggests a loss of confidence. You may be in despair at something you have done, and feel hampered by the circumstances.
2. To see someone else sinking would suggest you are aware of a difficulty which perhaps needs your help.
3. If you dream of sinking an object signifies that you may feel you are losing ground within a relationship or situation, something you must address urgently.
4. A sinking feeling in dreams usually suggests worry or fear. Emotionally you are unable to maintain your usual happiness. You may feel that you are not in control, and that you cannot maintain forward movement.
5. Both spiritually and physically, to be sinking is to be getting into a situation where you are unable to see clearly or to perceive the best course of action.

SIREN

1. To dream of hearing a siren, as in an ambulance or fire engine, is to be warned of danger.
2. To dream of sounding a siren suggests deception and distraction of man from his purpose.
3. In a woman's dream, to be sounding a siren signifies that she may appear to be destructive.

SISTER
See Family

SIZE

1. To be conscious of size in a dream highlights how you feel in relation to a person, project or object. Big might suggest important or threatening, whereas small might indicate vulnerability or something "less than" your own personal value.
2. To dream of a big house would be an awareness of the expansion of oneself, whereas a small house would indicate an intensity of feeling.

3. Spiritually size is irrelevant. It is more the appreciation of feeling that becomes important. A "big" feeling is something that consumes you, whereas a "little" perception may be only part of what really exists.

SKELETON
1. To dream of a skeleton represents a past action or shame you wish to hide.
2. If you dream of a dancing skeleton is an awareness of the life you have lived or are living. Usually you will have to assess whether you are not involved, or approve of fraudulent activities.
3. To dream of digging up a skeleton signifies that you may be surprised to learn something which you totally believed the contrary.
4. To dream of being frightened by a skeleton signifies that you may be a victim of future sarcastic remarks.

SKULL
1. To see a skull in your dream signifies that you may learn of some events which will require additional analysis for you to get the full sense.
2. To be conscious of one's own skull in dreams is to appreciate the structure that you have given your life.
3. To dream of talking to a skull is recognising the need to communicate with those who are lost to you.
4. If you dream of a skull talking to you, a part of you which you have rejected or denied is beginning to come back to life.

SKY
1. In dreams the sky can represent the mind. It can also signify your potential.
2. To dream of floating or flying in the sky can be ambivalent, since it can mean trying to avoid the mundane, or exploring a different potential.
3. If the sky is dark it may reflect your mood of gloominess; if it is bright, your mood of joy.
4. The sky signifies the unattainable. Whatever effort you make you can never make the sky tangible.

SMELL
1. To be conscious of a smell in a dream usually means that you are trying to identify an object or digging for additional information.

2. A pleasant smell could represent happy times or memories, whereas a bad smell can hold memories of particularly traumatic times.

SMOKE

1. Smoke in dreams suggests that there is a feeling of danger around, especially if you cannot locate the fire.
2. If you are smoking signifies that you are trying to control anxiety.
3. If you smoke in real life, but recognise in dreams that you no longer do so, you will overcome a difficulty.
4. If smokers give it up in everyday life, they will often have many dreams focused around the issue of smoking.
5. Spiritually smoke signifies prayer rising to heaven, or the raising of the soul to escape from space and time.

SNAIL

1. The snail appearing in dreams may engender a feeling of repulsion in some people. It does, however, also represent vulnerability and slowness.
2. From a psychological point of view, the snail suggests steadiness and self-containment.
3. To be moving at snail's pace suggests direct planned, careful movement.

SNAKE

See Serpent in Animals

SNOW

1. To see snow in your dreams signifies that you have the ability to make viable achievements but you have to be aware that you need to take extreme measures to make it last.
2. To dream of melting snow is a warning that you are about to lose authority over something.
3. Sometimes, snow in dreams can suggest emotional coldness or frigidity.
4. If you dream of being trapped in snow conditions signifies delays in official duties.

SOAP

1. Soap in dreams suggests the idea of being cleansed. You perhaps need to create an environment of cleanliness, both of physical cleanliness and appropriate behaviour.

2. Soap can also indicate a need to clean up your act. You may feel a sense of having been made dirty by an experience and situation, and your dream mind is alerting you to the fact that you need to deal with it.

SON
See Family

SOUP
See Food

SOUTH
See Position

SOWING
1. Sowing, in the sense of planting seed, is a symbol which has certain basic images attached to it. It can signify the sexual act, as well as suggesting good husbandry. It can also represent the beginning of a new project.
2. To dream of sowing can also signify that you are in the process of laying down a framework for success.
3. To dream of ground preparations for sowing suggests that you need to look at circumstances around you and decide what you can gain most.
4. Sowing in a spiritual sense suggests creating the correct environment in which growth can take place. It is the creative act.

SPACE
1. To be aware of space in your dream suggests a sense of freedom. You may be relieved of something which has been bothering you for some time.
2. To dream of being in what you consider to be confined space is a warning that you have to make the best use of opportunities.

SPADE
See Shovel

SPARK
1. A spark in a dream represents a beginning. Being aware of a spark is to be conscious of what is going to make things possible. From a

physical perspective it is a small thing which gives rise to a greater one.

2. The spark of an idea suggests the germ of a creative potential which, given the opportunity, will become much bigger.

3. The spark suggests fire and therefore love. It is the vital principle in life, without which you will die.

SPEAR

1. If you dream of seeing a warrior with a spear is a sign of aggressiveness. You may have to take steps against this.

2. To dream of throwing a spear suggests that perhaps you need to be aware of your more primitive aspects, or you may need to resort to primitive ways to reach accomplishment.

3. If you dream of using a spear with the intention to hurt other people signifies the need to be conscious to avoid nonsense and get straight to the point.

SPECTACLES
See Glasses

SPEED

1. Speed in dreams identifies an intensity of feelings which is not usually available in waking life. Because everything is happening too quickly, it engenders anxiety in the dreamer which creates problems.

2. To dream of travelling at high speed suggests trying to achieve a fast result.

3. Speeding, as in a traffic offence, suggests being too focused on an end result, and not on the method of getting there.

SPIDER

1. To dream of a spider signifies deviousness.

2. If you dream of being frightened by a spider is a sign that you may be unaware that you are being investigated in certain ways.

3. If you dream of a spider weaving its web signifies that you should take steps to develop a level of creativity to enable you reach attainment.

4. If you dream of killing a spider signifies that you have fears that you are reluctant to face. You may have to avoid embarrassing situations.

SPIRAL
See Shapes

SPIRITS

1. At its very basic level, you all have fears and feelings about death, and the appearance of Spirit helps you to come to terms with these. It will depend on the dreamer's own belief as to whether he or she feels they are actual spirits or not.
2. When spirits appear in dreams, their function may be to help you through various states of transition. While you cope with everyday fears there are many unconscious memories and feelings which can surface unexpectedly.
3. To dream of a frightening apparition of a spirit signifies that you may face a level of entrapment which may be very annoying.

SPITTLE

1. To dream of spittle signifies that you may soon face situations which contain elements of disgust.
2. If you dream of spitting out something unpleasant signifies good faith and a relief sooner rather than later.
3. If you dream of someone spitting on you is a warning that you may be unaware that you may be pulled down in some sort of ranking status.
4. To dream of spitting on someone signifies that you may resort to abuses when faced with frank discussions. This attitude may lower your self-esteem.

SPLINTER

1. To perceive a splinter in your dreams may represent a situation where you may face painful words or ideas.
2. To dream of being pricked with a splinter is a warning that you may be holding on to ideas which cause negative feelings. A careful analysis of your ideas may be useful at the moment.
3. To be part of a splinter group in a dream suggests feeling sufficiently strong about something to break away from mainstream thought.
4. To dream of hitting something which splinters, is to recognise that you need several parts of different things in order to make something complete.

SPRING

1. Springtime in a dream can suggest new growth or opportunities. Perhaps there is a fresh start in a relationship.
2. To dream of a spring of water suggests fresh energy, whereas a bedspring or other type of coil would indicate your dormant power.

3. To dream of walking with a spring in one's step is to be looking forward to something. The saying "spring forward, fall back" is also applicable in psychological terms, since effort is required to progress.

SPRINKLE

1. To dream of sprinkling something is a symbol which suggests an attempt to make a little go a long way. Perhaps you need to get the best out of situations around you, by putting a little effort into many things.
2. If you dream of someone sprinkling something on you suggests the symbolism of impregnation, of conception and gestation. You may need to develop your creative side in order to make considerable progress fast.
3. To dream of sprinkling something on somebody else signifies that you may tend to take care of other peoples' affairs before handling yours.

SQUARE
See Shapes

SQUIRREL
See Animals

STAB

1. To dream of being stabbed indicates that you are vulnerable not only to be hurt but also you have to be cautious against being conned.
2. For a man to dream of stabbing someone signifies the possibility of your desire to go to the extreme over forcing somebody to comply to your demands.
3. In a woman's dream, to be stabbed is a warning to avoid connections which may lead to aggressive masculine sexuality.
4. If you dream of stabbing at something rather than somebody would suggest the need to break through some kind of shell or barrier.

STAFF

1. A staff, in the sense of a stick, is a support mechanism, staff as in office staff, a support system. Dreaming of either should clarify your attitude to the support you require in life.
2. If you dream of using a staff for the purpose of pointing or giving directions signifies magical power in the form of a wand.

3. If you dream of somebody else using a staff signifies that you need support in order to attain the level of authority which is required for self-fulfilment.

STAGE

1. To be on stage in a dream is to be making oneself visible. An open-air stage suggests communication with the masses rather than a selected audience.
2. If you dream of being on a moving stage signifies the need to keep moving even with limited progress.
3. To dream of being on a stage, yet being apprehensive signifies that you lack the framwork necessary to reach great heights.

STAKE

1. To dream of having a stake in something signifies that you may face a risky commitment.
2. If you dream of putting stakes in the ground suggests marking out one's territory.
3. To dream of buying stakes is a warning against being framed into doing something you know you should not.

STAIRS
See Buildings

STAR
See Film Star and Shapes

STATION
See journey

STATUE

1. Dreaming of a statue is an alert that you may be worshipping or loving someone and not getting any response. You should take the necessary steps immediately to clarify your position.
2. If you dream of a statue which suddenly moves signifies that you may get new ideas about something but may not be appreciated by others.
3. If you dream of somebody you know suddenly turned into a statue signifies the end of a relationship you have been enjoying up to now.

STEALING

1. To dream of stealing suggests you are taking something without permission. This may be love, money or opportunities.
2. To dream of someone you know stealing from you may signify that you need to work out how much you value your trust in people in general.
3. If it is by someone you don't know, it is more likely that there is a part of yourself that you don't trust.
4. To dream of being in a gang of thieves, then you should look at, and consider, the morals of the peer group you belong to.

STEAM

1. Steam in dreams can suggest emotional pressure. You are passionate about something without necessarily knowing what it is.
2. Because it is two substances uniting into one, steam suggests transformation. It also suggests a transitory experience, since steam also melts away.
3. If you dream of being burnt by steam signifies that you may go through a successful but erratic transition.

STEPS

1. Steps in dreams almost invariably suggest an effort made to succeed. Going up the steps suggest trying to make things better and improve them, whereas going down means having to go into the past to shed light on something at present.
2. If you dream of steps which are too high to allow comfortable climb or descent signifies that you need self-determination to accomplish something, despite intense discouragement by other people.

STERILISE

1. To dream of sterilising something suggests that you wish to get rid of hurts or traumas and are prepared to put in the effort to do so.
2. Mostly, in a man's dream, sterilisation may suggest sexual dissatisfactions or doubts about his self-image.

STIFFNESS

1. Stiffness in dreams would suggest some anxiety or tension is present. There is a holding back of energy that is causing rigidity.
2. To dream of being stiff with someone is to be reserved and withdrawn, probably through shyness but possibly through anger.

308

3. To dream of facing a stiff task or challenge signifies that you have the strength to handle a present difficult assignment and you will do it well.

STONE

1. Dreaming of stone can suggest stability and durability, but also a loss of feeling.
2. To dream of carving stone or buying stone carvings signify your attempt to establish a long-term project or relationship which will have valuable influence on others.
3. To dream of a smashed stone is a warning to be careful about your present actions because you may be badly hurt emotionally.
4. If you dream of being turned into stone would suggest that you have had to harden up your attitudes.
5. If you dream of being stoned could either mean that you may be punished for misdemeanours or you may be under external influences which is driving your life at the moment.

STORM

1. In dreams a storm indicates a personal emotional outburst. You may feel you are being battered by events or emotions. It can also signify a warning to guard against anger.
2. If you dream of being caught up in a storm is a warning that you may soon face difficulty with regards to a relationship.

STRANGER

See People

STRANGLE

1. To dream of strangling someone is an attempt to stifle your emotions. It may not be physically healthy to hold your emotions. It will be very helpful to talk to someone.
2. To dream of being strangled is to be aware of one's difficulty in speaking out one's emotions. This may be mostly as a result of inhibition.
3. To dream of witnessing someone strangling someone else suggests that you may face a situation in which you may have to give sensitive advice.

STRAW

1. Straw in dreams highlights weakness and emptiness. This signals the need to make the effort to ensure that you see physical results, and this will raise your moral as a result.
2. To dream of a straw house, would suggest a state of impermanence is present in your life.
3. When you say something is built on straw, you are aware that it does not have a proper foundation. You need to look at what you feel is impermanent in your life and build on it.
4. Straw appearing in a dream can often reveal that you feel there is a lack of support, or that the support you do have seems to be rather dry and brittle.

STREAM

1. Dreaming of a stream suggests the awareness of the flow of your emotions. To be in a stream suggests being in touch with one's sensuality.
2. Emotionally if you are to function properly you must feel loved and appreciated. To be in the stream of things suggests being part of a social group, which will enable you to interact with people.
3. To dream of being trapped in a stream signifies that you have to guard against an emotional let down, e.g. someone you trust may be lying to you.

STRING

1. String appearing in dreams signifies some sort of binding, perhaps to make something secure. It may also represent trying to hold a situation together.
2. In a psychological sense, string like rope, can be seen as a link between two objects.
3. If you dream of an abnormally long string signifies that you have to look for a firm relationship which is actually within your surroundings.

SUBMARINE

1. To dream of a submarine signifies that you need to look at the subconscious depths for enlightenments on rather complicated issues at present.
2. To dream of being on board a submarine signifies that you may be hiding deep feelings about something or someone.

310

SUCKING

1. If you dream of sucking something such as a lollipop alerts you to a need for oral satisfaction in the sense of comforting yourself.
2. To dream of sucking a finger can suggest that you have a physical need.
3. To dream of trying to suck out an object which is stuck into something else, by the use of a sucker, signifies that there may be unfulfilled desires or the need to be whole and complete.

SUFFOCATION

1. If you feel of suffocating in a dream, it may be that your own fears are threatening to overwhelm you. It can also indicate that you are not in control of your own environment.
2. To dream of suffocating someone may mean you have the intention to overpower someone by using illicit means.
3. Mostly, in the case of women, to dream of being suffocated signifies fears about sexuality or doubts about a relationship.

SUICIDE

1. Dreaming of suicide alerts you to a violent end to something, perhaps a project or relationship.
2. To dream of committing suicide signifies a sign of anger against something you may have done or said and you may have to be careful to prevent the end of a business or business relationship.
3. Emotionally, when dreams of suicide occur, you may have come to the end of your ability to cope with a particular situation in your life. It does not actually mean that you are suicidal. It simply marks the end of a phase.

SUITCASE
See Baggage and Luggage

SUMMER

1. To be aware in a dream that it is summer suggests that it is a good time in your life, or good times are around the corner. You can look forward to success in projects you have around you.
2. To dream of being on a leisure holiday during a nice summer time signifies that you have the ability to make the most of what you have done to date.

311

3. To dream of having limits to enjoy the most of a summer time signifies that actually, you may be facing unfavourable limits which you can do something about them.

SUN

1. The sun in dreams suggests warmth and conscious awareness. A sunny day suggests happiness or you may soon be happy about something.
2. To dream of being in the sun indicates that you are looking for enlightenment regarding a subject which may have got to do with fertility.
3. Because the sun is such a powerful image on its own as a life source, it can also appear in dreams as a symbol for other life energy. This often represents unawareness of opportunities.

SURGERY

1. To find yourself in a surgery in dreams would indicate that you should be looking at your health and health matters.
2. Dreaming of undergoing a surgery indicates the need to accustom yourself to changes which may initially be difficult, but ultimately are better for future relations and functions.
3. Often times when you dream of witnessing a surgery signifies that you may have too much to deal with. The alarm bells are warning you to take a break or else you risk your health.

SWALLOW
See Birds

SWALLOWING

1. Swallowing in a dream suggests you are taking something in. This could be knowledge or information.
2. Dreaming of swallowing one's pride signifies the necessity for humility, while something being hard to swallow shows that you have a need to overcome an obstacle.
3. If you dream of having to swallow an emotion in your dream signifies that you have to be on your guard against acts of suppression which can be harmful.

SWAMP
See Marsh

SWAN
See Birds

SWASTIKA
See Shapes

SWEEP

1. To dream of sweeping suggests being able to clear away outmoded attitudes and emotions. To be sweeping up suggests putting things in order.
2. To dream of sweeping somewhere which does not get cleaner as you do so, signifies that you have to be prepared to stand firm against forthcoming blames which may be levelled against you.
3. To dream of sweeping unknown places signifies that you should pay more attention to details in your daily matters as something is prone to go wrong.

SWEETS
See Food

SWIMMING

1. To be swimming upstream in a dream would indicate that the dreamer is going against his own nature. Be extremely careful not to do or say things which will turn out to be disadvantageous.
2. To dream of a swimming fish can have the same symbolism as sperm, and therefore can indicate the desire for a child.
3. To dream of swimming in clear water indicates that you may be spared from a complicated argument which will help clean your name as a result.
4. To dream of swimming in dark water could symbolise the possibility of depression or discouragement.
5. To dream of being a good swimmer shows the ability to be able to handle emotional situation well, whereas being a poor swimmer in a dream could indicate the need to learn how to handle your emotions in a more positive way.

SWINE
See Pig in Animals

SWORD

1. The sword in dreams invariably suggests a weapon of power. You may have the ability to create power and use energy properly through your beliefs.

2. The sword symbolises justice and courage as well as strength. For the image of a sword to appear in a dream indicates there is an element of the warrior in you, and that you are prepared to fight for your beliefs.
3. Spiritually the sword signifies the power of authority and protection. In dreams to be given a sword signifies that you have the protection of the sacred. You are able to make your own decisions.

SYRINGE

1. In dreams the syringe suggests an awareness of the influence that other people can have over you.
2. Dreaming of a syringe can indicate that when you are attempting to influence other people, you need to be conscious of the way you do it. You can be very specific and hit the right spot, or you can have a more "scatter gun" approach.
3. If you dream of a non-functioning or blocked syringe signifies that you may not be able to exert the necessary influence needed to persuade someone to comply with a request you may have in mind.

T

TABLE
1. A table in dreams is recognised as a symbol of decision-making. It is mostly a focal point in any building or room, hence its significance of importance.
2. To dream of sitting comfortably at a table signifies a sense of order. It represents your ability to create order out of chaos.
3. A table can represent spiritual judgment and legislation.

TABLET
1. Taking medicine in the form of tablets signify your recognition of your need to be healthy. You may need to "heal" something that is wrong.
2. If you dream of giving tablets to someone else suggests that you may be aware that their needs are not being satisfied. You may be in a helpful mood but guard against abuses of your generosity.

TAIL
1. To dream of a tail can signify some residue from the past, something you still carry with you. It can also indicate sexual excitement, or possibly, by association, the penis.
2. The tail in a dream can also be recognised as a means of adjustment in difficult circumstances.

TAILOR
1. As with other occupations, it is perhaps more important to decide what significance the tailor has to the dreamer before attempting an interpretation. Any professional person develops certain talents and competencies, such as, in this case, the ability to do precise work and to "fashion" something new. To dream of a tailor alerts you to these qualities within yourself.
2. To dream of being a tailor by career signifies that you may entertain changes which may soon appear in your social life.
3. If you dream of people from other professional careers being tailors, e.g. a priest or a lawyer, signals the need for adjustments in whatever plans which are active at the moment.

TALISMAN

1. A talisman is a protection against evil or difficulty. When one turns up in a dream, you are often aware of the fact that your own mental powers are not sufficient to protect you from fear and doubt.
2. If you dream of suddenly wearing a talisman signifies that you are in need of external help.
3. To dream of giving a talisman to somebody else with the intention to protect signifies that you possess active psychic powers compared to most people whose psychic powers are dormant.

TALKING

1. To be conscious of people talking in a dream gives a sense of being in contact with your own ability to communicate. You are able to express clearly what you feel and think, whereas in waking life you may not feel confident.
2. To dream of hearing someone else talking signifies that you are perhaps afraid of not being listened to, properly, and this may be causing a level of anxiety.
3. If you dream of talking to your own self signifies that you have the ability to develop psychic communication.

TAMBOURINE

1. Dreaming of a tambourine, or any such musical instrument, allows you to be in contact with your own basic rhythms and needs.
2. The tambourine can indicate that you have some control over the rhythm and noise in your life. Particularly, to dream of playing the tambourine in a group, you are accepting your ability to participate effectively in life.

TAME

1. To dream of taming an animal indicates your ability to develop a creative link with the instinctive aspects of yourself.
2. To dream of being tamed, as though you yourself were the animal, signifies the need for restraint in your life.
3. To find that something is extremely tame, in the sense of something dull and boring, suggests that you should reconsider the way you live your life.

TANGLED

1. Sometimes when you are confused in everyday life, you may dream of an object being entangled with something else.

316

2. To dream of something tangled in such a way that it looks so complicated suggests that you should be on the look out for hidden difficulties in your everyday life.
3. To dream of tangled hair suggests that you need to be aware that your self-image or projection is coming across to other people as distorted.
4. Dreaming of cutting through a tangle of trees or undergrowth is part of the Hero's journey. You have courage and strength to push through with whatever you may have at the moment.

TANK
1. Dreaming of a water tank is putting yourself in touch with your inner feelings and emotions.
2. If you dream of a war tank connects you with your own need to defend yourself, but you have to be aggressive at the same time.
3. If you dream of using a war tank to destroy something signifies that you are feeling threatened in some ways. You should physically certify if this is the case.
4. If you dream of being trapped in an empty water tank signifies that you should become aware of your need to overcome objections and difficulties.
5. To dream of a tank full of any type of liquid signifies that you have a wide range of ideas which will be very helpful if you could analyse every waking situation and put your ideas to use.

TAP
1. The tap is an image of being able to make available universal resources. It signifies that infinite energy can be harnessed for your well-being.
2. To dream of not being able to turn a tap either on or off highlights your ability, or inability, to control those things you consider to be rightfully yours.
3. Water is considered to be a symbol of emotion, so a tap is representative of your ability to use or misuse emotion in some ways. To be able to turn emotion on and off at will is indicative of great self-control.

TAPE
1. Dreaming of a measuring tape indicates your need to evaluate someone or something. This may be in the sense of analysing whether you are receiving the required results you should be getting.
2. If you dream of measuring something with a measuring tape signifies that you may be trying to create order in your life.

3. If you dream of a recording tape would suggest that you are aware that the way you express yourself is worth remembering.
4. Masking or parcel tape in your dream could be considered to be restraining, to create boundaries, within which movement becomes difficult. In dreams this is a warning of the limitation you impose on yourself in everyday life.

TAPESTRY
See Weaving

TAR
1. Dreaming of tar on the road would suggest the potential to be trapped as you progress. Dreaming of tar on a beach or any other inappropriate places, however, might suggest that you have allowed your emotions to become contaminated in some ways.
2. If you dream of using tar to mend a road might signify that you can be repairing wear and tear in your everyday life.
3. To dream of tarring a fence could mean you must protect yourself. It will be necessary to make careful observation to identify potential dangers in the form of physical dangers.

TARGET
1. Aiming at a target in dreams would suggest you have a goal in mind.
2. To dream of shooting at a bull's-eye could be interpreted as a search for perfection. This is something which is achievable in limited areas of activities.
3. To dream of aiming at a person could suggest either hatred or sexual desire.
4. In a work sense a sales target might suggest that your goals are imposed on you by others.
5. On a more personal note if you were setting someone else a target in dreams, you would need to understand that the other person in the dream is a reflection of part of yourself.

TASTE
1. When something is not to your taste in a dream it does not conform to your ideals and standards.
2. To dream of having a bad taste suggests that whatever is signified by what you are eating does not nourish you.
3. To dream of recognising that your surroundings are in good taste suggests an appreciation of beautiful things.

TATTOO

1. On a physical level, a tattoo will stand for an aspect of individuality in the dreamer. He (or she) wishes to be seen as different.
2. A tattoo in dreams can also signify something which has left an indelible impression. This could be great hurt, but could also be a good memory. Sometimes, the image which is tattooed is worth interpreting if it can be seen clearly.
3. If you dream of being aware of a process of tattooing part of yourself signifies that you may be too radical to push for a change in your life.

TAU

1. To dream of a Tau as a T-shaped cross signifies supreme power. You may soon reap the benefits of enjoying a position which places you above all others but you should not be abusive.
2. Spiritually, this cross signifies the key to supreme power and living a truly successful life.

TAX

1. In everyday life, a tax represents a sum of money exacted from you for the right to live a certain lifestyle. In dreams, therefore, having to pay a tax suggests some kind of a penalty for living the way you choose.
2. Dreaming of car tax, for example, would indicate that greater effort is needed to move forward.
3. To be paying income tax suggests that you may feel you owe a debt to society.
4. To be paying property tax may suggest that you feel you have to pay for the "space" in which you exist.
5. To dream of refusing to pay any taxes suggests an unwillingness to conform.

TAXI

1. In a dream, calling a taxi signifies recognition of the need to pay a price or to make a sacrifice to progress, to get somewhere.
2. A taxi is a public vehicle in the sense that it is usually driven by someone unknown to you. You therefore have to trust the driver's awareness and knowledge. In dreams, therefore, a taxi can suggest having the ability to get somewhere without knowing how.
3. To dream of driving a taxi signifies that you are attempting something very challenging in real life but you may face limited knowledge to properly handle it.

TEA

1. To dream of having a warm cup of tea signifies comfort in the near future in terms of physical comfort.
2. To dream of handling tea as raw materials in a tea factory signifies that you will accomplish something to do with regards to your career but you may need initial preparations.

TEACHER

1. To dream of anyone who is either, or have been your teacher before, suggests that it is of importance for you to seek enlightenment on a subject which may be puzzling you at the moment.
2. To dream of somebody considered as a head teacher is a sign that you may need guidance in something which you are attempting at the moment.
3. To dream of being a teacher yourself signifies that you may face an embarrassing situation whereby you may have to give advice on subjects which are sensitive and may hurt people you are well acquainted with. It can also mean that you may have to lead others towards objectives which you yourself are not sure of.

TEARS

1. Tears in dreams can indicate an emotional release and cleansing. If you are crying you may not feel you are able to give way to emotion in everyday life.
2. To dream of someone else in tears signifies that you perhaps need to look at your own conduct to see whether you are not in undesirable practices, as far as you may be concerned.
3. To dream of being in tears and then to wake up and discover that you are actually crying, suggests that some hurt or trauma has come sufficiently close to the surface to enable you to deal with it on a conscious level.

TEASE

1. To dream of being teased suggests that you are becoming aware that your own behaviour may not be appropriate. You may have to be self-conscious and take actions accordingly.
2. If you dream of teasing someone to the point of anger signifies that you may actually need to work on certain indecisive qualities which you may have.

3. Teasing can be a form of bullying, of becoming a victim. You need to understand your requirement to have power over someone, rather than helping him or her.

TELEGRAM

1. To dream of a priority means of communication such as the telegram suggests that you may have to guard against losing your patience regarding something which is moving fast enough but you are finding it slow-moving.
2. If you dream of receiving a telegram suggests that you may receive valuable information from a trustworthy source.
3. To dream of a telegram of wedding congratulations may signify the dreamer's wish to be married.
4. On the other hand, a telegram bearing bad news may be alerting you to something of which you are already aware on a subconscious level.

TELEPHONE

1. To dream of using a telephone suggests the ability to make contact with other people and to impart information you feel they may need.
2. To dream of being contacted by telephone suggests there is information available to you which you do not already consciously know.
3. When you are aware of the telephone number you are ringing, it may be the numbers that are important. Please see *Numbers*.
4. To dream of searching for a telephone number suggests that you are having difficulty in coordinating your thoughts about your future actions.

TELESCOPE

1. Using a telescope in a dream is a warning that you need to take a closer look at something but do be careful not to take a one-sided view.
2. If you dream of somebody focusing on you in a telescope, signifies curiosity. There are no elements of spying but others may be curious about your activities.
3. Interestingly enough, a telescope in spiritual terms can signify the art of clairvoyance, the ability to perceive the future from an immediate perspective.

TEMPLE

1. Often in dreams a temple can signify your own body. It is something to be treated with reverence and care. It has the same significance as

a church, since it is an object built to honour and pay respect to a god or gods.
2. Psychologically, wherever there is a temple there is a sense of awe associated with creativity. Perhaps the biggest significance in dreams is the fact that it takes a lot to build one temple. This links with your awareness of the many facets of your personality which go to make a coherent whole.

TEMPTATION

1. Temptation is a conflict between two different drives. For instance, in dreams you may experience a conflict between the need to go out into the world and the need to stay safe at home.
2. Temptation is yielding to that which is easiest and not necessarily the best course of action.
3. Intellectually, when presented with options of action you may tend to go for a result which gives short-term satisfaction, rather than long-term. The idea of giving in to temptation suggests that it is bigger or more powerful than you are. Often, dreams can show you the course of action you should be taking.

TENANT

1. To dream of being a tenant suggests that you do not want to take responsibility for the way you choose to live. You do not want to be burdened by having full responsibility for your living space.
2. To dream of having a tenant signifies that you are prepared to have someone live in your space. This may be the type of dream that occurs as you are preparing to become involved in a full-time relationship.
3. To dream of a commercially related tenant denotes that you will have some insights into how you handle such activities with financial implications.

TENT

1. A tent in a dream would suggest that you feel you are on the move, and not able to settle down the way you feel you should.
2. A tent can also signify that you perhaps need to get away from everyday responsibilities for a time, and rediscover your relationship with natural forces. There is benefit to be gained by being self-sufficient and not dependent on anyone.
3. If you dream of a tent, which is not providing the required shelter to be comfortable, signifies that there will be limitations in your attempt to settle down into a stable relationship.

TERROR

1. Terror in a dream is often the result of unresolved fears and doubts. Please evaluate what is causing you such fears and face these difficulties bluntly.
2. To dream of someone else being terrified signifies that you need to work out what course of action should be taken to avoid unnecessary hostility.
3. If you dream of terrorising someone, or having the attempt to cause terror to others signifies that you have unaccomplished goals and you should be warned against resorting to cheats.

TESTS

1. Dreaming of any forthcoming tests of any sort, signifies that you need to make a self-evaluation of the way you handle your daily events. There may be a far better way to do so.
2. To dream of a medical test may be alerting you to the need to watch your health.
3. If you dream of a driving test would suggest a need to be confident in your next endeavour.
4. Testing something in a dream suggests that there has been some form of standard with which you must adhere.

TEXT

1. For a piece of text to appear in your dream would signify the need for encouragement and perhaps wisdom.
2. Text from a book or a text of a play would indicate the need for the dreamer to carry out instructions in a particular way in order to achieve success.
3. A spiritual text is an encouraging message to enable you to progress.

THAW

1. In dreams to be conscious of a thaw is to note a change in your own emotional responses. You no longer have a need to be emotionally distanced as previously.
2. Psychologically you have the ability to "warm up" a situation, and to melt coldness away. If you are aware of coldness within yourself, on an emotional level you need to discover what the problem is or was, and why you have reacted as you did.

THEATRE

1. To dream about a theatre, it will depend which part of the theatre is highlighted. If it is the stage, then a situation that the dreamer is in at this particular moment is being drawn to his attention.
2. If it is the auditorium, then his ability to listen is significant.
3. If you are not involved in the action, it indicates you are able to stand back and take an objective viewpoint.
4. To be in the spotlight, for instance, might signify your need to be noticed.

THERMOMETER

1. To dream of a thermometer is an indication that you have to keep a close watch over your feelings. It is very important not to jump to conclusions in any situation. Listen first to both sides of the story.
2. To dream of a clinical thermometer would portray your emotional generosity, whereas an external thermometer would suggest your intellectual abilities.
3. Psychologically you sometimes need an external evaluation as to where you are coming from. A thermometer would be a reassurance device.

THIEF

1. Dreaming of a thief links with your fear of losing things, or of having them taken away. You may be afraid of losing love or possessions.
2. When a thief appears in dreams, you are aware of a part of your personality which can waste your own time and energy on meaningless activity. It literally steals from you.
3. To dream of being a thief *see stealing*.

THIRST

1. Dreaming of being thirsty suggests that you have an unsatisfied inner need; you may be emotionally at a low ebb and need something to give you a boost.
2. To dream of quenching your thirst indicates that you are capable of satisfying your own desires.
3. Thirst can also signify that you need to look very carefully at either what you are being denied, or what you are denying yourself in waking life.

THISTLE

1. To be conscious of thistles in a dream is to be aware of some discomfort in waking life. A field of thistles would suggest a difficult road ahead.

2. To dream of a single thistle would indicate minor difficulties.
3. The thistle has a meaning of defiance and vindictiveness. When dreaming of a thistle you may be being made aware of those qualities, either in people around you or in yourself.

THORN
1. To dream of being pierced by a thorn or splinter signifies that a minor difficulty has gotten through your defences.
2. To dream of being pricked by a thorn to the point of drawing blood signifies that you need to look at what is happening in your life which could make you vulnerable.
3. In a woman's dream a thorn could represent the sexual act, or rather, fear of intercourse.
4. The thorn, also associated with Christ, may signify that you are dedicating yourself to some element of your spiritual quest. The crown of thorns indicates suffering for your beliefs.

THREAD
1. In terms of your ordinary everyday life you perhaps need to follow a specific pattern in your daily activities right through to the end.
2. To dream of threading a needle has an obvious sexual reference. It can also, because of the perceived difficulty in threading a needle, suggest incompetence in ways other than sexual activities.
3. To dream of a tangled thread suggests a difficulty which needs unravelling.
4. If you dream of a spool of thread suggests that you need an ordered existence.

THRESHOLD
1. Crossing a threshold in dreams indicates that there are new experiences ahead.
2. To dream of being lifted across a threshold may suggest marriage, or in this day and age, a new relationship.
3. When you are about to take on new responsibilities you can dream of standing on the threshold.
4. To dream setting thresholds suggest that you may be moving into a new life, or perhaps a new way of living.

THRONE
1. When you dream of sitting on a throne, you are acknowledging your right to take authority.

2. If you dream of an empty throne signifies that you are not prepared to accept the responsibility for who you are. It may be that you are conscious of a lack of parenting.
3. To dream of someone else on a throne, you may have passed over authority unnecessarily to others.
4. A throne is a seat of authority or power. In dreams it can represent your ability to belong to groups, or even to society. You may need to take the lead in a project or scheme.

THUNDER

1. Hearing thunder in a dream can give a warning for the potential of an emotional outburst. You may be building up energy which eventually must reverberate.
2. To dream of hearing thunder signifies that there is still time to gain control of a potentially difficult situation.
3. Thunder has always been a symbol of great power and energy. In conjunction with lightning, it was seen as a tool of the gods. It could bring doom and disaster, but also cleansing.
4. Spiritually, the rumblings of thunder can demonstrate deep anger, or in extreme cases, Divine anger.

TICKET

1. To dream of a ticket will generally mean that there is a price to pay for something.
2. If you dream of a bus ticket would indicate that there is a price in the form of a sacrifice for moving forward, and this applies to train tickets as well.
3. A theatre ticket may suggest that you need to take a back seat and be objective over a part of your life.
4. Tickets to a football match might mean that you will have to pay for some area of conflict in your life.

TIDE

1. Dreaming of a tide signifies an attempt to go with the ebb and flow of life, or, rather more specifically, with your emotions.
2. As a tide also removes debris, the symbolism of cleansing is relevant. A high tide may symbolise high energy, whereas a low tide would suggest a drain on your abilities or energy.

3.   In waking life there are two times in the year when there are very high tides, the spring and the autumn. Hence to dream of an exceptionally high tide might signify the attainment of limitless power.

TIGER
See Animals

TIMBER
See Wood

TIME
1.   For time to be significant in a dream signifies that there is usually the necessity to measure it in some ways, or to use a period of time as a measurement for achieving the target to something at present.
2.   To dream of the time during morning hours will suggest that you should have an easy way in achieving whatever you need in your conscious waking life.
3.   **Afternoon:** This is a time of life when you can put your experience to good use.
4.   **Evening:** The end of life highlights your ability to be more relaxed about your life and activities.
5.   **Mid-day:** To dream of being conscious of mid-day suggests you are fully conscious and aware of your activities.
6.   **Night:** may be a period of depression or secrecy. You may be introspective or perhaps simply at rest.
7.   **Twilight:** can indicate in dreams a period of uncertainty and possible ambivalence in so far as your direction in life is concerned. It may also suggest a period of transition such as death.
8.   To be early for an appointment in a dream suggests having to wait for something to happen before you can carry on with other things.

TITANS
1.   Titans in dreams appear as huge god-like figures, sometimes overbearing, sometimes just large. In this context they represent the forces within you which allow things to manifest, or to happen.
2.   Psychologically you probably use about ten percent of your available energy. Those Titanic forces which can arise in dreams are those parts of yourself that are urging to make use of more of your resources in the form of exerting more energy in your endeavours. When used properly, you can create a world of your own.

TOAD
See Reptiles in Animals

TOBACCO
1. To dream of tobacco will have different meanings depending on whether the dreamer is a smoker or not. If he or she is a smoker, then tobacco, in the dream, is probably a comfort tool.
2. If not, then the symbolism has probably more to do with the idea of using tobacco to achieve a particular state of mind.
3. If the dreamer is smoking a pipe, there may be issues of masculinity to deal with.
4. Some cultures use tobacco to drive away bad spirits, and it is true that initially tobacco will give the person a mood lift. In dreams it is this symbolism of change which is the meaningful one.

TOILET
1. To dream of a toilet signifies the notions of privacy, and the ability to reach a state where you can release your feelings in private.
2. Something wrong with the toilet could suggest that you are emotionally blocked.
3. To dream of going to an unfamiliar toilet suggests you are in a position where you do not know what the outcome to a situation will be.
4. To dream of cleaning a dirty toilet suggests you are losing your relaxed and controlled attitude.

TOMB
1. To dream of going into a tomb suggests going down into the darker parts of your own personality. You may be fearful to begin with, but later more at ease.
2. To dream of finding yourself in a tomb suggests you are ready to face your fears of death and dying.
3. If you are trapped in a tomb in a dream denotes that you may be trapped by fear, pain or old outdated attitudes in your waking life.
4. To dream of being in a tomb where there are bodies, there are usually parts of yourself you have not developed.

TOOLS
1. Tools in dreams suggest the different ways and means that you have at your disposal for enhancing your lifestyle. It is a question of whether you are making the most of it.

2. Each tool will have its own significance. A drill suggests working through emotions and fears as well as attitudes which have become hardened.
3. A hammer provides the energy to break down old patterns of behaviour and resistances.
4. A saw suggests being able to cut through all the rubbish you have accumulated in order to make something new.

TOP
See Position

TORCH
1. In dreams, a torch can represent self-confidence. It can also suggest the need to be able to move forward, but at the same time carry your own light.
2. Dreaming of a lighted torch shows you can have the confidence to know that because of your own knowledge you have the ability to see the way forward.
3. You may feel that you need some spiritual guidance, and this can sometimes symbolise as a torch.
4. If you dream of a torch with difficulties to light up, signifies that the more you are thinking about something which is drawing nearer, the more your self-confidence reduces.

TORNADO
1. A tornado appearing in a dream is a symbol of violent energy of one sort or another. Often it is emotions and feelings against which you feel powerless.
2. To dream of sheltering a tornado signifies a symbol of energy which has turned in on itself, and therefore is a warning of forthcoming destruction.
3. To dream of having survived a tornado signifies that you have the potential at your hands for a new life or a new beginning to something which is extremely important to you.

TORPEDO
1. The torpedo, because of its shape, has obvious connections with masculine aggressiveness. You may have to watch against using your power in destructive forms.

2. To dream of using a torpedo signifies that you are on target with whatever you are attempting at the moment.
3. A torpedo is symbolic of spiritual directness. The dreamer should be aware of correct action in the circumstances he finds himself in.

TORTOISE

1. The tortoise for most people suggests slowness but also perhaps thoroughness. It also in dreams signifies a shell, which perhaps you, or others around you, have put up in order to protect or defend yourself.
2. The tortoise may of course simply be an image of a pet as an object which is loved. It may also however, be a symbol for long life.

TORTURE

1. When an image connected with torture appears in a dream, often you are trying to come to terms with a great hurt. This does not need to be on a physical level, it hardly ever is. It is more likely to be emotional or mental pain.
2. If you are being tortured in your dream symbolises that you may tend to put yourself in the position of a victim without realising it.
3. If you dream of torturing somebody else signifies that you have impatience which if you cannot control, will backfire on your own self in the form of mental stresses.

TOURIST

1. A tourist is someone who does not know his way around. If, in your dream you are the tourist, then you need to look at that aspect within yourself.
2. To dream of someone else being the tourist indicates that you need to be aware of what help you can give to other people.
3. To play the tourist in a dream is to be aware that you have the necessary information to do what you want, but you are choosing not to.

TOWER

1. A tower in a dream usually represents a construction which you have developed in your life. This may be an inner attitude or an outer life.
2. To dream of a tower with no door suggests you are out of touch with your inner self and common sense.
3. To dream of a tower with no windows signifies that you are unable to see and appreciate either your external good points or your inner qualities.

4. If you dream of an ivory tower suggests an innocent approach to something.
5. **A square tower:** signifies a practical approach to life.
6. **A round tower:** You should develop more spiritual awareness.
7. **To be in a tower with shallow steps:** would indicate that to explore your inner self may be easy.
8. **Complicated steps:** may indicate that you are a fairly private individual.
9. **If the door is barred:** You are not ready to explore your unconscious self.
10. **If the door is closed:** You must make an effort to get past a present difficulty.
11. **If inside the tower is dark:** You are still afraid of your subconscious functions.

TOWN
See Places

TOY
1. To dream of toys around you demonstrates an awareness of children around you, or of your more childlike attitude.
2. To dream of playing with toys signify the creative side of yourself, and the more playful innocent part.
3. To dream of playing with uninteresting toys signify that you may be mulling over new ideas or new ways of doing something over and over again.

TRACK
See Path and also Train, in Journey

TRAIN
See Journey

TRAITOR
1. To dream of a traitor suggests that you are subconsciously aware of deviousness. This may be in someone else, or it could be a part of your personality which is letting you down.
2. When, in a dream you are betrayed by others and believe them to have let you down, you are perhaps aware that it is through shared belief in waking life that they have let you down. This would mean they are traitors.

3. If you dream of becoming a traitor to somebody else, signifies that you still have more effort to do in your attempt to eradicate some bad practices.

TRAMP

1. To dream of a tramp in the sense of a decrepit old wanderer links you back to the part of yourself which is not expressed fully in real life. You have to guard against irresponsibility.
2. The tramp personifies in yourself the wanderer, the freedom lover. In dreams he will often appear at a time when you need freedom, but can also show that that need can bring difficulty and sadness if you are not careful.

TRANSFORMATION

1. A dream where obvious changes occur and things are transformed into something else suggests an increase in the level of your awareness.
2. A landscape may change from dark to light (negativity to positivity); a person may change from masculine attitudes to that of the feminine; or one image may change into another.
3. Once the dreamer understands the change is for the better, he is able to accomplish changes in his own life.
4. As the growth to maturity takes place, there are many transformations which occur. These are often depicted in dreams as immediate changes, like a speeded-up camera filming an opening flower.

TRANSPARENT

1. When something is transparent in your dream signifies that you may be feeling vulnerable, but may also be aware of insights you would not normally have.
2. To be inside a transparent bubble, for instance, would suggest visibility and vulnerability in your life, perhaps taking on new responsibilities.
3. For someone else to be behind a transparent shield suggests they are somewhat remote and unavailable to you.
4. When you are aware in dreams that things around you are transparent, you gain the ability to "see through" things. You are able to be discerning in your judgment.

TRAP

1. To be in a trap in a dream signifies that you feel you are trapped by external circumstances.
2. To be aware of trapping something or someone is attempting to hold onto them.

3. To be trapping a butterfly or other flying species or even insects indicates your attempt to be trying to capture the inner self.
4. When you feel trapped in dreams, you are not usually able to break free of old patterns of thought and behavior. You need outside help.

TRAVEL
See Journey

TREASURE
1. Treasure in dreams always represents something which is of value to you. It is the result of personal achievement and effort.
2. To find buried treasure in your dream signifies that you may find something you have lost, perhaps a part of your personality.
3. To dream of burying treasure is to be trying to guard against the future, and potential problems.
4. To dream of finding a box of treasure is to have some understanding that you must break through limitations before you find what you are looking for.
5. To dream of a treasure hunt suggests the finding of earthly goods or material gains which will not necessarily be good for you.

TREE
1. The tree is symbolic in dreams of the basic structure of your inner life. When one appears in your dream it is best to work with the image fairly extensively. A tree with wide branches would suggest a warm loving personality.
2. **A small close-leafed tree:** Would suggest an uptight personality.
3. **A well-shaped tree:** Would suggest a well-ordered personality.
4. **A large, messy tree:** Would suggest a chaotic personality.
5. **An oak tree:** Represents strength.
6. **A tree with spreading roots:** Would indicate an ability to relate well to the physical elements of life in order to achieve.
7. **A deep-rooted tree:** Would suggest a more self-contained attitude.
8. **A rough trunk tree:** Suggests obviously a rough and ready personality, whereas a smoother trunk would indicate more sophistication.
9. **To dream of climbing the tree:** Suggests you are looking at your hopes and abilities, in order to succeed.

TRESPASSING

1. To dream of trespassing signifies that perhaps you are intruding on someone's personal space. This may also suggest that there is a part of you which is private and is vulnerable. You should respect those boundaries.
2. To dream of others trespassing on your property indicate that you need to look at your own boundaries. Sometimes it is interesting when interpreting the dream to find out whether the trespasser is there voluntarily or involuntarily. You can then work out whether you are the victim or not.

TRIANGLE
See Shapes

TRICKSTER

1. In dreams, the trickster is literally that part of yourself which can create havoc in your life. When under stress this personage can present himself in dreams as the character who points one in the wrong direction, answers questions with the wrong answers, etc.
2. Psychologically, if you have been too rigid in your attitude to life, for instance, struggling to be good the whole time or continually taking a moral stance, the trickster can appear in dreams as a counterbalance.
3. This is the spiritually irresponsible part of your nature. You have not yet put yourself on the correct spiritual path, and need to do so.

TRIPLETS

1. Spiritually triplets appearing in dreams suggest that events or situations should be looked at carefully in terms of physical wants, emotional needs and spiritual requirements. Then there would be development of spiritual stability.

TROPHY

1. Dreaming of a trophy is to recognise that you have done something for which you can be rewarded.
2. To dream of a trophy in the form of a cup would suggest receptivity.
3. A shield: Will represent protection.
4. Formerly trophies such as animal heads were much sought after. This is no longer so, but the symbolism of overcoming one's basic fears in order to achieve still remains.

334

TRUMPET

1. A trumpet in a dream will most often suggest either a warning or a "call to arms." From a practical point of view it will be alerting you to some danger you have put yourself in or are facing.
2. To dream of blowing a trumpet represents the need to maximise one's potential. You should reach for the best within yourself in order to have the maximum effect in your life.

TRUNK

1. In previous times to dream of a trunk was supposed to foretell a journey, possibly a long one. Nowadays, as people tend to travel light, it is much more likely to represent a repository for old things and hence signify old outdated ideas.
2. When a trunk appears in a dream it is time to summon the courage to sort out what is still outstanding and what is also causing you fears.
3. To find jewels in a trunk indicates the good that can be found in doing a personal spring-cleaning.
4. Dreaming of a trunk indicates that spiritually you need to explore your hidden depths to get the best out of yourself.

TUG-OF-WAR

1. To dream of a tug-of-war suggests a conflict between good and bad, male and female, positive and negative. You may face a tricky situation to sort them out.
2. A tug-of-war may also indicate the need to maintain balance through tension between opposites. To be on the winning side suggests that what you wish to achieve can be achieved with help.
3. To be on the losing side requires you to identify the parallel situation in ordinary everyday life and decide whether to continue.

TUNNEL

1. A tunnel in a dream usually represents the need to explore something which may be going on right under your nose. You may have to make careful observations throughout your daily activities in order to detect where you may need to start.
2. To dream of perceiving a light at the end of the tunnel indicates that you are reaching the final stages of your ambition.
3. To dream of something blocking the tunnel signifies that some past fear or experience is stopping you from progressing.

TURF

1. To dream of being on turf ground signifies that you have a wish for supreme success.
2. Dreaming of one's association with a particular piece of ground can activate memories and feelings connected with happy times. This may, by recollection, help to clarify a particular problem or situation.

TURKEY

See Bird

TWEEZERS

1. Dreaming of tweezers suggest that you need to look at a situation in minute details. By grasping this detail properly, much good can be achieved.
2. In the sense that tweezers are tools, such a dream might suggest that you need to develop the correct tools for a job you may shortly undertake.

TWINS

1. To dream of seeing twins is a perfect example which warns you to avoid total confusion when you face situations where you are unsure of what your next action should be.
2. If you dream of meeting your twin brother or sister (even if you are not a twin pair in actual life), signifies that you should be on your guard against being confused by other people to take advantage over you.

TYPHOON

See Storm

U

ULCER

1. To dream of an ulcer is a warning that there is work which needs to be done to heal a situation which has been very hurtful.
2. It will depend on where the ulcer is, as to what needs healing. To dream of a stomach ulcer, for instance, would suggest an emotional difficulty.
3. If you dream of a mouth ulcer would suggest some problems with speech or making yourself understood to those around you.
4. If you dream of nursing someone else's ulcer signifies that you are aware that that person is not dealing with a dilemma in which you are involved.

UMBRELLA

1. To dream of an umbrella signifies that you may not have to worry too much about a particular difficult situation as you will instinctively strike the right cord towards an effective solution.
2. To dream of sheltering under an umbrella signifies the need for you to avoid forthcoming difficult circumstances which could be detected by close observations to other peoples' conversation around you.
3. To dream of an umbrella can also signify that you need to develop certain skills to cope with certain situations in your everyday activities.

UNCLE
See Family

UNDERNEATH
See Position

UNDERGROUND

1. To dream of an underground is an alert that you should take present opportunities to explore your own hidden depths. You cannot usually access the unconscious in waking life, and to dream of being underground will often allow you to come to terms with that side in a very easy way.
2. To be on the subway usually signifies the journeys you are prepared (or forced) to take towards understanding who you are.

337

3. The subconscious or the unconscious is often perceived in dreams as a cave or place underground.

UNDRESS
1. When you find yourself undressing in a dream signifies that you may be putting yourself in touch with your own sexual feelings.
2. Another situation is the possibility that you may also need to reveal your true feelings about a situation around you, and to have the freedom to be totally open about those feelings.
3. To dream of watching someone else undressing often indicate that you should be aware of that person's sensitivity.
4. If you dream of undressing someone else suggests that you are attempting to understand either yourself or others on a very deep level.

UNEARTH
1. To dream of trying to unearth something signifies that you are attempting to reveal a side of yourself which you do not yet understand.
2. If you dream of attempting to unearth something which personally belongs to you signifies that you may be trying to uncover aspects of your personality which you have consciously been hiding up to now.
3. If you dream of somebody else attempting to unearth something which you have deliberately hidden signifies that you should display a fair level of honesty in your every day activities.

UNEMPLOYMENT
1. Dreaming of being unemployed suggests that you are not making the best use of your talents, or that you feel your talents are not being recognised.
2. Unemployment is a fear that almost everyone has. When an event connected with unemployment occurs in a dream, your feelings of inadequacy are highlighted. You need to experience that fear in order to overcome it.
3. A sense of spiritual inadequacy and inability can translate itself into the image of unemployment. This is more to do with not being motivated enough to accept a spiritual task.

UNICORN
See Animals

UNIFORM

1. Dreaming of uniforms has to do with your identification with a particular role or type of authority. However rebellious you may be, a part of you needs to conform to the ideas and beliefs of the social group to which you belong.
2. Often in collective groups, the right to wear a uniform has to be earned. Dreaming of being in a group of uniformed people indicates that you have achieved the right to be recognised.
3. Identification of a common spiritual goal and an agreement as to "uniform" behaviour is an important aspect in spiritual development.

UNION

1. If you dream of a union, in the sense of a trade union, suggests that you need to make collective action which is for the good of all.
2. We all attempt to achieve unity from duality, to create a relationship between two parts or opposites. Dreaming of achieving union depicts this relationship. Psychologically, the human being is consistently looking for a partner.
3. To dream of a non-effective union or a union which is disintegrating signifies that you may lose grasp of your hold to a facility which recognises your authority.

UNIVERSITY

1. Dreaming of being in a university highlights your own individual potential and learning ability.
2. Since a university is a place of "higher" learning, you are being made aware of the breadth of experience and increase in knowledge available to you. You need to move away from the mundane and ordinary into specific areas of knowledge and awareness.
3. To dream of being an authority person in a university signifies that you need extra knowledge to handle a forthcoming responsibility effectively.

URINE

1. To dream of urine signifies that you may need a closer examination to new patterns of life you are about to embark, or to new ways of handling things.
2. If you dream of urinating in inappropriate areas signify that you may have to resist proposals to join a group of people, or close colleagues whose aim is to indulge in undesirable practices.

3. To dream of accidentally drinking urine, signifies that you may have to be cautious against being wrongly held liable to things which are not entirely your fault.
4. If you dream of somebody else urinating on you signifies that you should guard against inferiority.
5. If you dream of urinating on somebody else signifies that you have to watch out against exaggeration in justifying a forthcoming demand.

V

VACCINATION

1. To dream that you are being vaccinated suggests that you are likely to be hurt by someone (perhaps emotionally). What they are trying to do to you will, in the end, be helpful.
2. It is very easy for you to be influenced by other people. Vaccination indicates that you can be affected by other people's ideas and feelings.
3. If you dream of vaccinating someone signifies that you have a good intention to help but you should also take the necessary care not to impose conditions which may be extremely difficult to the recipient.

VAGINA

1. Many people have some type of inhibition over their sexuality or "bodily parts." Few, however, dream directly of the vagina itself. It usually symbolises femininity.

VALLEY

1. If you dream of going down a valley can signify that the easiest part to complete a task remains to be taken up.
2. If you dream of someone forcing you down a valley signifies depression and gloominess.
3. If you dream of tumbling down a valley signifies that you should search for new areas of productivity within you.
4. If you dream of being trapped in a valley signifies that you should not succumb to other peoples' authority, at least for the time being.

VAMPIRE

1. When heavy demands are made on you which you do not feel capable of meeting, a vampire can appear in your dream. You are figuratively being "sucked dry."
2. Often the fear of emotional and sexual relationships can be represented in dreams as a vampire.
3. If you dream of fighting a vampire signifies bravery and courage to stand firm against oppression.
4. To dream of defending others from the attack of a vampire is a warning for you to ensure that you are absolutely right in your doings before defending others.

VAN
See car in journey

VANISH
1. One of the most annoying things about dreams is that images will vanish unexpectedly. There is also the tendency for you to forget parts of the dream on waking. The reason is that the subject of the dream has not yet fully fixed itself in consciousness. Working with dreams can, in actual fact, help to "fix" the information your subconscious is attempting to give you.
2. Just as a child believes in the world of magic, so the dream state is one that is totally believable. When images vanish in a dream, they will very often become more tangible in the waking state.
3. The mind has a great capacity for magic, and to dream of things vanishing, and then possibly reappearing, highlights this.

VARNISH
1. To dream of varnish may signify that you may be covering something up in order to hide imperfections.
2. Dreaming of varnish can also mean that you have achieved some spiritual goals.
3. If you dream of varnishing something, may signify that you may be protecting yourself and attempting to present a better self-image.
4. To dream of somebody else varnishing something which belongs to you suggests that you are not happy with your original creation. It may need further work to preserve what you have already done.

VASE
1. As a holder of beautiful things, any receptacle such as a vase, water pot, pitcher or urn, tends to represent the intention and importance for you to improve either the façade of your house or most importantly your office.
2. If you dream of a vase which is holding beautiful flowers or plants signifies that you should really look intensively behind anything with an attracting appearance.
3. If you dream of a shattered vase signifies that you may end up in a dull situation for something which you have started so brightly.
4. If you dream of a vase holding very inappropriate things such as knives signifies deception.

VAULT

1. To dream of going down into a vault represents your need to explore those areas of yourself that have become hidden.
2. If you dream of being trapped in a vault signifies that you may have to pay particular attention to what you say regarding past happenings you are aware.
3. To dream of a damaged vault signifies that you may learn of an unexpected illness.

VD
See Sex

VEGETABLES
See Food

VEGETATION

1. Vegetation in a dream can often represent the obstacles that you put in front of you in order to grow. For instance, a patch of brambles can suggest irritating snags to your movement forward, whereas nettles might represent people actually trying to prevent progress.
2. While the obstacles you create may cause difficulty, there is also an underlying abundance and fertility that is available to you.
3. To be clearing vegetation, for instance in a vegetable garden, can suggest clearing away that which is no longer of use to you.

VEIL

1. When an object is veiled in a dream, there is some kind of secret which needs to be revealed. You may, as the dreamer, be concealing something from yourself, but you could also be being kept in ignorance by others.
2. The mind has different ways of indicating hidden thoughts in dreams. The veil is one of these symbols.
3. A veil can represent all that is hidden and mysterious, and this translates into aspects of the occult.

VELVET

1. It is usually the texture and quality that is relevant when a material appears in a dream. It is the sensuousness and softness of velvet which is significant. To dream of velvet is to dream of forthcoming harmony.
2. Spiritually velvet can depict richness and giftedness.

343

VERMIN
See Rat

VERTICAL
See Position

VICAR
1. Just as the priest was given spiritual authority over many, and was often a figure to be feared, so the vicar is also given this authority. To dream of a vicar signifies that you should be extremely careful to whom you give such authority as to collect important items on your behalf or the signing of important documents in your absence.
2. To dream of being a vicar yourself signifies that you need more knowledge of your spiritual qualities.
3. To dream of a vicar turned into a woman signifies that you may be subject to an investigation.

VICE
1. There are obviously two meanings to the word vice. One is a tool which clamps and the other a wrong action. Dreaming of a vice in its first sense may suggest that you are being constrained in some ways.
2. The second would indicate that you are aware of the side of yourself which is rebellious and out of step with society. You may in both cases need to make adjustments in your behaviour.
3. Often dreams allow you to behave in ways which are not those you would normally try in waking life. Being conscious of a particular vice, e.g. sloth, envy, apathy, etc. in your dream character may enable you to handle that tendency within yourself.
4. Forthcoming unacceptable behaviour may manifest in the form of vice.

VICTIM
1. To dream of having the feelings of being the victim of an unfair judgement is a warning that you should be more alert to debates which involve financial implications.
2. If you dream of making others become victims under your authority, signifies that you may indulge in greed which may later turn against you.
3. To dream of making others become victims by exerting physical harm or assault, signifies that you should avoid situations leading to frustration by making careful analysis before making vital decisions.

4. If you dream of being a victim of burglary, rape or murder can signify that you should take the necessary steps to preserve your personality which is weak at the moment.

VICTORY
1. To dream of others being victorious over you signifies that you may need to overcome difficulties which may shortly surface in your life.
2. If you dream of victory over other people signifies that you can reproduce in waking life. It gives you confidence in your own abilities.
3. Victory in a psychological sense is the overcoming of obstacles which you have set up for yourself.
4. If the dreamer has achieved a degree of spiritual success, it can show itself as a victory of some kind.

VILLAGE
1. For a village to appear in your dream signifies that you may have to integrate into a group to enable you to see real results for something you are attempting at the moment.
2. To dream of being in an unknown village signifies forthcoming oppression which may be felt in close relationships.
3. If you dream of being in a familiar village signifies that you may soon be in a relaxed and carefree mood.

VINE
1. The vine in dreams can suggest growth and fruitfulness. This can be of one's whole self, or the various parts.
2. To dream of the vine signifies that you are linking with the more spiritual side of yourself which has grown through shared, rather than individual, experience.
3. A vine or vineyard can symbolise growth of a spiritual nature. It can also represent fertility.

VINEGAR
1. Vinegar, because it is sour, is a representation of all that is problematic in taking in information. It can thus signify knowledge which is unacceptable.
2. Oddly enough vinegar is a symbol of life, both because it preserves, and also because it is something which is left after a change of its original state. In dreams this symbolism can come across very strongly.

3. If you dream of serving something with excess vinegar signifies that you may be subjected to stiff conditions in your endeavour to accomplish something.

VIOLENCE

1. Any violence in dreams is a reflection of your own inner feeling, sometimes about yourself, sometimes about the situations around you. Often the type of violence is worthy of notice if you are to understand yourself fully.
2. When you are unable, because of social pressures or circumstances, to express yourself properly, you can find yourself behaving violently in dreams.
3. To dream of others behaving violently towards you, you may need to take care in your waking life not to upset others.
4. A sense of spiritual injustice may be represented by scenes or acts of violence in a dream. The dreamer should equate this with recent spiritual events.

VIPER
See Serpent and Snake in Animal

VIRGIN

1. To dream of being a virgin suggests a state of innocence and purity.
2. To dream that someone else is a virgin highlights the ideals of integrity and honesty.
3. The virginal mind - that is, a mind that is free from deception and guile, is perhaps more important than physically being a virgin, and it is this aspect which often becomes evident in dreams.
4. In a woman's dream such a figure suggests she is in touch with her own psyche.

VIRGIN MOTHER
See Mother Mary in Religion

VISIONS

1. To dream of having visions signifies that you are being deliberately kept from vital knowledge.

VISIT

1. To be visited by someone in a dream can suggest that there is information, warmth or love available to you.

346

2. If it is someone you know then this may apply in a real-life situation. If not, then there may be a facet of your personality which is trying to make itself apparent.

3. To be paying someone else a visit in a dream signifies that you may need to widen your horizons in some fashion. This may be physically, emotionally or spiritually.

VITAMIN

1. Dreaming of taking vitamins indicate that you have a concern about health. You may be aware that you are not nurturing yourself properly, and require additional help.

2. On a slightly more different level, you are aware that you are not doing the best for yourself and need more out of life in order to function according to your true potential. There could be a situation in your life which needs a particular type of assistance.

3. Vitamins could also suggest that a higher vibration is needed in order to progress.

VOICE

1. The voice is a tool that is used to express yourself. You all have inner awareness of your own state which is sometimes difficult to disclose. Often in dreams you are able to use your voice in more appropriate ways.

2. A voice that speaks through or to one has two areas of significance. If one believes in the spirit realm, this is communication from a discarnate spirit.

3. More psychologically, when you suppress certain parts of your personalities, they may surface in dreams as disembodied voices.

4. The Voice of God is a term which is used to describe the energy of a spiritual summon.

VOID

See Abyss

VOLCANO

1. The image of a volcano in dreams is a very telling one, partly because of its unpredictability. To dream of a volcano being extinct can indicate either that you have "killed off" your passions, or that a difficult situation has come to an end. This may be one that has been around for some time.

2. To dream of an erupting volcano usually signifies that you are not in control of a situation or of your emotions, of which there may be a hurtful release.

3. If the lava is more prominent it signifies feelings which will run very deep.
4. If the lava has cooled it signifies that there has been a deep passion which has now cooled off.
5. If the explosiveness is more noticeable, anger may be more prominent.

VOMIT

1. To dream of vomiting suggests a discharge of disagreeable feelings and emotions. It would be a clearing of something within that makes you extremely uncomfortable.
2. To dream of watching someone else vomit indicates that you may have upset someone and need to have compassion.
3. Vomiting is a symbol of a discharge. This signifies that you may have held on to bad feeling for so long that it has caused your spiritual system some difficulties.

VORTEX

See Whirlwind

VOTE

1. Dreaming of voting in an election, whether general or within the workplace, highlights your wish and ability to belong to groups.
2. If you dream of voting in favour of something signifies that you should be sincere in your forthcoming decisions with regards to your social life.
3. To dream of voting against something signifies that you should guard against external influences to rebel.
4. To dream of being elected to a position of power signifies that you possess great inner strength which should be put to use in order to gain much needed respect.
5. If you dream of being voted out of a position of authority signifies that you have lost the drive to accomplish something important at present.

VOUCHER

1. A voucher in dreams can suggest your ability to give yourself permission to do something. If, for instance, it is a money off voucher you may not be valuing yourself properly, or alternatively you could be looking for an easy option.

2. A voucher has the effect of opening up one's opportunities. Because it is usually an exchange between two people, it can indicate the help that others can give you.
3. To dream of giving away a voucher to someone else signifies that you may soon have the tendency to exploit others for selfish gains.

VOYAGE
See Journey

VULTURE
See Birds

W

WAFER

1. A wafer, because of its extreme lightness, signifies that you may have to be extremely careful not to say more than what is necessary when participating in sensitive conversation or debate as you may end up into unnecessary arguments.
2. A wafer biscuit is constructed in many layers. It thus becomes a symbol for diversity. You may need to understand the various "stages" of your life in order to manage your life successfully.
3. To dream of eating a wafer signifies that you may shortly be a participant in an event which may not last due to a lack of a proper understanding of clear objectives.

WAFFLE

1. To waffle, in the sense of talking unnecessarily at length, can be translated by the dreamer as the need to control his self-expression.
2. To dream of someone else waffling, indicates that in real life the dreamer needs to listen very carefully to instructions.
3. To dream of eating a waffle suggests a need to approach life in a different way. You perhaps need to adopt a more down-to-earth, homely approach to achieve success in relationships.

WAGES

1. Wages are normally paid in exchange for work done. In dreams, to be receiving wages signify that you have done a good job even if your results are not yet available.
2. To dream of paying somebody wages imply that you owe something in the sense of either material things or an explanation.
3. To dream of receiving a wage packet suggests that your value is tied up with other things such as loyalty and duty.
4. Often when you are doing something that you do not want to do, or which you do not enjoy, the only payoff is in the wages you receive. To dream of wages may signify that you should not expect anything else in a situation in everyday life.
5. Spiritually, wages can represent recompense for your actions, and the reward you deserve coming your way.

WAIL

1. To dream of hearing someone wailing indicates that you have become conscious of someone else's sadness and that you may be called for assistance.
2. To dream of finding yourself wailing signifies that you may be allowing yourself an emotional release which would not be seen to be appropriate in everyday life.
3. Wailing is reputed to be a method of summoning the spirits. In dreams, therefore, it can suggest that you are trying to get in touch with a power that is greater than what you may be able to handle.
4. Grieving and the making of sounds is used spiritually to banish bad spirits. The dreamer should look at what he feels needs "banishing" from his life.

WAITER/WAITRESS

1. The interpretation of this dream depends on whether you yourself are waiting at table, or whether you are being waited upon. If you are in the role of waiter, you are aware of your ability to care for other people.
2. If you are being waited on, then you perhaps need to be nurtured and made to feel special.
3. To dream of the appearance of a waiter or waitress signifies that you may need to be conscious that for complete fulfilment in any task or responsibility you need to wait.

WAITING

1. To dream of waiting for somebody, or something, implies a need to recognise a sense of anticipation. You may be looking to other people, or outside circumstances, to help you move forward or make decisions.
2. To dream of waiting for something with impatience signifies that your expectations are too high.
3. If you dream of waiting patiently for someone or something signifies that there is the understanding that events will happen in their own good time.
4. When you become aware that something is expected from you, and other people are waiting for appropriate action, you may need to consider your own leadership qualities.

WAKE

1. A wake, in the sense of a funeral service, gives you an opportunity to grieve properly. When in dreams you find yourself attending such an

occasion, you need to be aware that there may be some reason in your life for you to go through a period of grieving.
2. To dream of other people attending a wake indicates that you may need support to overcome a disappointment.

WALKING
1. In a dream, walking indicates the way in which you should be moving forward. To be walking purposefully suggests you know where you are going and it implies the right direction as well.
2. To dream of wandering aimlessly suggests that you need to create goals for yourself.
3. To dream of using a walking stick is a warning that you have to recognise your need for support and assistance in certain areas of your life.
4. Walking may be used as a relaxation from stress, and it is this significance which often comes up in dreams. If you are alone then your walk can be silent and contemplative. If it is in company, then you can communicate and converse without fear of interruption.

WALL
1. In dreams, walls usually indicate the boundaries you have set yourself.
2. If you dream of building a wall purposefully to keep others from your premises signifies that you should keep a reasonable level of privacy regarding information you may have.
3. If you dream of facing a wall which is keeping you outside a specific premise indicates that you may not be aware that you are not being trusted by people whom you trust with confidential matters.
4. If you dream of jumping over a wall with the intention of intruding on other peoples' premises signifies that you have to take extra care when faced with your next decision involving privacy or private matters of other people.
5. To dream of being behind a wall which is imprisoning you indicates that you are being held prisoner by your own fears, doubts and difficulties.
6. If you dream of a wall which appears and disappears indicates that you have only partly dealt with your problem.

WALLET

1. To dream of a wallet signifies that you need to make provisions to open up facilities to enable you to improve in either financial means or respect that you rightfully need.
2. To dream of a bulging wallet signifies that you are on the right track towards fulfilling a goal which may be short term.
3. To dream of an empty wallet signifies that you need resources in the form of external help to enable you tackle whatever task you have at present.

WALLPAPER

1. For wallpapers to appear in your dream signifies that the time has come for you to make some necessary changes to move away from old-fashioned practices in either your job or at home.
2. To dream of putting up wallpaper signifies covering up the old self (possibly superficially), particularly if the old wallpaper is not removed.
3. Wallpaper in a dream can have the same significance as clothes on a character. You may want to make changes in your life but need to experiment, and get a proper understanding first.
4. Wallpaper can also mean that there is also the need for you to take a look at yourself and be sure that you are being true to yourself, as wallpaper often symbolises an outer facade of some kind.

WALNUT
See Nut

WAND

1. When you dream of using a wand indicates that you are aware of your influence over others and so you must take the necessary steps against abuses.
2. To dream of someone else using a wand indicates that you are aware of the power of suggestion, either for negative or for positive within a situation.
3. Conventionally the wand is an instrument of supernatural forces, and it is often this image which is the most important. You are aware of some force external to yourself which needs harnessing.
4. Obviously a wand works in tandem with magic, so to dream of a wand can symbolise "magical" powers which may influence you.

WANDERER
See Tramp

WANT

1. To dream of wanting something indicates that you are suppressing either certain facilities or material things which you need to complete self-satisfaction.
2. If, in dreams, you find you want to do, or be somebody different, you are aware of the potential within you either to achieve success or to change your life.
3. To dream of wanting something belonging to other people is a warning to avoid being implicated in fraudulent activities.

WAR

1. In dreams war always denotes conflict. It has a more global effect than one-to-one combat, and would suggest that you need to be more conscious of the effect your actions will have on others.
2. War in dreams signifies that you also need to be aware that you are taking part in conflict which is deliberately engineered rather than spontaneous.
3. To dream of playing a specified role in a war signifies that you should take the necessary care not to be forceful in your demands for anything you may need, although your desire may be so.
4. War is a symbol of spiritual disintegration. You may need to be aware of what is disintegrating within your life.

WARDEN

1. A warden in a dream is often a manifestation of the guardian or the keeper. You may have a part of your personality which acts as monitor or attempts to suppress other parts of your personality, and this appears as a warden.
2. In working with dream images you will often recognise aspects of the Spiritual Self which protect you from outside influence and this also can appear as a warden.

WARDROBE

1. A wardrobe, often because it is large, can have the same significance as a passage, and therefore suggests a period of transition. Because it houses your clothes, it also suggests how you deal with your self-image.

WAREHOUSE
See Buildings

WARMTH
1. Warmth in a dream touches your "feel good" factor and enhances your sense of comfort and well-being.
2. Psychologically, feelings of cheerfulness and hopefulness can create an awareness of warmth and can be interchangeable.
3. A feeling of warmth in a dream can symbolise that most sought-after prize-unconditional love. The dreamer can afford to move positively in search of this.

WARNING
1. To receive a warning in a dream suggests that you are aware that either internally or externally something needs attention. You may be putting yourself in danger.
2. To be warning someone in your dream highlights your ability to be aware of difficulty and danger, either to others or to hidden parts of your personality.
3. To receive a written warning indicates you may be behaving badly. A warning in this case can actually be showing you the way toward being a more intuitive person.

WARRANT
1. A warrant represents permission from a higher authority, either spiritual or physical. It will depend on the type of warrant as to what action the dreamer needs to take. For instance, a search warrant suggests looking at one's motives, whereas a warrant for arrest indicates that you need to stop carrying out a particular action.
2. When you are unable to make decisions, dream images can often help you. The warrant opens up possibilities of which you may not have been aware.
3. The dreamer may be seeking spiritual permission for some reason, and this can be symbolised by a warrant.

WARTS
1. To dream of warts indicate that you have a distorted view of your environment. You may have to analyse whether you are a victim of deceit.
2. If you dream of warts on your own body signifies that you are often distressed by anything which is out of the ordinary or wrong.

WASHING

1. Dreaming of washing either yourself, or for instance, clothes, suggest getting rid of negative feelings. You may need to change your attitude, either internally or externally.
2. Since water is a symbol for emotion and the unconscious, washing stands for achieving a relationship with your emotional self and dealing successfully with the results.
3. To dream of washing something which appears not to become cleaner signifies that you may face recurring problems or hiccups. You may have to unsettle several other people to secure a long-term solution.

WASP

See Insects

WASTE

1. Waste in dreams signifies matter or information you no longer need.
2. Waste can also suggest a misuse of resources, you may, initially be using too much energy on a particular project.
3. If you are being wasteful in dreams signifies that you need to reassess how you are running your life. You may be giving too much in relationships, or trying to make things happen.
4. If you dream of other people wasting your resources signifies that you may have to look to where there is most likely to be an exaggeration in demands placed on you.

WATCH

See Time

WATCHING

1. To dream of watching over something signifies that you may soon undertake a task which you must put a lot of concentration in order to achieve the best result.
2. To be aware of someone watching you in a dream suggests that you feel threatened by someone's close interest in you. This may be in a work situation, but could also be in personal relationships.
3. To dream of watching other people with the intention to catch them at something wrong signifies that there is a need for you to monitor your actions, particularly if new forms of spiritual discipline have recently been taken on.

WATER

1. Water is usually taken in dreams to symbolise all that is emotional and feminine. It is a mysterious substance, given that it has the ability to flow through, over and around objects. It has the quality of being able to wear away anything which gets in its way. Water can also stand for the dreamer's potential and his ability to create a new life in response to his own inner urgings.
2. Water also represents cleansing, being able to wash away the contamination that you may experience in everyday life. In baptism, water is a cleanser of previously held "sins," often also those inherited from the family. Entering water suggests beginning something new.
3. To dream of being immersed in water can suggest pregnancy and birth.
4. **Flowing water:** Signifies peace and comfort.
5. **Rushing water:** Indicates passion.
6. **Deep water:** Suggests unawareness of close events.
7. **Shallow water:** Represents a lack of essential energy.
8. **Going down into water:** Indicates a need to renew one's strength, to go back to the beginning.
9. **Coming up out of the water:** Suggests a fresh start.
10. **To be on the water:** (as in a boat) can represent indecision or a lack of emotional commitment.
11. **Bathing:** Suggests purification.
12. **Canals:** symbolises the birth process.
13. **Dams:** Signifies that there are conscious attempts to control your emotions.
14. **Diving:** Represents attempts to find the parts of yourself which you have suppressed.
15. **Floods:** Represent the chaotic side of you, which is usually uncontrollable, hence, you should be on the look out.
16. **Fountains:** Suggest womanhood.
17. **Lake:** A lake, like a pool, can signify a stage of transition between the conscious and the spiritual Self.
18. **To be reflected in a pool:** Indicates the dreamer needs to learn to accept that there will be a part of himself that he does not like very much but, when harnessed, can give much energy for change.
19. **Rivers or streams:** Always represent the dreamer's life and the way that he is living it. It will depend on the dreamer's attitude as to whether he sees his life as a large river or a small stream.

20. **If the river is rushing by:** Suggests that you may feel that life is moving too quickly for you.
21. **If the river is very deep:** Suggests that you should perhaps be paying attention to the rest of the world, and how you relate to it.
22. **Crossing a river:** Indicates great changes.
23. **If the river causes fear:** Suggests that you are perhaps creating an unnecessary difficulty for yourself.
24. **If the water in the river appears to be contaminated:** Suggests that you are not doing the best you can for yourself.
25. **Sea or ocean:** Signifies that you have not harnessed certain powers within your reach.
26. **A shallow sea:** Suggests superficial emotion.
27. **The waves in the sea:** Represent emotion and lust.
28. **A calm sea:** Suggests a peaceful existence.
29. **A stormy sea:** Signifies passion, either negative or positive.
30. **Rise and fall of the tides:** Suggests to be conscious both of the passage of time and of the rise and fall of your own emotions.

WATERFALL

1. To see a waterfall in your dream warns you against any display of emotion that is forceful and yet somewhat controlled.
2. Whenever any emotion reaches the stage where it must "spill over" in order to become manageable it can be represented as a waterfall in dreams.
3. A waterfall shows that some degree of spiritual power is around, and the dreamer should look to make use of it.

WAVES
See Water

WAX

1. Dreaming of wax signifies that you need to allow some flexibility in order to make something achievable. You should be prepared to give way, but also to be firm when necessary.
2. Wax can also to be taken to represent insincerity. It is something that is consumed by the flame, for instance, of a candle, and therefore can be moved and changed into something else with qualities that it did not initially have.
3. If you are a person in authority, wax may signify the need to move away from rigidity to enable you to facilitate certain practices.

358

WEALTH

1. Dreaming of being wealthy is to dream of having in abundance those things that you need. You may have possibly come though a period where you have put in a lot of effort and to dream of having a great deal of wealth indicates that you have achieved what you have set out to do.

2. Wealth and status usually go naturally together, so often when you are having problems in dealing with your own status in life you will have dreams about wealth.

3. Wealth in dreams can also often indicate the resources that you have or that you can use from other people. You have the ability to draw on your experiences or feelings and to achieve a great deal within the framework of your life.

4. There is a "wealth" of spiritual knowledge to be gained, and to dream of this indicates that it is within the dreamer's grasp.

WEAPONS

1. To dream of weapons usually suggest your desire to hurt someone. This is a warning against actually having to deal with such circumstances in everyday life.

2. Depending on the weapon that you use you may get a fairly good idea of what the real problem is, in the waking self.

3. **An arrow:** Indicates being pierced by some kind of powerful emotion, of being hurt by someone else through words or actions. You need to turn your attention inward in order to make yourself feel better.

4. **Gun or pistol:** Represents male sexuality.

5. **If a woman dreams of being shot:** Indicates either her wish for sexual intercourse or fear of sexual aggression.

6. **If you are shooting the gun:** Indicates that you may be using your masculine abilities in quite an aggressive way, in order to defend yourself.

7. **A knife:** Represents the ability to cut through debris, to "cut into" whatever is bothering you and to cut out the hypocrisy that perhaps is prevailing in a situation.

8. **The sword:** Because of its hilt, which is a cross shape, it often represents a system of belief which is used in a powerful way. Equally it can be used to suggest spiritual strength, creating an ability to cut away the unnecessary more powerfully than the knife.

9. **To have a weapon used against you:** Means that you have to look at how you are party to people being aggressive around you. It may be

that you have done something to upset others which may result in aggression.

10. Various weapons can suggest varying degrees of spiritual power. The dreamer should use this power with relevant caution.

WEASEL
See Animals

WEATHER

1. Weather, as being part of the "environment" of the dream, usually indicates your moods and emotions. You are very much aware of changing external situations and have to be careful to adjust your conduct in response to these.

2. Weather also can indicate your internal responses to situations. If, for instance, there was a storm in your dream your emotions would be stormy, perhaps angry and aggressive.

3. If there was a clear blue, unclouded sky, you may recognise that you have the ability to keep the situations that you are in under control.

WEAVING

1. Weaving is a very basic symbol and suggests the need to take responsibility for your own life. To be doing any handicraft shows that you have situations in hand.

2. Weaving is taken to signify life itself, and often your attitude to the way you run your life.

3. Weaving is one of the strongest spiritual images there is. In most cultures there is an image of your fate being woven in a particular pattern. You are not supposed to be in control of that pattern, but must accept that God knows what is best.

WEB

1. For a web to appear in your dream signifies that you may be caught up in a situation that could trap you and not quite know which direction to move.

2. If somebody else makes deliberate moves to trap you in a web in your dreams signifies that you may face a situation which is extremely complex which you may have no idea which way is going to be most advantageous for you.

360

WEDDING
See Marriage

WEDDING RING

1. To dream of a wedding ring signifies your desire to achieve something eternal.
2. To dream of losing one's wedding ring would very often symbolise a problem within a marriage or a love relationship.
3. To dream of finding a wedding ring might well indicate that a relationship is being formed which could result in marriage.
4. To dream of wearing a wedding ring on the finger which represents the heart, that is, the fourth finger of the left hand, suggests that you may soon make romantic promises.
5. To dream of a wedding ring being on any other finger than that particular finger mentioned above may indicate that you may make false promises or you feel your relationship to be a constriction or an entrapment in a certain way.

WEDGE

1. Dreaming of a wedge often indicates that you need to open up situations around you. You need to put something in position which means that you can be open and truthful at all times.
2. Since the wedge is also a symbol of support, it may be that you need to be aware that in situations around you, you might need increasing assistance. You would also need to guard against becoming too dependent on that kind of support.
3. If you are feeling somewhat isolated, a wedge will symbolise the spiritual support that you have been seeking.

WEED

1. To dream of weeds may indicate misplaced trust, misplaced energy or even misplaced attempts at success.
2. To dream of clearing weeds on your own premises signifies that you should make a positive attempt to make a careful analysis of what is preventing you from making progress because at the moment you are not moving the way you should be.
3. To be digging up weeds would show that you are aware that, by freeing your life of the nonessentials, you are creating space for new growth and new abilities.

4. Mental attitudes which clog you up and do not allow you to move forward, and old patterns of behaviour can very often be shown in dreams as weeds.
5. Weeds, by courtesy of their irritating qualities and refusal to be quickly eradicated, symbolise spiritual difficulties.

WEEPING

1. To dream of either yourself or someone else weeping is to show that there needs to be a discharge of an emotion somewhere. You may be sad over certain events or fearful of forthcoming events.
2. To dream of weeping can also signify that you have created difficult situations for yourself which you may be regretting up to this day.
3. Something exuding moisture so that it seems to be weeping is often deemed to be miraculous, and this dream can appear quite often in stages of transition as you are moving from one state of awareness to another
4. Weeping suggests mourning for some spiritual quality you have lost.

WEIGHING

1. To be weighing something in your dream is to be assessing its worth. This image connects with the calculation of your needs and what is of value to you, whether materially or spiritually.
2. To dream of weighing something by balancing the scales indicates that you are looking for justice within a situation.
3. Weighing something in your dream may also signify that you have to be clear of your own spiritual worth.

WEIGHT

1. To dream of experiencing a weight signifies that you should be conscious of your responsibilities and you should also assess the importance and seriousness of what you are doing.
2. Weight in a dream may well indicate the need to be practical and down to earth. You need to keep your feet on the ground.

WELL

1. A well is a way of assessing the deepest resources of feeling and emotion that you have. If there is something wrong with the well, e.g. you cannot reach the water, then this suggests that you are not able to get in touch with your best talents.

2.	The image of a well in a dream suggests your ability to be "well." You have the ability to be healed and to fulfil your dearest wish, if you so desire.

3.	A well can symbolise a form of contact with the depths, possibly the depths of emotion.

WEST
See Position

WET
See Water

WHALE
See Animals

WHEAT
See Grain

WHEEL

1.	A wheel in a dream indicates the ability and need to make changes, to move forward into the future without being thrown off course.

2.	To lose a wheel from a vehicle signifies to lose motivation or direction to be thrown off balance. You should guard against this, as it will hamper progress.

3.	A large wheel, such as the Ferris wheel in a fairground, suggests that you should be aware of life's ups and downs, hence, not to be discouraged by small delays.

WHIP

1.	As the whip is an instrument of torture, for it to appear in your dream indicates that you may soon have to make a decision for either the need to control others or to be controlled by them. You have to balance your advantage carefully and choose your best course of action.

2.	Because the whip is an instrument of punishment, you need to be aware that in trying to force things to happen, you may also be creating problems for yourself.

3.	A whip suggests corrective punishment and self-flagellation.

WHIRLPOOL/WHIRLWIND

1.	Both these images are symbols of the vortex, a representation of life and natural energy. There are usually conflicting energies in both.

When they appear in dreams you are aware of the quality of power you have within. The whirlpool will more properly represent emotional energy.

2. The whirlwind will suggest intellectual power.

3. Intellectually you may know that you have control over your life, but are caught up in an endless round of activity which appears to be unproductive but in fact contains a tremendous amount of energy.

4. A whirl of creativity lies ahead. You must "roll with it" and fully take advantage.

WHISKEY
See Alcohol

WHISPERING

1. To hear whispering in a dream suggests that you need to listen to someone or something very carefully.

2. To dream of someone whispering in your ears signifies that you may not have the full information available to you about a situation in your waking life.

3. Sounds in dreams can often manifest as the opposite quality to that which is required. Thus, whispering could be interpreted as a shout for attention.

WHISTLE

1. To hear a whistle in a dream is a warning to alert you to a particular event. You need to pay attention to the most significant activity going on at present because it is most probable that you may take essential advantage of it.

2. As a means of controlling and training, it may be relevant as to how it is blown. For instance if it is blown harshly, you may being made aware that you have transgressed a known code of conduct.

WHITE
See Colours

WIDOW

1. For a woman to dream of being a widow can suggest loss and sadness.

2. To dream of being in the company of a widow highlights your ability to be free and use your own innate wisdom.

3. In a man's dream a widow may signify a deeper understanding of a woman's needs. He may recognise that all women do not necessarily become dependent on him. This will, as a result, be necessary for him

to give more domestic responsibility to the woman and will generate more trust.

WIFE
See Family

WIG

1. In previous times, covering the head was considered to be a way of hiding the intellect, of giving a false impression or of indicating wisdom. A judge's wig can suggest all of these. A hairpiece or toupee highlights false ideas or an unnatural attitude.
2. Sometimes a wig highlights the fact that you have something to hide. You are perhaps not as competent, as youthful or as able as you would like others to believe.

WILD

1. To dream of a wild animal will stand for that aspect of your personality which has not yet committed itself to using rational thought. You may need to learn a little more about your personality.
2. To dream of anything which grows wild may signify anarchy and lack of stability. In its more positive sense there is profusion and promise in whatever you are trying to do.
3. In a dream, to be or feel wild often suggests a lack of spiritual control.

WILL

1. To dream of a will or any legal document symbolises the way in which your subconscious side can push you into taking notice of your inner needs.
2. To be making a will is to be making a promise to yourself over future action. It may also have overtones of attempting to look after those you love and care about.
3. To inherit from a will means that you need to look at the habits, characteristics and morals you have inherited from your ancestors.
4. Because for many, making a will is a very final action, in dreams it can indicate a recognition that you are entering a new phase of life.

WILLOW
See Tree

WIND

1. To dream of for instance, a breeze would suggest gentleness and pleasure. An idea or concept you have is beginning to move.

2. A gale might indicate a principle you feel passionately about, whereas a north wind might suggest a threat to your security.
3. On a slightly more psychological level, wind in a dream can suggest the beginning of a new deeper awareness of yourself.

WINDMILL
1. The image of a windmill in dreams can suggest the correct use of resources. Because wind often suggests intellect it is therefore the use of intellectual assets.
2. To dream of a windmill in full working motion signifies that you should make a move to use your naturally-possessed resources and make a bold move to push an idea forward.
3. To dream of a damaged or partly-damaged windmill signifies that you should take the necessary steps to consider the feelings of others in more details before making vital decisions.

WINDOW
See Buildings

WINE
See Alcohol

WINGS
1. Because wings make you think of flight, to dream of, for instance, birds' wings would suggest attention is being drawn to your need for freedom.
2. A broken wing indicates that a previous trauma is preventing you from "taking off."
3. Wings can also be protective, and this symbolism often appears in dreams. An angel's wings would depict the power to transcend your difficulties, as also would the wings of a bird of prey.

WINTER
1. In dreams, winter can represent a time in your life which is unfruitful. It can also represent old age, a time when your energy is running down.
2. At a period in your life when you are emotionally cold, images associated with winter, such as ice and snow can highlight the appropriateness, or otherwise, of the way you feel. In clairvoyance,

the seasons can also indicate a time of year when something may happen.

WISDOM

1. To dream that you are wise indicates the potential you have to run your life successfully and to relate meaningfully to other people.
2. Any figure of wisdom appearing in dreams usually indicates that you should think more carefully before proceeding with present decisions and actions.
3. Confirmation of the dreamer's spiritual integrity is represented by the presence of wisdom in a dream. It may often appear in the guise of a Wise Old Man.

WITCH

1. To see a witch in your dream signifies that you may soon face a situation where you may need information to enlighten a situation.
2. To dream of consultation with a witch signifies your need for inner knowledge in the sense that you need to learn more about spiritual aspects of life. This will, as a result, impart wisdom which in essential at present, to guide you more appropriately.
3. To dream of being a witch yourself signifies that you should refrain from being influenced by the decision of other people to participate in "shady" activities.

WITNESS

1. When you find yourself in the position of being a witness to, for instance, an accident, it may be that your powers of observation are being highlighted. You need to take very careful note of what is going on around you. Your interaction with authority may also be being called into question.
2. Dreaming of testifying as a witness suggests that you feel you are being called to account for your actions or beliefs. You may feel somewhat insecure until you have been accepted by your peers.
3. To dream of somebody else testifying against you signifies that you should take a closer look among your peers to discern who may be working purposefully against your efforts.

WOLF
See Animals

WOMAN
See People

WOOD

1. Dreaming of wood, in the sense of timber, suggests your ability to appreciate the past and to build on what has gone before. You are capable of building a structure, which may or may not be permanent.
2. Dreaming of, for instance, a wooden toy highlights your connection with the more natural side of yourself. You may not have to "fit" yourself into being somebody else to make effective impressions. Just proceed naturally with whatever you have to do.
3. To dream of everything suddenly being made out of wood is a warning not to be rigid.

WOOL

1. How you interpret wool depends on whether the image you have is of lamb's wool. Lamb's wool may stand for blurred thoughts and feelings. You have not really sorted out your thoughts and may still be indecisive.
2. Wool has, from earliest times, represented warmth and protectiveness. Nowadays it particularly represents gentleness and mothering.
3. Wool is symbolic of Spiritual Protection. "Pulling the wool" over someone's eyes, though generally accepted as devious, can also be a protective act. There may be things, which the dreamer does not wish, or need to spiritually see at the present time.

WORK

1. Dreaming of being at work highlights issues, concerns or difficulties you may have within the work situation. You could be actively trying to make changes in your life and these changes, in dreams, become reflected into the work situation.
2. Often, what you do as a job bears no relation to what you consider to be your real work. Dreams can very often help you to change your situation by giving information as to your real talents and gifts.
3. When you dream of working at something which does not have a place in your ordinary everyday life, it may be worth exploring the potential within that line of work.

WORKSHOP

1. A workshop is a place that is productive. In dreams it symbolises the part of yourself which creates projects which then become profitable for you, though not necessarily financially.

2. A workshop may often be where you meet others of like mind, people who are creative in the same way as you are. It therefore represents group interaction and talent.
3. A workshop often holds within it creative outlets. This creativity can be used for the dreamer's spiritual progression.

WORM

1. Depending on the dreamer's attitude to sexuality and gender, there may be a sense of threat. The worm is not necessarily seen to be particularly clean.
2. The worm in dreams can also highlight your feelings of ineffectiveness and insignificance.
3. If the worm is bigger than you are, then this would suggest that your own sense of inferiority is a problem.
4. If you are particularly conscious of a worm cast, that is, the earth the worm has passed through its body, then this is a transformation image, and indicates you are capable of changing your life into something more fertile.
5. Being given to the worms is a metaphor for death, so you need to be aware that on a spiritual level, changes may shortly take place.

WORSHIP

1. Dreaming of being in a situation where you are worshipping something such as an idea, a person, a concept or an object is to be opening yourself up to its influence. You may soon reap the benefits of something.
2. If you are not particularly religious but find yourself in the middle of an act of worship, you may need to look at how you deal with a common belief system or set of principles in your everyday life.
3. To be worshipping an object which is not a religious image may suggest that you are paying too much attention to whatever that object represents. For instance, you may be too materialistic, be paying too much attention to sex or other ordinary aspects of life.

WOUND

1. Any wound or trauma in dreams will signify hurt feelings or emotions. If you are inflicting the wounds it signifies your own aggression and mistrust.
2. If the wounds are being inflicted on you, you may be making yourself into, or being, the victim.

3. The type of wound will be important in interpreting the dream. A large ugly wound will suggest more violence, whereas a small one may indicate a more focused attack.

WREATH

1. A wreath in a dream can suggest honour. The shape will be important, as often it is circular, signifying continuity and completeness, as well as everlasting life.
2. Dreaming of being given a wreath suggests being singled out, perhaps for some honour.
3. Dreaming of giving someone else a wreath validates your relationship with that person.
4. A wreath in dreams can have the same significance as any of the binding symbols such as harnesses and halters. It forms a bond which cannot be broken, or a sacrifice which must be accepted.

WRECK

1. Dreaming of a wreck, such as a car or shipwreck, indicates that your plans may be thwarted in some ways. It is necessary to decide whether you are at fault for the failure of your plans or someone else is.
2. Since a wreck can happen due to circumstances beyond your control, such a dream can indicate a greater need for control, or management of resources.
3. A wreck of some kind symbolises a defeat. The dreamer, though frustrated on this occasion, should continue to "battle" through to reach his intended goal.

WRITING

1. To dream of writing is an attempt to communicate information that one has. Sometimes the instrument you are writing with is important. For instance, a pencil would suggest that the information is less permanent than with a pen, whereas a typewriter or word processor would suggest business communication rather than personal.
2. Writing as a creative art is meaningful, and as a form of self-expression perhaps allows you to communicate when spoken words are inadequate. In dreams you may learn how to communicate with others in differing ways.
3. The dreamer may not be consciously aware of his spiritual progression. Dreaming of writing suggests a subconscious record is being kept.

X

X

1. If an X appears in a dream, you are usually "marking the spot." It can also represent an error or something that you particularly need to note.
2. If a cross appears in the shape of an X, this usually represents the idea of sacrifice or perhaps of torture.

X-RAYS

1. Dreaming of X-rays can be significant in a number of ways. There may be something influencing the dreamer's life on an unconscious level which needs to be revealed.
2. If the dreamer is carrying out the X-ray it may be necessary to look more deeply into a situation. There may also be a fear of illness, either in oneself or others.
3. Within waking life, it may be that there is something you need to see through. This can be a play on words, in that you need to finish something off, or you may need to have a very clear view of a situation around you.

Y

YACHT
See Boat in journey

YARDSTICK

1. To dream of a yardstick formerly represented correctness and rigidity. But nowadays, it has less significance. It still, however, represents good judgment. .

2. The yardstick represents the measurement of acceptable standards. In dreams this may represent standards of behaviour, belief or conformity

3. Spiritually a yardstick symbolises the standards that you have set yourself. You may wish to be reassured that you are maintaining these standards fully.

YARN

1. Yarn in the sense of knitting yarn or twine often signifies your ability to create order out of chaos.

2. A yarn, as in a tale or story, has most often to do with your sense of history, or of continuity. To be being told a yarn or story links with your need for heroes and heroines, and perhaps your need for a mentor.

3. The myths and stories of the old heroes who undertook their own spiritual journey can help you identify a strategy for life.

YAWN

1. To dream of becoming conscious of yawning can indicate boredom and tiredness. You may also be attempting to say something, but have not yet thought through what you wish to say. Be prepared.

2. A yawn in dreams may also be a way of controlling your own or other's abusive behaviour.

YEAR
See Calendar

YEARN

1. A need which may be perfectly manageable in ordinary everyday life becomes a yearning and seeking in dreams. Such a dream would highlight an emotion which you may need to look at in order to understand.

2. If you have suppressed your needs through long habit or self-denial, an urgency may emerge in dreams for the very thing you have consciously denied.
3. The dreamer may have become impatient in his seemingly never-ending search for his spiritual self. This is often symbolised by a yearning feeling in a dream.

YEAST
1. Yeast is accepted as a substance which both lightens food and makes it palatable. At the same time it changes the substance and texture. In dreams it represents ideas or influences which can irrevocably change your life or situations, often for the better.
2. Yeast ferments and thus it becomes one of the symbols of growth and unconditional love.
3. Yeast can be symbolic of the steady growth towards the realisation and beauty of natural love.

YES
1. Occasionally in dreams you become aware that you have "said" yes. This is an instinctive acceptance or acknowledgment of the validity of whatever has been happening.
2. Often, before you are able to make changes in your ordinary everyday life, you need to give yourself permission on an unconscious level. Recognising this in the dream state can be an important part of your growth process.
3. You are being given permission to spiritually grow and flourish. With this permission, the dreamer can look toward a more directed lifestyle.

YEW
See Tree

YIELD
1. To yield in a dream is to be aware of the futility of confrontation. To understand this you may need to look at situations within your life.
2. Yielding is one of the more feminine attributes and signifies your need to let go and simply "go with the flow."
3. The dreamer may have been contemplating the idea of a more spiritual existence for some time, and has now finally yielded, or submitted to the notion.

YOGI

See Guru

YULE LOG

1. In pagan times a log was decorated and burnt in order to clear away the Old Year. In dreams it will be seen as a symbol of light and new life.
2. In modern times, the Yule log is symbolised as a celebration cake. Therefore it tends to suggest the New Year in dream language.
3. A Yule log represents a spiritual offering or sacrifice, particularly at the time of a spiritual or religious celebration, when you pay homage to the gods.

Z

ZEBRA
See Animals

ZERO
See Numbers

ZIGZAG
1. When you see a zigzag in dreams you are looking at the potential to be hit by disaster, such as in a bolt of lightning. An event will occur which brings about a discharge of energy. Circumstances will then be brought back into balance.
2. In a psychological sense, you will achieve a new level of awareness, perhaps even a revelation.

ZIPPER
1. A zipper appearing in a dream may indicate your ability, or difficulty, in maintaining relationships with other people.

ZODIAC
1. Everyone has a fascination for horoscopes, without necessarily understanding the significance of the zodiac wheel. It is often only when you begin the journey of self-discovery that images and symbols from the zodiac will appear in dreams.
2. Frequently, the animal or creature associated with your own star sign will appear, almost as a reminder of basic principles. The way you deal with that image will give you insights into how you really feel about yourself.
3. The zodiac wheel is symbolic of your relationship with the universe. Sometimes the signs of the zodiac are used in dreams to demonstrate time or time passing, and also suggest courses of action you might take. For instance, if you dreamed of a girl riding a goat you might have to seek perfection (Virgo) through tenacity (Capricorn). Each sign also rules a particular part of the body, and often a dream alerts you to a possible imbalance.

The spheres of influence as described below are:

1. **Aries:** The symbol is the Ram and it governs the head. The colour associated with the sign is red; its specific gemstones are amethyst and diamond.
2. **Taurus:** The symbol is the Bull and it governs the throat. The colours associated with the sign are blue and pink; its specific gemstones are moss, agate and emerald.
3. **Gemini:** The symbol is the Twins (often shown as masculine and feminine) and it governs the shoulders, arms and hands. The colour associated with the sign is yellow; its specific gemstones are agate and beryl.
4. **Cancer:** The symbol is the Crab and it governs the stomach and higher organs of digestion. The colours associated with the sign are either violet or emerald green; its specific gemstones are moonstones and pearls.
5. **Leo:** The symbol is the Lion and it governs the heart, lungs and liver. The colours associated with the sign are gold and orange; its specific gemstones are topaz and tourmaline.
6. **Virgo:** The symbol is the Virgin and it governs the abdomen and intestines. The colours associated with the sign are grey and navy blue; its specific gemstones are pink jasper and jade.
7. **Libra:** The symbol is the Scales and it governs the lumbar region, kidneys and skin. The colours associated with the sign are blue and violet; its specific gemstones are opal and lapis lazuli.
8. **Scorpio:** The symbol is the Scorpion and it governs the genitals. The colours associated with the sign are deep red and purple; its specific gemstones are turquoise and ruby.
9. **Sagittarius:** The symbol is the Archer and it governs the hips, thighs and nervous system. The colours associated with the sign are light blue and orange; its specific gemstones are carbuncle and amethyst.
10. **Capricorn:** The symbol is the Goat and it governs the knees. The colours associated with the sign are violet and green; its specific gemstones are jet and black onyx.
11. **Aquarius:** The symbol is the Water Bearer and it governs the circulation and ankles. The colour associated with the sign is electric blue; its specific gemstones are garnet and zircon.
12. **Pisces:** The symbol is The Fishes and it governs the feet and toes. The colours associated with the sign are sea-green and mauve; its specific gemstones are coral and chrysolite.

ZOO

1. Dreaming of being in a zoo suggests the need to understand some of your natural urges and instincts. You perhaps need to be more objective in your appraisal than subjective.
2. There may be an urge to return to simpler, more basic modes of behaviour. Some people are natural observers, and you may be being alerted to the fact that you also need to be capable of participating in conduct appropriate to the group to which you belong. You also, of course, may be conscious that you yourself are being observed, perhaps in the work situation.
3. Dreaming of a zoo can alert the dreamer to the necessary and appropriate customs and behaviour in an impending situation.